The Primitive Church
in the Modern World

The Primitive Church
in the Modern World

EDITED BY
Richard T. Hughes

University of Illinois Press · URBANA AND CHICAGO

© 1995 by the Board of Trustees of the University of Illinois
Manufactured in the United States of America
1 2 3 4 5 C P 5 4 3 2 1

This book is printed on acid-free paper.

Library of Congress Cataloging-in-Publication Data

The primitive church in the modern world / edited by Richard T.
    Hughes.
        p.   cm.
    Includes bibliographical references and index.
    ISBN 0-252-02194-0 (cloth : alk. paper). — ISBN 0-252-06492-5
(pbk. : alk. paper)
    1. Primitivism—Religious aspects—Christianity. I. Hughes,
Richard T. (Richard Thomas), 1943– .
BR1661.P75   1995
270.8—dc20   95-5366
                                                                        CIP

Contents

Acknowledgments

I wish to express appreciation to the following: the Pew Charitable Trusts, whose generous support made possible both a conference, "Christian Primitivism and Modernization: Coming to Terms with Our Age," held at Pepperdine University in the summer of 1991, and this book, which grew directly out of that conference; Dr. and Mrs. Terry Koonce, whose generosity made possible the publication of this volume; Lori Glenn, a graduate student in the Religion Division at Pepperdine University and my assistant, who handled the logistical details of the conference in a magnificent way; and Sue Bauer, director of the Word Processing Center at Pepperdine University, and Dora Pember, word processing specialist, who rendered invaluable assistance in the preparation of this manuscript.

The Meaning of
the Restoration Vision

RICHARD T. HUGHES

The study of Christian primitivism, broadly conceived, is a relative-ly new field, and theoretical studies of Christian primitivism in the American context are newer still. Franklin H. Littell pioneered in the larger discipline with his 1952 book *The Anabaptist View of the Church,* later published as *The Origins of Sectarian Protestantism.*[1] There, Lit-tell explored sixteenth-century Anabaptism as a restorationist or resti-tutionist phenomenon.

When my mentor at Abilene Christian University, Everett Fergu-son, called my attention to Littell's book in 1966, I found the world Littell described immensely familiar, though it was a world separated from my own by some 450 years. I found it familiar because I was raised in a primitivist or restorationist tradition—the Churches of Christ—and understood almost by instinct the impulses and perspectives Lit-tell described. I was so intrigued by Littell's work that I focused my M.A. thesis, written under the supervision of Professor Ferguson, on a comparison of the restoration vision as adopted by key evangelical Anabaptists, on the one hand, and by Thomas Campbell and Alexander Campbell, early founders of the American-born Churches of Christ, on the other.

Now that many years have passed, I realize how that M.A. thesis placed me on a life-long quest to understand the meaning of that vi-sion. In keeping with that quest, I organized at Abilene Christian Uni-versity in 1985 a conference that explored the meaning of the restora-tion vision in a variety of Christian traditions and that resulted in the book *The American Quest for the Primitive Church.*[2] While that conference shed considerable light on the meaning of the restoration ideal in *particular* contexts, it did little to help scholars develop a comprehensive understanding of the term *restoration*. Indeed, after reading a number of the papers from that conference, Henry Bowden concluded that "the meaning of the term [*restoration*] is relative to different people who appropriate it, to what they say it means, and to what activities they pursue under its aegis. Based on historical usage of institutional, doctrinal and biblical categories, there is no meaning intrinsic to the title, and we can find no common agreement on any set of organizational forms or ideas."[3]

Many scholars agreed, however, that one central theme threads its way through all primitivist movements: a rejection of any sense of history. Bowden therefore compared restorationists to German New Testament scholars of the nineteenth century whose search for the historical Jesus "produced only the reflection of a Protestant face at the bottom of a deep well."[4] Grant Wacker concurred: "I shall use that word [*primitivism*] in a broadly generic manner to refer to any effort to deny history, or to deny the contingencies of historical existence, by returning to the time before time, to the golden age that preceded the corruptions of life in history."[5] Without question, a profound "sense of historylessness"[6] often characterizes self-proclaimed restorationist or primitivist movements. Indeed, I and a colleague, C. Leonard Allen, devoted an entire book to this sense of historylessness and the "illusions of innocence" it often engenders.[7]

But is this all that can be said about the restorationist project? Can we conclude, simply, that restorationism and primitivism are fuzzy terms that point to no specific content other than the naive attempt to avoid the power of history and culture?

The Meaning of the Restoration Vision

The first thing to be said is simply this: restorationism involves the attempt to recover some important belief or practice from the time of pure beginnings that believers are convinced has been lost, defiled, or corrupted. Restorationism further assumes that at some point in Christian history a fall or apostasy occurred. Without a fall, a loss, or an apostasy, the notion of restoration is simply unintelligible. On these points, all restorationists agree. This simple set of commitments separates restorationists from a variety of Christian believers who are uncomfortable speaking of an apostasy or a fall, who do not view the founding age as more normative than other periods in Christian history, or who think the founding age important but self-consciously interpret its meaning in the light of later events and developments. Put another way, restorationists seek to apprehend some particular dimension of the founding age, unmediated through subsequent understandings. Someone speaking from a modern perspective might well contend that such a quest is illusory. To convinced restorationists, that objection carries little or no weight. To them, the founding age exercises an exclusive claim on their allegiance, a claim they are unwilling to give to any other period in Christian history.

To argue that such a view is naive or constitutes a rejection of the power and significance of history does not diminish the fact that such movements exist and have always existed in American life and culture. Yet, historians of American religion have persistently sought to understand primitivists as something other than what they really are. If historians wish to subsume primitivists under the labels "evangelical," "conservative," or "fundamentalist"; if they wish to view the restoration impulse as nothing more than a function of the democratic sentiment; or if they want to insist that all Christians are, at certain levels, primitivists, then these historians simply guarantee their own inability to understand the meaning of restorationist movements and their place in American life and culture.

Beyond the exclusive allegiance primitivists pledge to the founding age, Bowden was right when he argued that "the meaning of the term [restoration] is relative to different people who appropriate it, to what they say it means, and to what activities they pursue under its aegis." In other words, restorationists clearly differ on those aspects of the first age they find important and normative. Some focus on theology and doctrine, some focus on issues of lifestyle and ethics, some focus on early Christian experience, while still others seek to recover the forms and structures they think characterized the ancient church. Some of these believers do careful historical and exegetical work in order to determine as precisely as possible what the founding age was like and are therefore less susceptible to charges of historical naivete than are others. On the other hand, some blatantly and uncritically project their own contemporary concerns onto the first age and, unwittingly, find their own reflection staring back at themselves from deep within the well of Christian history. Finally, in each of these categories, restorationists disagree among themselves. Nonetheless, all who appeal to the first age in any of these ways qualify as restorationists.

I do not find helpful efforts to deal with the bewildering variety of believers who appeal to the first age by distinguishing between primitivism and restorationism. Grant Wacker and George Marsden, for example, both propose in essays in this volume just such a distinction as a way of clarifying the reversional orientation among pentecostals. For example, Wacker writes that "among early pentecostals primitivism was not simply restorationism. . . . The latter suggested a rather self-conscious effort to sit down, figure out what the New Testament blueprint called for, then quite rationally reproduce it in the modern world. Campbellites, Mormons, Landmark Baptists, and other so-called restorationist sects of the nineteenth century readily come to mind. Pentecostal primitivism certainly included all of that, but it was more." Wacker goes on to explain how pentecostal primitivism had more to do with experience than mere rational reconstruction. Thus, "first generation [pentecostal] stalwarts sought to reenter that [primitive] world as literally as possible by breathing its holy air, smelling its sacred fragrances, and luxuriating in its spiritual delights."

The problem with such a proposal is that while scholars currently employ only two, or perhaps three, operative terms to describe such movements—*restorationism, primitivism,* and sometimes *reversion*[8]—this proposal co-opts one of those terms to privilege one single movement out of a vast array of similar phenomena.

In my judgment, it is far more productive to use *primitivism* and *restorationism* as roughly synonymous and therefore interchangeable terms, as I have done in this essay, but then work out a series of descriptive labels to designate the type of restorationism or primitivism one has in mind. Thus, for example, one might well describe Mormons and pentecostals as experiential primitivists, chiefly concerned with replicating a presumed spiritual dimension of the first age; Holiness advocates and sixteenth-century Anabaptists as ethical primitivists, mainly concerned with conforming themselves to ethical norms found in the teachings of Jesus and elsewhere in the New Testament; and the American-born Churches of Christ as ecclesiastical primitivists, chiefly concerned with reproducing the forms and structures they think characterized the most ancient churches.[9]

Primitivism, Fundamentalism, and Modernization

Since restorationism includes such a diversity of movements and emphases, it is impossible, in my view, to articulate a comprehensive definition of the phenomenon beyond the most basic observation that restorationists place supreme value on the founding age and seek to recover specific dimensions of that age in their own time. One can, however, turn the restorationist project in slightly different directions so that it catches light from different angles. In this way, we might discover dimensions of this vision that heretofore have escaped careful examination. This was precisely the purpose of the conference that convened at Pepperdine University in 1991, "Christian Primitivism and Modernization: Coming to Terms with Our Age," resulting in the present book.

As it turned out, this second conference did highlight a theme important to many restorationist believers: their tendency to define their most fundamental values and commitments by the ancient norms of the Christian faith, however perceived, and only then—if at all—by the norms of modernity or modernization. In other words, genuine primitivists judge the modern world by the standards of the ancient faith, not the other way around.

In exploring this relationship, a comparison of restorationism and fundamentalism turned out to be crucial. R. Scott Appleby, former associate director of the Fundamentalism Project at the University of Chicago and now director of the Cushwa Center at Notre Dame, lifted this comparison out of the narrow confines of American Christianity and into the broader framework of Hinduism and especially Islam. Appleby finally concluded that fundamentalists are not primitivists and that primitivists are not fundamentalists. If he is right, his point is important, since scholars and journalists alike often place primitivists squarely in the fundamentalist camp.

In Appleby's judgment, fundamentalists are essentially modernists who, indeed, look like primitivists, but only because they make rhetorical use of primitivist themes in their effort to control the modern world. On the other hand, genuine primitivists exhibit little interest in political power. Instead, they seek mainly to conform their lives and their religious organizations to the norms of the first age, regardless of the values and interests of the modern world and its politics. "The world they [the primitivists] seek to restore," Appleby concludes, "does not sit easily with the ambition of modern world conquerors." Instead, primitivists often exhibit a "prophetic stance toward the very kingdoms and nation-states that the fundamentalists seek to conquer."

Brimming with implications, Appleby's essay raises a number of other considerations. In the first place, if Appleby is correct, then genuine restorationist movements are always sects, never denominations. A religious movement that has embraced the values of modernity and modernization and by virtue of that embrace has come to terms with the culture in which it lives is by Appleby's standards no longer an authentically restorationist movement. Seen from this perspective, all the traditions represented in this book began their careers with a strong restorationist emphasis, but virtually all have now abandoned their restorationist moorings for a modern project that renders the restoration vision essentially powerless. While many of these traditions continue to claim for themselves a place in the restorationist orbit, as the reader will see in some of the essays that follow, one suspects that these claims are fundamentally rhetorical, not substantive.

Primitivism as a Countercultural Project

This does not mean, however, that there are no longer spokespersons for the restoration vision. Indeed, one feature both of *The American Quest for the Primitive Church* and of the present volume is the presence of voices that speak from within the restorationist circle. In *The American Quest for the Primitive Church,* that voice belonged to David Edwin Harrell Jr. Here, those voices belong to Franklin H. Littell, John Howard Yoder, and James Wm. McClendon Jr.

Inclusion of these documents represents a deliberate strategy. While other essays in this book provide readers with secondary scholarship *about* restorationist movements, these three essays perform a different task. While critical and reflective analyses in their own right, these essays are also primary documents that originate from within a restorationist perspective and especially from within that perspective most commonly associated with Anabaptism. From that vantage point, these essays assess the meaning and power of the restorationist vision and explore ways in which that vision can be articulated with greater clarity.

A striking feature of all three of these essays is the way they fit the basic framework developed by Appleby in his comparison of primitivists with fundamentalists. For example, when Appleby writes that primitivists often exhibit a "prophetic stance toward the very kingdoms and nation-states that the fundamentalists seek to conquer," he implicitly suggests that primitivists sometimes turn their energies in profoundly countercultural directions.

As the keynote address for the conference, Franklin H. Littell's essay explores the countercultural potential of the restorationist ideal and provides the basic structure for the vision these three essays, taken together, seek to explore. Indeed, Littell speaks clearly of "decline" and "apostasy" and argues that primitivist/restorationist movements, by definition, enshrine the first age as a transcendent norm and, on that basis, stand in judgment on the contents of modern culture. For that reason, primitivists typically resist all forms of *Kulturreligion* that are built around the importance of nation, folk, or race.

In a companion piece, John Howard Yoder concurs. An "apostasy" began, Yoder claims, when Christian apologetes, eager to commend their faith to "antiparticular pagan generality," abandoned the highly particularistic Jewish foundations of the Christian religion. This philosophical transition, in turn, made it possible for Christians after Constantine to accept the premise that the empire, representing the universal rather than the particular, was now the fullest incarnation of the Christian faith.

Littell further contends that when restorationist programs embody genuine ethical power, they root themselves not in the ancient story alone, that is, the tale of what once was, but in an apocalyptic orientation as well, that is, the tale of what will be. Primitivism apart from apocalypticism, Littell suggests, grows wooden, dry, and stale.

As an example, Littell points to the restoration movement led by Alexander Campbell in the nineteenth century. Campbell's movement built its restorationist agenda on the grid of Scottish Common Sense Realism, apart from any serious apocalyptic orientation other than a postmillennial sentiment informed by popular civic piety. Here was a millennial vision informed not by anticipation of the coming kingdom of God but simply by the spirit of the age. Of Campbell, Littell writes,

> I think that the bone that stuck in the throat, methodologically, was the insistence that the religious program qualify by the norms set by Scottish Common Sense philosophy. The secure ground of a powerful myth or root metaphor was left behind, and vigorous minds entered into the intellectual controversies of the age as modernity defined them. To "stick to the facts," to proclaim Bible "facts," to authenticate religious "truth" by grafting it onto "the scientific method"—these are rules more readily related to vital civil life in nineteenth-century America than they are to what could be known and reclaimed from the life of early Christians at Corinth and Antioch and Ephesus. The stance of primitivism, which looks backward for its norms, was replaced by the spirit of modernity, looking blithely toward a future of progressive and orderly change.

By implication, Littell suggests that Campbell left to his restorationist heirs—Christian Churches and Churches of Christ—a legacy greatly impoverished by his scientific approach to the restorationist task.

James Wm. McClendon Jr. therefore concludes this trilogy of primary documents by asking how an authentic restorationist vision might best be conceptualized. He concludes that restorationists might serve themselves best through narrative theology that, on the one hand, employs an imaginative use of types or images and that, on the other hand, combines a restorationist orientation with an apocalyptic worldview. "History that is more than chronology and necrology," McClendon writes, "appears only when it is viewed with . . . eyes that can see how this is that, how storied past and prophetic future converge upon this present."

Are Restorationists Biblicists?

Finally, if primitivists are not fundamentalists, we must ask if they are biblicists. George Marsden raises this issue when he writes, "Much of what passes for primitivism is virtually synonymous with a simple biblicism, or an effort to follow biblical rules as the highest rule for church practice and for life."

While there is merit in Marsden's proposal, there are problems as well. First, as we have seen, restorationism involves far more than simple biblicism. For example, Marsden himself points out that many evangelicals, especially fundamentalists, "often claim to stand for 'the historic Christian faith' and claim the traditions of nineteenth-century evangelicals, of Whitefield, of Wesley, and of the Reformation." In other words, fundamentalists self-consciously filter the ancient faith through the norms of a later Protestant orthodoxy. This means that fundamentalists can hardly be accused of historical naivete, a charge that can be leveled against many primitivists. But it also means that fundamentalist biblicism is a radically different phenomenon than primitivism.

Second, by confusing primitivism with biblicism, Marsden's proposal virtually robs the primitivist perspective of its countercultural potential, the very drive that Appleby, Yoder, and Littell find so central to the primitivist project. As Marsden himself observes, far from resisting the values and norms of modernization, biblicism—especially its Reformed variety—is fully capable of embracing modernization. Indeed, Marsden finds that in the Reformed tradition, biblicism was an important tool for the reformation of "the whole of society," not simply for the reformation of the church, and therefore pointed toward the future, not toward the past. For that reason, he argues, "biblicism and modernization might go hand in hand."

Marsden has illumined, however, an important paradox in the Reformed tradition and one with which we must come to terms. With its emphasis on the sovereignty of God over all of life, the Reformed tradition can work in two radically different directions. First, it can and does sustain a powerful drive to reform all of society and to impose its vision upon all the earth. In this sense, Marsden is correct when he sees the biblicist side of the Reformed tradition as a modernizing impulse pointing not toward a sacred past but into a future dominated by the rule of God.

At the same time, it is crucial to remember that many restoration-ists in American history have descended from that very same Reformed tradition. One thinks here of the Separatist Puritans, of the Separate Baptists, or of people like Barton W. Stone in the early nineteenth century. In each of these instances, Reformed Christians despaired when society failed to conform to the sovereign will of God. When that happened, they often focused their energies not on the construction of the kingdom of God for a future age but on a restoration of the ancient order in their own time and place. Such efforts sometimes prompted separation from the larger society and often generated a strong, countercultural resistance to the world and its values. If one asks, therefore, if primitivists and modernizers could emerge from the same Calvinist fountain, the answer most certainly is yes.

Conclusions

Finally, it must be said that while the Reformed tradition was an important source of restoration endeavors, it was not the only source. In addition, as the following pages make clear, restorationist movements emerged especially from the Radical Reformation of the sixteenth century and from the Wesleyan tradition of the eighteenth century.

Today, restorationist movements continue to emerge, but the vitality of this tradition is found neither in the so-called mainline nor in the older restorationist movements that now have made their peace with the modern world. As Littell points out in his essay,

> Some prosperous movements, once restitutionist and hopeful, until now called "mainline" with increasingly dubious justification, have settled down to acceptability as denominations. But a strong wind is arising in another point on the compass. Dean Kelley, in his great book *Why Conservative Churches Are Growing,* has shown very clearly that there is another path from accommodation and decline, one that offers hope, "separation," discipline, and the power of the Word of God. Powerful new movements of restorationist orientation are growing rapidly in both North and South America. And in the United States restitutionism is alive and well. Only, like so many millions of Americans during the last half century, a multitude of those looking for a recovery of New Testament Christianity have changed their ecclesiastical place of residence.

This new "ecclesiastical place of residence" is one of the horizons to which scholars interested in the restorationist phenomenon must now direct their attention.

Notes

1. Franklin H. Littell, *The Origins of Sectarian Protestantism* (New York: Macmillan, 1964).

2. Richard T. Hughes, ed., *The American Quest for the Primitive Church* (Urbana: University of Illinois Press, 1988).

3. Henry Warner Bowden, "Perplexity over a Protean Principle: A Response," in Hughes, ed., *American Quest*, 176.

4. Ibid.

5. Grant Wacker, "Playing for Keeps: The Primitivist Impulse in Early Pentecostalism," in Hughes, ed., *American Quest*, 197.

6. Sidney E. Mead uses this phrase in *The Lively Experiment: The Shaping of Christianity in America* (New York: Harper and Row, 1963).

7. Richard T. Hughes and C. Leonard Allen, *Illusions of Innocence: Protestant Primitivism in America, 1630–1875* (Chicago: University of Chicago Press, 1988).

8. See Theodore Dwight Bozeman, *To Live Ancient Lives: The Primitivist Dimension in Puritanism* (Chapel Hill: University of North Carolina Press for the Institute of Early American History and Culture, 1988).

9. Two efforts to work out typologies of restorationist movements include Samuel S. Hill Jr., "A Typology of American Restitutionism: From Frontier Revivalism and Mormonism to the Jesus Movement," *Journal of the American Academy of Religion* 44 (Mar. 1976): 65–76, and Richard T. Hughes, "Christian Primitivism as Perfectionism: From Anabaptists to Pentecostals," in Stanley Burgess, ed., *Reaching Beyond: Chapters in the History of Perfectionism* (Peabody, Mass.: Hendrickson, 1986), 213–55.

Introduction

Primitivism and Modernization: Assessing the Relationship

MARTIN E. MARTY

Children growing up in the homes of historians may on occasion have given voice to frustration as some of mine sometimes did when they asked apparently simple questions. Most historians do not believe that most questions or any answers can be simple. They, we, take long running jumps back into history, trace nuances and subtleties along the way, hedge their bets, insert reserve clauses, avoid extremes, and . . . Finally, the child is likely to say something like one of mine did: "You make everything more complex than it is."

The reader of this book on primitivism and modernization is likely to respond similarly: primitive is primitive, so movements designed to restore the primitive or return it should be simply that. Modern is modern, so modernization should simply be defined and isolated as it affects the various religious movements discussed in these chapters. However, I do not find a single one of them that lets matters be as simple as that polarity suggests.

Why the difficulty?

First, because people may live by ideals and relate to forces, but they never do so simply. They fail to agree on defining the ideals or living up to them; they are often acted upon by forces they cannot name or fully understand. There is great variety within movements. Attachment to a movement or a force is only a part of the life of even the most devoted adherents or self-conscious respondents. They are surrounded by others who do not agree with them on the ideals or share them; they are impinged upon selectively by forces, depending upon where and how they live and how insulated or fortified they choose to be or can be. Somehow, they all negotiate with elements in their environment, and their negotiations are never neat and they never follow stable patterns. If they did, we would find that only robotologists would need to study them. Historians study worlds of ill-defined ideals, contingency, chance, compromise, victimage, heroism, clarifications, partial victories, survivals: in short, worlds of stories. Numbers of them are in this book.

The concept of "primitivism" and its cousins, "restoration" and "restitution," can be defined with some measure of accuracy, chiefly because founders of movements made quite clear what they were rejecting and what they were affirming. If they wanted to run up flags to see who would salute or wanted to be leaders, they had to make clear what ensign was on the flag. Self-conscious primitives in American culture were clear.

The concept of "modernization," however, is much less easily defined and it is hard to get agreements on a definition. It is a name for complex and often contradictory trends colored by the persons who use it. In a sense both "primitivism" and "modernization" are what Max Weber called "ideal types," used as pure forms for measurement, even though history never gives us pure forms in all their purity.

The use of such types allows the historians in this book to shed light on issues that become ever more urgent for the believing communities and scholarly academies alike. Each author has been free to range between the poles of "primitivism" and "modernization," and they all do. I want to anticipate the sequence of essays and then, having shown what the concept of the example can mean, revisit many of them to illustrate.

Three authors are allowed grand-scale observations. George Marsden, as well as anyone in the book, shows how there is something of the primitive in modern movements and more of the modern in putative primitivisms—Puritanism, for example—than often thought. Some might say that he confuses the issue: he intends to. He creatively proposes the notion of "biblicism" as the operating "ism" in many movements called primitive. R. Scott Appleby compares fundamentalisms that want to come across as restorationist because they return to "fundamentals" but are often agents of modernization and at home with the trappings of modernity. Finally, John Howard Yoder argues that while the primitivist outlook may appear to legitimate modernity or "the way things are," that need not be the case. The primitivist model, Yoder claims, can help establish authentically Christian norms.

The focus narrows when authors concentrate on particular religious movements. In the Stone-Campbell tradition, for example, David Edwin Harrell Jr. discusses the way the embrace of the modern by some Disciples and their cohorts led to compromise or selling out of the very ideal of being primitivist Christians.

Primitivism was both a spontaneously combusting and a contagious movement in the nineteenth century; one way for historians to test a vision is to see how it is acted upon in different communities. So the Wesleyan, Holiness, and pentecostal eruptions—significant variations on a significant set of themes—deserve and demand treatment. Susie C. Stanley polarizes restitution as a reform movement and modernization as a threat and then sees "holiness" as a means of negotiating between them. But Stanley also grants much to the seductive and embracing powers of modernity—her use of the "dancing" metaphor or image serves her well—to show how it is inescapable and has to be and will be related to however much tension—her choice of terms—such relating generates.

The subtleties that go with sorting out the primitive and the modern and then seeing them interrelate receive subtle treatment from Grant Wacker, who suggests that the pentecostal polarity is between "primitive" and "pragmatic," the second of which, one notes, is often associated with an aspect of modernity. These are opposites, says Wacker, but they both attract and they both appear in pentecostalisms.

Then come the Mormons. Thomas G. Alexander shows how Mormons successfully negotiate as they pick and choose their restorationist way through modernity. Still another set of communities are here coded as "Mennonite." Theron Schlabach picks up the theme of "discipleship" as the Mennonite way of paralleling primitivism, over against arguments from John Howard Yoder.

By the end, one may well be awed by the variety and complexity that characterize the theme of "primitivism" and by the ways scholars have tried to do justice to partly contradictory, sometimes overlapping, and occasionally congruent subcommunities in American religion. Where does that leave us? There is already enough complexity and confusion in the world. Do we need more exemplifications of this, more blurrings of lines, more stirrings of complacencies in matters of consensus? Answer: We do. But that does not mean that we have to be left in a shadowy thicket. The authors are not here to confuse but to clarify; it happens only that what they are out to clarify eludes simple straitjacketing. I want to stress the ways in which they deal with examples and the exemplary.

On Defining "Primitivism" and "Modernization"

"Primitivism" and "modernization" elude simple definition, and the
contributors to this volume certainly do not agree on definitional issues. Rather than complicate further an already complicated scene, it
seems more profitable to ask at this stage, Why care? Why put energy
into connecting two elusive and protean concepts, especially using a
further problematic one—the "denomination"—as an instrument for
doing the connecting?

The motive behind the inquiries concerning "primitivism" is very
clear. It happens that millions of Americans belong to church bodies
whose vision and program can somehow be connected with concepts
such as "the primitive" and "restoration" or "restitution." Something
of their outlook finds a match in other religious movements and the
larger culture. Why does this impulse exist and why do people act upon
it? One way to address such questions is to hold that impulse up against
another concept, "modernization." That is a code word for a complex
of events and phenomena that surround these church people and their
contemporaries.

The people who call for a response to "primitivism" and those who
do the responding are seldom interested in defining "modernization."
They may only rarely use the term or in only a few cases be familiar
with what it means. Instead we can hypothesize that they are doing
what people have always had to do: they are trying to make sense of
the reality around them so that they can live their lives as they will and
must. They must reach somewhere beyond themselves for reference
points, models, and patterns.

The conventional term for the object of their search for a mode
of Christian existence is *paradigm*. The etymological reference behind that term (*paradeiknunai*) is "to exhibit beside, show side by
side"; the result is "a pattern, exemplar, example." However, in the
case of primitivism, the restoration of "the ancient order of things,"
a different word with, of course, a different etymology is more appropriate since it brings out the singularity of the pattern. This is *exemplum*. Behind it is *eximere*, "to take out; . . . the primary sense is
thus 'something taken out.'"

Now for a metaphor relating to "modernization." In medieval Latin, we learn, the taking out associated with *exemplum* meant "a clearing in the woods." In 1883 Charles de Fresne Du Cange, in his *Glos-
sarium mediae et infimae latinitatis*, gave as the second of three
definitions of *exemplum*, "woods or brush cleared for cultivation."[1] We
picture modern life as the figurative woods, the set of circumstances

surrounding Alexander Campbell, Barton Stone, Joseph Smith, and various other nineteenth-century leaders and their heirs as well as their followers at the end of the twentieth century. They found themselves in a dark wood, a bewildering thicket, a mix of secular lures and sacred competitors. They must find their way or their place. Since these leaders set out to persuade others, by spoken or written word, to adopt the *exemplum* that they found persuasive, we profitably see their use of "the primitive," or restoration to "the ancient order of things," as a rhetorical device or strategy.

John D. Lyons developed the medieval sense of the *exemplum* for our modern application; the often forgotten sense of the term as "a clearing in the woods"

> sheds light on many characteristics of the rhetorical figure, example. Only the clearing gives form or boundary to the woods. Only the woods permit the existence of a clearing. Likewise, example depends on the larger mass of history and experience, yet without the "clearings" provided by example that mass would be formless and difficult to integrate into any controlling systematic discourse. Most of all, the clearing, the *exemplum,* posits an inside and an outside—in fact, the clearing creates an outside by its existence.[2]

To apply the metaphor or historical circumstances at once: "the larger mass of history and experience" was the rich but confusing set of options among competitors for the claim that each alone possessed Christian truth. Alexander Campbell and his contemporaries found it urgent to settle the issue; they needed a clearing provided by example so that they could integrate experiences and then proceed with their believing and living.

For Aristotle, the use of example was one of only two ways to argue rhetorically, the other being "enthymeme." In matters of faith there was no way to produce logically certain truths, as the use of enthymemes would have intended—though in his rationalism Alexander Campbell sometimes suggested reliance on such proof—so example alone was effective. Again, for Aristotle there were two sorts of examples to adduce: the invented or fabulous or fictional on one hand and, on the other, "one which consists in relating things that have happened before." Cicero elaborated on this relevant one by locating examples in *historia,* "an account of actual occurrences remote from the recollection of our own age."[3]

Campbell and company were not interested in being historians, in narrating remote actual occurrences for the sake of narration. They and their followers had a more desperate agenda, which we have just described as acts of interpretation for the living of life. Lyons throws further light that we can apply to their quest when he says that "the term *exemplum* reveals the importance of the idea of reproducivity in example, for *exemplum* denotes both the model to be copied and the copy or representation of that model."[4]

For a second time we move from an instant application of the metaphor of *exemplum* as "clearing in the woods" to the circumstances and rhetorical task of the pioneer American denominational primitivists. They used the primitive Christian church as they learned of it and grasped its outlines in the New Testament and most particularly in the Acts of the Apostles. That church was reproducible; it was "the model to be copied" and the contemporary primitivist congregations were a "representation of that model."

The use of primitive Christianity as a model for reproduction and representation was at the heart of the Campbellite, Stoneite, and other pure primitivist movements. In the medieval metaphor: these helped the followers determine what was "outside"—in this case, all the denominations that allowed for complexity and postprimitive history and tradition(s)—and what was "inside"—the nondenomination or movement of Disciples of Christ who reproduced in pattern and represented in rhetoric that earliest Christian church.

If primitive Christianity was to be the *exemplum,* the "clearing in the woods," everything outside the circle of reproduction and representation was the woods itself. In this volume it passes under the code name *modernity* or *modernization.* All other Christians than those in their clearing, argued these primitivists, were outside, wandering, wayward, or lost. If they wanted to escape the darkness of the woods and the loss of definition they experienced with it, they had to be "taken out" or to "come out" of the woods; the reference to "come-outers" is frequent in these essays. Staying in the woods, not following or being the *exemplum,* was impermissible for those who would be Christians. Sooner or later all would-be believers who possessed goodwill must themselves come out into the clearing to share the benefits of early Christian life as reproduced in modern times.

The Complication: The Fall into the Hermeneutical Circle

If what E. M. Cioran has called "the fall into time," what Mircea Eliade spoke of as "the fall into history," what classic American historians thought of as what we might call a "fall into complexity" had concerned the primitivist rhetoricians, though they may not have used the terms associated with those three "falls,"[5] they themselves were not aware of another kind of fall. They certainly would have resisted being seen as part of it. This is what we might call, a bit inelegantly, the fall into hermeneutics, into the hermeneutical circle. Such a fall means, as numbers of essays on irony point out here, that they were unwitting and unwilling victims of one feature of modernity: the realization that all interpreters bring something to interpretation. They bring preunderstandings to the understandings they draw from texts, precedents, models, and *exempla* off which they would live.

Each of these primitivist groups saw everyone outside its clearing in the woods as being colored by its assumptions. The restorationists simply did not see and would not recognize that they also brought their own. As several essayists here point out, numbers of these preunderstandings derived very directly from the Enlightenment. To paraphrase Langdon Gilkey, the restitutionists were to their belief structure about reason what the Greeks were to Hellenism. Their belief structure created an envelope around them from which they could not escape.

The nineteenth-century rhetorical and denominational woods were full of clearings, *exempla,* that were designed to attract respondents and followers. The primitivists who did the clearing were convinced that in modern times believers could, and that their particular set of believers did, authentically replicate whatever was important in the early church as narrated in the Acts of the Apostles. Everyone else to some degree strayed into the figurative woods of history, tradition, complexity, modernity, or even intentional faithlessness. Latter-day Saint prophet Joseph Smith thought the Campbellites did this; the Campbellites in turn thought the Mormons did so; both considered that all nonprimitivists, nonrestorationists, a priori thus wandered and were lost.

The Irony of It All

Various essayists here speak of the consequent ironies of primitivist situations. The Disciples of Christ turned their back on history yet they made one grand exception for the New Testament accounts, not realizing all the historical baggage that came with these. They did not want to be fallen into history, but they made history and became part of its stream. They bade others come into their clearing but soon fell out with each other and fought over the boundaries and definitions of their *exempla.* They did not want to see denominationalism thrive and ended up creating new denominations. The authors of essays on these themes now and then warn lest later interpreters treat the primitivists with condescension because of these ironies; yet few can resist pointing to their existence.

About one thing these observers or critics seem to be agreed: none of the primitivists wanted to live "back there" in New Testament times or thought they could have if they wanted to. To draw models from some other time, as everyone does reflectively or reflexively, does not mean that they could move back to primitive days. They used the past for the sake—of what? Many of the debates over primitivism in the restorationist denominations, and between them and others, have to do with futures. This is not the place to recount all the discussions of pre- and post- and a-millennialism or apocalypticism among people of the primitivist persuasion. Even the founding leaders of the Disciples of Christ or the Churches of Christ and their most noted successors did not agree on these futures or even on their relative importance.

Of course, as people of faith and hope they looked to God's future prepared for them. But the adducing of the experience of other denominational traditions in this collection shows how determinative eschatology was for these others, while it was a relatively arbitrary element among the themes of the core primitivist tradition.

What they were concerned with, I gather is the consensus of these authors, was the present: living in the now, making sense of the woods around them. Some radicals among them may have carried "come-out-erism" to extremes, as David Edwin Harrell Jr. finds some of the socially alienated doing. They wanted to be world-deniers who would turn their back on concerns of the nation, the workaday world, or culture. But far more of them celebrated life in America in the nineteenth and twentieth centuries, in the circles of Disciples, Churches of Christ, or the fundamentalist, Holiness, pentecostal, Mormon, and Radical Reformation groups that inhabited the penumbra of primitivist clearings. They were not escaping to the pristine past but trying to replicate it in the present. That is why so many authors find it congenial to speak of people in all these traditions as being "moderns," albeit of peculiar sorts.

The Comparativist Illumination

This book is dedicated to the notions accompanying comparativism in history. One can study the elements of primitivism in isolation from the rest of the world and certainly from each other. The comparative attempt (and, of course, all historical reference is somehow comparative) consciously sets things side by side—now we *are* talking about "paradigms" in the etymological sense—in order to illumine features that might otherwise escape notice. Etymology helps us again: *paradeiknumi* picks up on *deiknumi,* which means "to bring to light, to show

forth." Comparativism ill serves the historian if it provides straitjack-
ets, Procrustean beds, brushes for tarring with guilt by association, or
motives for lumping together common enemies to produce a better
target for opposition. It seeks a kind of light and showing.

R. Scott Appleby in his comments on fundamentalism, as already
noted, reflects the main motifs of comparative studies in the Fundamentalism Project he codirected. These are pursued not so that our
scholars can suggest that the Gush Emunim on the West Bank in Israel is "just like" the Muslim Brotherhood in Egypt or Bob Jones University in South Carolina. These studies instead try to bring to light
and show forth elements that otherwise might go overlooked. For just
one sample, Appleby has effectively shown that primitivism does not
equal fundamentalism and is not always fundamentalist, and that fundamentalism does not equal primitivism and is not always primitivist.
From such evidence drawn from comparative studies we have been able
to help correct widely held notions that fundamentalists are premodern fossils, leftovers from earlier stages of human development, mis-
interpreters of the signs of the times, static reactionaries. They tend
instead to be creatures of modernity, emergent in contemporary conditions, excellent readers of the signs, dynamic, and reactive.

So it is with primitivisms when compared across the boundaries of
denominational families. Denominations are often neglected or despised in public life by observers of American culture and even by sociologists of religion and theologians of an ecumenical age that is clut-
tered with parachurches. But if we think of denominations as "clearings
in the woods," attempts to find *exempla* for measuring what is inside
and what is outside, for establishing some sort of boundaries, it becomes
clear that comparing their attitudes toward the primitive will tell much
about how particular groups of people relate to modernity.

Some have done so with more reference to specific futures than have
the primitivists. This is the case with premillennial fundamentalists, as
George Marsden has depicted them. Others have done so with more
reference to developing and not so specifically defined futures. This is
the case with the definitely primitivist Mormons, as Thomas G. Alexander sees them. The Latter-day Saints' understanding of progressive
revelation kept them from relying on the single *exemplum* of the early
church.

In a conference paper Grant Underwood quoted E. R. Dodds on
early Christianity and related that experience to the Latter-day Saint
experience to find an *exemplum* for Mormonism's "exclusiveness," its
refusal to concede any value to alternative forms of worship. Of course,
this meant a figurative "clearing in the woods": such exclusiveness in

early Christianity and in Mormon times "lifted the burden of freedom from the shoulders of the individual: one choice, one irrevocable choice, and the road to salvation was clear."[6]

However, the Mormon *exemplum* package was not as restrictive as that of the Disciples of Christ. The Mormon *exemplum* included in its primordium the accounts of ancient Israel, especially in the Exodus but also with reference to sacrifice and plural marriage and, more drastically, "modern prophetic pronouncement," the speeches and writings of Mormon leaders since the time of Joseph Smith. One hardly needs the arts of subtle comparativists to see how different Mormon primitives were from Campbellite and Stoneite sorts. Thus Underwood: "Mormons are as committed as any primitivist to the proposition that the word of God proclaims the divine will, but for them the word of God was meant to be continuous rather than confined to past pronouncement."[7] Thus the Saints had what the Disciples did not have and did not want: "both the relevancy of modern revelation and the normativeness of divine decree." Underwood saw that this combination enabled Mormons to cope with modernization; thus functionally it served as the primitive *exemplum* did for the Disciples and the Church of Christ: it helped situate them in the present.

The comparativist historian notes similarities and differences in a fresh way by lifting out the primitivist element in the Holiness and pentecostal traditions as well. In a conference paper Melvin E. Dieter pointed to a significant pentecostalist departure, one that the Disciples and Church of Christ rejected: the claim that their movement was a "'de novo' act of God." The point for Disciple primitives was precisely that their movement was not something new; instead it was a replication and reliving of the old act of God that was the early Christian church in the Acts of the Apostles. Thus the Holiness movement, for all its love of the pure and simple and early, was "reformationist and traditionalist" more than "primitivist/restitutionist." Yet Dieter also saw the two movements webbed and somehow wedded. The Holiness movement was "a tradition torn between the two polarities of restitution and reform." It was ecclesiastically primitive with a vengeance, but its experiential primitivism led Holiness to offer something new, something that seemed to appeal to later constituencies with more efficiency and effectiveness than the purer and more restrictive primitivists have been able to do around the world.[8]

Similarly Susie C. Stanley rejected the notion that the Wesleyan/ Holiness movement was antimodern or countermodern or, by fossilizing definitions, fundamentalist. Poised as it must be between its "primitive heritage" and its "education, which has been shaped by modernity," the movement loses some people to modernity and holds others who avoid the pull of modernity. Still others use the Wesleyan/Holiness theme to engage in "questioning modernity's assumptions from a postmodern perspective." No doubt that can be done by more dedicated primitivists as well.

As for pentecostalism, the move beyond the *exemplum* of ecclesiastical primitivism is even more bold. One might say, on Grant Wacker's evidence, that what speaking in tongues symbolized was the real "clearing in the woods" taken from early Christianity and projected into the present and the future. For pentecostals, modernity is not, in Wacker's terms, a "package deal"; one might also say from his portrayal, neither is pentecostalism. To extend the figure: pentecostals evidently tolerate a less defined, less bounded clearing in the woods than do pure primitivists. They are more ready than these restorationists to improvise interpretations of the early Christian experience and to set out to realize them in surprising ways. Wacker sees in pentecostals a combination of primitivist and pragmatist strains that may very well have analogues in Disciples of Christ and Church of Christ bodies. But the pentecostals use a "whatever the cost" approach to receive charismatic gifts and experience pentecostal experiences in the present and the future. They therefore do not simply "yearn" somehow to return to a time before time, to a space outside of space in the "ancient order of things." Wacker's essay contributes to the definition of what isolates the denominational primitives from others who share something of the primitivist vision.

We are left, then, with a mix of denominational traditions, all of which share a passion for primitive Christianity, but none of which does with it quite what the various strands issuing from Campbell, Stone, and others do. The essay by David Edwin Harrell Jr. points to some of these variations. Harrell lets us in on arguments over the interpretation of primitivism from within the clearing, thereby illustrating some of the complexity about the notion of a simple return. Like almost every contributor to this volume, Harrell shows that the pioneer rhetoricians he treats were anything but antimodern. They lived in the woods of modernity, but simply chose a particular clearing by referring to the early Christian *exemplum*. His Disciples negotiated with modernity by being extremely individualistic, but always in the context of that primitivism. Harrell depicts how extreme liberalism and modernism, *Christian Century* style, culturally adaptive seekers of respectability, and the socially alienated could all find help from primitivism as they defined the inside and the outside of their common life by reference to this *exemplum*. So there could be, Harrell says, ill-defined pre- and post-

and a-millennial interpretations. Only one common element mattered: a return to the past for the sake of the present was at issue for these early modern people. And if Stanley thought the Holiness people could be postmodern, Harrell carried the game further by pointing to post-postmoderns at an Abilene Christian University conference.[9] Many primitivist scholars seem to have landed squarely in the hermeneutical circle after their fall.

Harrell ends with a reference to contemporary diversity of an order that exceeds the nineteenth-century diversity that he had noted earlier. At the root of everything, the only important uniting element, is "the movement's primitivist plea." It is quite clear that this plea is not the root of the other movements however congenial they found primitivism to be. The modernist Disciples abandon true primitivism; others celebrate the America that is, making only nominal reference to their *exemplum*, while still others use it to keep their clearing clear since the woods of modernity around them are full of hostile forces.

Can the Primitivist Center Hold, the Impulse Remain?

If division on the lines of this threefold set of interpretations threatens the demise of the primitivist stronghold, one wonders where next it will find its pure form of expression. Few of the contributors think that the impulse will go away; it is simply blended elsewhere with other elements by people who need different strategies and devices for coping with and transcending the modernity that they, and we, cannot easily define. The questions for ecclesiastical primitivism are: Can the center hold? Will the restitutionist *exemplum,* in its purest and thus most impelling form, survive to invigorate the others—by example?

Notes

1. Quoted by John D. Lyons in *Exemplum: The Rhetoric of Example in Early Modern France and Italy* (Princeton: Princeton University Press, 1989), 3, 241; I depend on Lyons for further development of the rhetorical concept.
2. Ibid., 3.
3. Ibid., 6–8. Lyons quotes Aristotle, *Rhetoric* 1.2.1356b and 2.20.1293a–b, and Cicero, *De inventione* 1.19.
4. Lyons, *Exemplum,* 11.
5. E. M. Cioran, *The Fall into Time,* trans. Michael Howard (Chicago: Quadrangle Books, 1970); on the fall into history, see "Autobiographical Fragment," in Norman J. Girardot and Mac Linscott Ricketts, *Imagination and Meaning: The Scholarly and Literary Worlds of Mircea Eliade* (New York:

Seabury, 1982), 124; David W. Noble, *Historians against History: The Frontier Thesis and the National Covenant in American Historical Writing since 1830* (Minneapolis: University of Minnesota Press, 1965); in the fall into history George Bancroft, Frederick Jackson Turner, Charles A. Beard, Carl Becker, Vernon Parrington, and Daniel Boorstin are pictured as being devoted to "innocence" over against urban-industrial (European) complexity.

6. Grant Underwood, "Primitivism and the Latter-day Saints," paper presented at the conference "Christian Primitivism and Modernization: Coming to Terms with Our Age," Pepperdine University, Malibu, Calif., 1991.

7. Ibid.

8. Melvin E. Dieter, "Primitivism in the American Holiness Tradition: Historic Strengths and Weaknesses," paper presented at the conference "Christian Primitivism and Modernization: Coming to Terms with Our Age," Pepperdine University, Malibu, Calif., 1991.

9. David Edwin Harrell Jr., "Epilogue," in Richard T. Hughes, ed., *The American Quest for the Primitive Church* (Urbana: University of Illinois Press, 1988), 239–45.

PART 1

Primitivism and Fundamentalism

Primitivism as an Aspect of Global Fundamentalisms

R. SCOTT APPLEBY

Given my role in developing a series of conferences and publications that attempt to analyze a broad range of disparate phenomena—diverse, religiously inspired reactions to modernity—by organizing their presentation around a term as problematic and potentially misleading as *fundamentalism*,[1] I came to this project on *primitivism* with a great deal of accumulated sympathy for others who would attempt such an enterprise. In his introduction to *The American Quest for the Primitive Church*, Richard T. Hughes adopted the terms *restorationism* and *primitivism* in much the same way as we used *fundamentalism*. That is, he hoped the terms, as he employed them, would be "more suggestive than prescriptive" and thus "add depth and texture to the possible interpretations of this theme in American history." Hughes thus provided but "minimal definitions at the outset and sought to allow various definitions and distinctions to be drawn by the practitioners within the various groups that we would explore." It would then be left to specialists in the individual traditions "to make sense of the variety of ways in which the reversional orientation has been employed and nuanced in 350 years of American history."[2]

To his credit Hughes cited Henry Bowden's somewhat disheartening evaluation of the results of this strategy: "The meaning of the term [*restoration*] is relative to different people who appropriate it, to what they say it means, and to what activities they pursue under its aegis. Based on historical usage of institutional, doctrinal and biblical categories, there is no meaning intrinsic to the title, and we can find no common agreement on any set of organizational forms or ideas."[3] This is the comparativist's worst nightmare: the analytical constructs will die the death of a thousand qualifications and thus be rendered useless for the task of developing a coherent and coordinated view of disparate but nonetheless clearly related phenomena.

I do not agree that this fate has befallen either *primitivism* or *fundamentalism*. At this stage of the research such a verdict would be pre-emptive of the process required in order to form valid conclusions about this particular comparative method. Whether or not the respective terms can be given sufficient nuance so as to enhance our overall understanding of modern religion depends in part upon a sustained commitment to the process of examining various movements and denominations according to informed hypotheses about what they may hold in common. This process requires project directors to proceed exactly as Hughes has done, that is, by commissioning essays on separate movements or denominations in their particularities, while providing a flexible, not to say elastic, "definition" of the controlling construct.

Two qualifying comments are necessary regarding my use of the term *fundamentalism*. First, I will refer primarily to manifestations of fundamentalism in various religious traditions after 1970, not to its historical manifestations in the nineteenth century or the earlier part of the twentieth. In this period, I argue, one side of a historical dialectic within fundamentalism (the political-activist) has been emphasized at the expense of the other (the primitivist-separatist). Second, I will not focus on American Christianity as the primary point of reference. In the study of global fundamentalisms the American Christian variant is, surprisingly, something of an anomaly. This is true in large part because American fundamentalism has developed in the most modernized and vital democracy in history—one with a powerful set of civil institutions serving as a buffer between individuals or social movements on the one hand and the government on the other. Such an environment has presented American fundamentalists with a set of choices and possible paths of development—opportunities as well as constraints—unlike any other around the world.

Employing *fundamentalism* and *primitivism* in the general hypothetical senses described above requires the comparativist constantly to revise his or her working definition as valid specific objections are raised about any one of the generalizations upon which the general model is based. At this juncture in the research, a suitable working definition of global fundamentalism built upon case studies of comparable movements within Islam, Christianity, Judaism, Hinduism, Sikhism, and Buddhism includes the following elements:

> Global fundamentalism has emerged in this century as a tendency, a habit of mind, found within religious communities and par-

adigmatically embodied in certain representative individuals and movements. It manifests itself as a strategy, or set of strategies, by which beleaguered believers attempt to preserve their distinctive identity as a people or group. Feeling this identity to be at risk in the contemporary era, they fortify it by a selective retrieval of doctrines, beliefs, and practices from a sacred past. These retrieved "fundamentals" are refined, modified, and sanctioned in a spirit of shrewd pragmatism: they are to serve as a bulwark against the encroachment of outsiders who threaten to draw the believers into a syncretistic, areligious, or irreligious cultural milieu. Moreover, these fundamentals are accompanied in the new religious portfolio by unprecedented claims and doctrinal innovations. By the strength of these innovations and the new supporting doctrines, the retrieved and updated fundamentals are meant to regain the same charismatic intensity today by which they *originally forged* communal identity from the formative revelatory religious experiences long ago.

In this sense contemporary fundamentalism is at once both derivative and vitally original. In the effort to reclaim the efficacy of religious life, fundamentalists have more in common than not with other religious revivalists and primitivists of past centuries. But fundamentalism intends neither an artificial imposition of archaic practices and life-styles nor a simple return to a golden era, a sacred past, a bygone time of origins—although nostalgia for such an era is a hallmark of fundamentalist rhetoric. Instead, religious identity thus renewed becomes the exclusive and absolute basis for a recreated political and social order that is oriented to the future rather than the past. By selecting elements of tradition and modernity alike, fundamentalists seek to remake the world in the service of a dual commitment to the unfolding eschatological drama (by returning all things in submission to the divine) and to self-preservation (by neutralizing the threatening "Other"). Such an endeavor often requires charismatic and authoritarian leadership, depends upon a disciplined inner core of adherents, and promotes a rigorous sociomoral code for all followers. Boundaries are set, the enemy identified, converts sought, and institutions created and sustained in pursuit of a comprehensive reconstruction of society.[4]

From this working definition I will advance a general thesis about the relationship between global fundamentalism and primitivism. While there is a primitivist impulse within fundamentalist movements, it is not the defining characteristic of these movements. Fundamentalisms are not primarily concerned with, or committed to, a restoration of the time of origins and pristine purity (what Arthur O. Lovejoy and George Boas term a "chronological primitivism"); nor are the various programs of fundamentalists in different religious traditions an expression of a "cultural primitivism" proceeding from "the yearning of the civilized for a simpler, less complex world."[5] (By invoking both of these types of primitivism I mean to indicate that I am using the term in its broadest sense to include any reversionist orientation, whether one is reverting to the time of origins or to a subsequent time of purity, or "golden age.") Fundamentalists by and large do not call for or attempt the unmodified or "pure" reappropriation and reapplication of the norms of a privileged historical, or prehistorical, moment; nor is their *primary* concern a return to biblical times or norms. They are not, that is, strict primitivists or strict "biblicists."

This is not to say that the primitivist-restorationist and fundamentalist programs are unrelated. In certain areas of fundamentalist corporate religious life and behavior, primitive or scriptural norms may be applied and sanctioned; in some traditions, these retrieved norms often seem to function as a kind of qualifying test for membership in the inner circle or hard-core cadre of leaders and decision makers. Both fundamentalisms and primitivisms sustain a critique of the present religious order and direct the reform of religious life and practice by drawing upon sacred sources of revelation and law. Both privilege the communities to which these sources were entrusted and see these communities as normative (although, as we shall see, in different ways). Both fundamentalists and restorationists-primitivists tend to interpret these sacred sources and normative traditions in such a way as to preserve and, indeed, stridently emphasize their transcendent character (which is thereby scandalous to modern sensibilities). Both believe that modernity and modernization processes have introduced a corrupting and disfiguring element into traditional religious life. Both fundamentalism and primitivism (if not restorationism, as defined above) may in fact also privilege certain historical moments within the now-eroded traditional way of life.

Despite these affinities, however, fundamentalists differ substantively from primitivists and restorationists in regard to the understanding and diagnosis of modernity (including its scope and its essential nature); the programs of action to be followed by religiously responsible agents living within modernity and under the impact of modernization; and the strategies for achieving those programs. These basic differences proceed from different understandings and interpretations of the modernizing process and from different convictions about its long-term consequences.

Fundamentalism as a Modern Construct

Fundamentalists are neither traditionalists nor primitivists; rather, contemporary fundamentalists may be seen as latter-day modernists. That is, fundamentalists may be seen as late twentieth-century inheritors and transformers of the programs of religious modernism that were attempted (and failed miserably, say the fundamentalists) at an earlier phase of the modernizing process, in the late nineteenth century and the early twentieth. Indeed, fundamentalisms formed initially in reaction to these modernisms. Modernism has been variously defined, but it may be summarized as an attempt to establish a viable synthesis between "the ancient faith and modern thought"[6] in order to preserve a vital and meaningful role for religion within traditional societies that have been exposed to, and at least partially transformed by, critical historical consciousness, scientific rationality, and other elements of the Enlightenment.

The first generation of modernists, it is now clear, privileged the contributions of modernity in the attempt to build the synthesis. Many of them did so self-consciously. In this sense contemporary fundamentalists would recoil at being seen as modernists, since it is religion rather than modernity that they aim to privilege. However, they are clearly involved in constructing a synthesis between the two. And the results of these efforts demonstrate that, once again, modernity is setting the terms for religious adaptation. Fundamentalists are agents of modernization; the religion of the modernizing fundamentalist is often a hybrid rather than a synthesis of modernity and tradition.

Fundamentalists are preoccupied with modernity, they are among its shrewdest and most perceptive observers, and they are growing exceedingly skilled in imitating its behavioral patterns and appropriating its instrumentalities. Thus, when contemporary fundamentalists privilege primitive norms and supernatural revelation, they do so within the context of some level of commitment to this rapprochement with modernity. Forewarned by the failures of the earlier generation of modernists, fundamentalists must live with the consequences of those failures even as they try to undo them by constructing a new synthesis that privileges, rhetorically and sociopolitically, the fundamentals of religious faith that the earlier modernists allowed historical criticism and secular rationality to erode.

In Islam the situation is summarized by the word *West-toxification*, a malady that infected the Westernized Muslim elite who uncritically followed the path of early Islamic modernists.[7] According to this diagnosis, a too-ready accommodation to the West amounted in practice to an abandonment of *dar 'ul-Islam* and led to the poisoning of the religious-traditional wellsprings of authentic Islamic life. A crisis of identity ensued with the failure of substitutionary secular and nationalist ideologies such as pan-Arabism, Nasserism, and revolutionary Marxism. In articulating the depths of this crisis and in responding initially to it, the first generation of Islamic fundamentalists across the Arab world (1930–65) did speak a kind of primitivist language: "the crisis may be met effectively only by a re-ordering of society according to Islamic principles." But this primitivist impulse was tempered in the second generation (1965–95) by the requirements of Muslim political accommodation in Algeria, Egypt, Pakistan, Iran, and even postwar Iraq. Since the Iranian revolution of 1978–79, Muslim politicians have become aware firsthand of the myriad complexities and ambiguities involved in governing a modern "Islamic state," or even a discrete Islamic society, while preserving structurally a meaningful fidelity to the norms and laws found in the Qur'an and in the Sunna of the Prophet.[8]

A somewhat similar evolution began in the 1960s at an accelerated pace among Hindu "fundamentalists" (also referred to as "communalists" or "Hindu nationalists"). Within a generation, these religious activists journeyed from the margins to the center of Indian political life by virtue of their participation in the World Hindu party (or VHP [Vishwa Hindu Parishad]), a cultural organization, and the Bharatiya Janata party (BJP), a powerful political party. In the 1990s Hindu activist leaders attempted to moderate the exclusivist and doctrinaire stance that undermines coalition politics. Yet, the hard-core leadership continued to sustain a rhetoric of purification and "Hinduness" drawn from selected epics and legends.[9]

In asserting that fundamentalists are committed to transforming the "world," therefore, one must recognize that this "world" includes the reality beyond the local church, mosque, or temple and even beyond the larger religious community (the Islamic *umma* or the Christian church). Furthermore, the very comprehensiveness and ambition of this impulse demands that fundamentalists attempt to remake the outside world not in the image of the pristine religious community (although scriptural and traditional "blueprints" revealed to this community are privileged resources) but along the lines of an envisioned order that appropriates the opportunities, and eliminates the dangers, of modernity by a very specific kind of fidelity to "primitive truths." The "discourse of primitivism" has in the past played an important limiting role in the construction of this new order; that is, it has established barriers to innovation, boundaries within which modernization may proceed.[10] Whether the primitivist discourse can survive increasing levels of participation in the discourse of modernization remains to be seen.

As latter-day modernists, fundamentalists are oriented not to the past but to the future. The coming time of redemption does not, however, require a withdrawal into a protective cocoon of pristine religiosity, but rather an active and progressivist engagement with the world that is being destroyed and rebuilt. "Return" is not an option or even a desideratum; even effective separation or withdrawal in anticipation of the final vindication became increasingly difficult in the previous generation, so much so that the generation of fundamentalists living in the 1990s—within Islam, Judaism, Hinduism, Sikhism, and Christianity—was more directly engaged with the outside world and working within its structures and on its terms than was any previous generation.[11] Separatism, fundamentalism, and primitivism are an increasingly unlikely trio. I shall return to this point.

Fundamentalists thus wish neither to escape modernity nor to repudiate it, but rather to shape it according to their own understanding of the role of a "privileged past" within a remade modern world. They are hegemonic in ambition but often accommodationist in practice, a situation that tends to weaken primitivist impulses.

Primitivism and Fundamentalism within Islam

To illustrate these patterns let us take the most prominent, widespread (and perhaps most controversial) example of a religious fundamentalism by considering the variegated efforts of Islamic movements across the Middle East and South Asia. In such movements contemporary Muslims seek to establish the Shari'a, the code of Islamic law, within nation-states resistant or openly hostile to religious law as a framework for political and legislative decisions, as well as social and cultural life. Described as "reactive" in their original inspiration, Islamic fundamentalisms are said to initially adopt a confrontational mode in response to what is experienced as the threat to the values and norms of a traditional way of life, whether that threat comes from a secular Westernized regime or from modernizing agents within the religious tradition. The fundamentalist response thus falls into a more generalized pattern of oppositional movements that strive to create an alternative order by which to compete with, or withdraw from, a threatening external order. Specifically, fundamentalists look to religious precepts, doctrines, and laws in creating and sanctioning the new order they seek to build. This pure and whole "new order" is also intended to be comprehensive, reaching into all aspects of life. This stated intention of many modern fundamentalisms also presents them with their greatest source of frustration within the irresistibly pluralist social, economic, and international contexts in which fundamentalists, as others, must operate today.

These reflections lead to two conclusions relevant to the discussion of Islamic fundamentalisms. First, Islamic fundamentalisms may share many traits of Islamic revivalisms, but the two phenomena are not identical. Fundamentalisms may indeed arise within, or in other cases lead to, a religious revival that features a general cultural and social but not explicitly political return to Islamic paradigms and juridical sources. There are movements within Islam that have exclusively followed what may be called a primitivist impulse; the best example perhaps are the *salafiyya* (pious ancestors) movements found across the Middle East and also in parts of central Asia and northwest China that seek self-consciously to return to the lifestyles and norms of the pious ancestors, the first generation of the Prophet and his followers.

It is important to note that the salafiyya and revivalist movements are not fundamentalisms. Fundamentalisms ultimately move toward the fundamentals, the determining principles and doctrines, not only of religious belief and practice, but especially of the polities in which they find themselves. Unlike the salafiyya movements, they are inherently political. Islamic fundamentalist political expression is varied; it may be evident in the politics of the enclave seeking to preserve itself within an alien temporality, in the politics of the democrat seeking to amass popular support for Islamism from below, or in the politics of the revolutionary seeking to impose the new/old order from above.

In each of these political expressions, it must be emphasized, fundamentalisms are necessarily involved in compromise and accommodation—often to the extent that, after a time, they can hardly any longer be described as "fundamentalist" in the sense of the original exclusivist, dogmatic, and confrontational mode that was central to the formative experience of the movement. Fundamentalisms inevitably become involved in modern political life and in so doing they participate in a common discourse about modernization, development, political structures, and economic planning. They may add nuances and modify the terms of that discourse; they may successfully or unsuccessfully try to redirect or reinvent aspects of it; but they are contained within it and find any hope of even a partial return to pristine Islam, much less the construction of a "purely" Islamic form of modern polity, well out of reach.[12]

This leads to a second consequence of considering Islamic fundamentalisms from a more generalized perspective. Fundamentalisms born in this century find themselves in a situation quite different from the one that gave rise to Saudi Arabia, the prototypical fundamentalist state in that it established a polity based on the Shari'a. Wahhabism, the religio-ideological basis of the Saudi state, originated and thrived within the framework of a traditional collaboration between the *ulama* (religious scholars) and the ruler, both of whom shared the basic goal of restoring pristine Islam. In this eighteenth-century context the Wahhabis were able to retrieve and shape whole a comprehensive system of jurisprudence that became a stable foundation for a conservative Islamic state. Unavoidable compromises with modernity were negotiated by a partnership of ulama and ruler. Contemporary fundamentalist movements—Islamists in Egypt, Algeria, Pakistan, and Jordan, for example—find themselves unable to contemplate the construction of such a state, for they are engaged fully in a continual round of negotiations with and accommodations to both the secular state and the revived and variegated Muslim populace. They live and move within the framework of twentieth-century secular rationality, even if they do not fully endorse it; their version of political Islam is necessarily a hybrid of Shari'a and selected elements of modern political ideologies ranging from democratic capitalism to Marxism.[13]

The Jamaat-i-Islami and the Tablighi Jamaat, the two most important Islamic movements of the south Asian subcontinent in the twentieth century, represent the divergence between fundamentalism and forms of revivalism based on a primitivist or restorationist impulse. The Jamaat-i-Islami places primary emphasis on the resacralization of political life and the establishment of an Islamic state with the Qur'an and the Sunna as its constitution and the Shari'a as its basic law. The Tablighi movement focuses its activities on the moral and spiritual uplift of individual believers, asking them to fulfill their religious obligations irrespective of whether there is an Islamic state or not. Both movements hold to a literalist interpretation of the Qur'an and the traditions of the Prophet and evince hostility toward Islamic liberalism; both claim that they are ultimately working for the revival of pristine Islam. Both are regarded as equally legitimate Islamic responses to the challenges of modernity and are thus mainstream rather than fringe movements. Both of them enjoy enormous support in certain important sectors of Indian, Pakistani, and Bangladeshi societies, and their influence has reached far beyond the country of their origin.

Apart from these similarities, there are important differences in their ideologies, organizations, and methods of *dawa'* (call)—differences that suggest that the Jamaat-i-Islami comes closer to a fundamentalist paradigm, while the Tablighi Jamaat approximates a "primitivist" or "resto-

rationist" orientation.[14] The Jamaat-i-Islami's emphasis on the Islamiza-
tion of politics and state has tended to transform the movement into a
modern cadre type of political party, while the Tablighi Jamaat's program
of strengthening the spiritual moorings of individual believers has helped
it retain its character as a da'wa (evangelical) movement. The Jamaat-i-
Islami is a highly structured, hierarchically organized, bureaucratic organization that has established a clear line of authority and a huge network of functional departments and nationwide branches; the Tablighi
Jamaat, on the other hand, is a free-floating religious movement with
minimal dependence on hierarchy, leadership positions, and decision-
making procedures. Although both are primarily lay movements with
minimal participation by the ulama, the Tablighi Jamaat is closer to traditional forms of Islam than is the Jamaat-i-Islami, which in its own self-
perception represents a synthesis of tradition and modernity.

According to the political scientist Mumtaz Ahmad, at its beginning
the Jamaat-i-Islami in Pakistan and elsewhere in the Muslim world
adopted Western ideas of organization, made full use of modern publishing technology, and accepted the Western premise of instrumental, if not substantive, rationality. They were thus able to communicate
with the large number of young people who had or were obtaining
Western education. Their strategy was not that of adaptation to the
West but of equality with and independence from the West, without
jeopardizing the prospects of using the technological benefits the West
had to offer. They wanted socioeconomic changes in their societies, and
in their pursuit of a share in political power were driven to radicalism.

The Jamaat-i-Islami does seek to restore the original teachings of
the Qur'an and the Sunna and to recreate the socioreligious system
established under the direct guidance of the Prophet and his first four
successors—"the rightly guided caliphs." At least in theory it tends to
reject the later developments in Islamic theology, law, and philosophy
as well as the institutional structures of historic Muslim societies that
evolved during the period of empires. In actual practice, however, like
most of the other fundamentalist groups, it does not deny outright the
legitimacy of historical Islam insofar as the legal-religious structures
of Islamic orthodoxy are concerned. The Jamaat-i-Islami upholds the
right to *ijtihad* (individual interpretation) and fresh thinking on matters not directly covered in the teachings of the Qur'an and the Sunna
and have shown a readiness to accept fresh thinking in the implementation of the socioeconomic and political teachings of traditional Islam:
political parties, parliaments, elections, and so forth. Their demand for
the establishment of an Islamic state and the introduction of an Islamic
constitution is their trademark. They criticize the conservative ulama

and the Tablighi Jamaat for reducing Islam to the five pillars—profession of faith, prayer, fasting, almsgiving, and pilgrimage. Islam is a complete system and a comprehensive way of life that covers the entire spectrum of human activity, be it individual, social, economic, or political. They present Islam as a dynamic and activist political ideology that must acquire state power in order to implement its social, economic, and political agenda. Ahmad writes,

> This brings us to one of the most important defining characteristics of the Jamaat-i-Islami and other Islamic fundamentalist movements: *unlike the conservative ulama and the modernists, the fundamentalist movements are primarily political rather than religio-intellectual movements.* While both the ulama and the modernists seek influence in public policy-making structures, the fundamentalists aspire to *capture* political power and establish an Islamic state on the prophetic model. They are not content to act as pressure groups, as are the ulama and the modernists. They want political power because they believe that Islam cannot be implemented without the power of the state. Finally, as lay scholars of Islam, leaders of the fundamentalist movements are not theologians but social thinkers and political activists. The main thrust of their intellectual efforts is the articulation of the socio-economic and political aspects of Islam.[15]

The Jamaat-i-Islami's founder, Maulana Maududi, gave a new language—a political language—to Islamic discourse. Terms and phrases first used by Maududi, such as "the Islamic system of life," "Islamic movement," "Islamic ideology," "Islamic politics," "the Islamic constitution," "the economic system of Islam," and "the political system of Islam," have now become common parlance for Muslim writers and political activists everywhere.

In contrast the "primitivist" Tablighi movement is a Muslim missionary response to militant Hindu efforts to convert Muslims in northern India. According to the historian Barbara Metcalf, the Tablighi Jamaat seeks to "purify" the borderline Muslims from their Hindu accretions by putting them in touch with pristine Islam; the focus of the movement is on making Muslims better and purer Muslims.[16] Tablighi workers are extremely rigid in following the orthodox rituals and do not approve of what they consider the "modernist" and lax attitudes of the Jamaat-i-Islami. They emphasize both the form and the spirit of the religious practices. Their insistence on conformity to Shari'a is uncompromising. They strongly believe in the seclusion of women and regard any secular education of girls as unnecessary and un-Islamic. They are

also very particular about preserving all outward forms of Islamic culture and following the Sunna of the Prophet to the letter. Most of them,
for example, keep the beard to its proper Shari'a length, wear their
trousers above their ankles, and cover their heads. The exclusive focus
of attention is the individual; they seem not to concern themselves with
issues of social significance, including the reform of political and social institutions. Political formulations of the basic Islamic beliefs and
concepts undermine the authentic religious core of Islamic values and
rob them of their spiritual significance.

While Islamists in Iran, Pakistan, and Egypt consider the acquisition
of political power and the establishment of an Islamic state a basic pre-
requisite for creating a truly Islamic society, the Tablighi Jamaat believes
that political power does not in itself ensure the effective organization
of an Islamic social order. It insists that political change must be preceded by, and consistently augmented with, the moral transformation of
individuals and society. Muslims have been called upon by the Qur'an
and the Prophet to organize themselves for religious purposes. An Islamic social organization is thus essentially a religiously based organization and is not necessarily an Islamic state. The task of organizing Muslims for religious purposes such as regular attendance at prayers,
collection and distribution of zakat, and the systematic propagation of
Islam need not depend on the establishment of an Islamic government
or a state; these are obligations that have to be undertaken by individual Muslims. Muslims may form local-level religious organizations and
appoint community leaders to supervise the observance of religious du-
ties, but the aims of such organizations will be fulfilled only if they are
carried out without the coercive and external power of the state.

How Modernity Draws Fundamentalisms away from Primitivism

The debate between these two Islamic movements, both initially
formed in order to preserve and "restore" pristine Islam, is a debate
about the nature of modernity, the modernizing process, and the appropriate response of would-be restorationist religious movements.[17]
These movements seek to resacralize land, space, and time; to reclaim
communities and whole nations for God. But fundamentalisms, unlike
primitivisms, are characterized by a religiopolitical response to modernization, that is, they seek to resacralize secularized territories by first
delimiting and controlling them politically.

My thesis—that fundamentalists are modernists and that this modernism relegates primitivist impulses to a secondary role in the social
construction of the movement—has a corollary. Fundamentalists have

sensed and understood the internal logic and the consequences of modernity in a way that restorationists have not. Rightly, it seems, they have interpreted the modernizing process as disruptive of particularized communities, that is, as destructive of human solidarities constructed upon "primordial" ties of ethnicity and religion. The British social philosopher Anthony Giddens, not writing on behalf of fundamentalists, nonetheless echoes the concerns of their treatises when he describes the consequences of modernity as entailing "the separation of time and space and their recombination in forms which permit precise time-space zoning of social life; [this leads to] . . . the disembedding of social systems—lifting them out from local and traditional contexts of interaction—and the self-reflexive ordering and reordering of social relations in light of continual inputs of knowledge affecting the actions of individuals and groups."[18] Modern technology, Giddens observes, relocates individuals across time and space and reconstitutes communities according to "continual inputs of knowledge" rather than according to traditional ties and norms. Modernization has shattered those traditional boundaries.

Self-proclaimed modernists have and continue to see this as a benevolent step toward universal harmony, a global community, the end of sectarianism. Fundamentalists are not convinced this is a good thing; they seek to direct the modernizing process differently by restricting its undisciplined interventions. Fundamentalists want to reestablish boundaries and often use scriptural or traditional norms ostensibly as a guideline in so doing. Set firmly against globalization and universalizing tendencies, the fundamentalist countertrend leads toward particularization, segmentation, partition.

A shrewd use of the instrumentalities of modernization plays an important role in this fundamentalist program. As control comes through the consolidation of power, fundamentalists perceive modern instrumentalities, as do we all, as exceedingly powerful and power-bequeathing. Modernity concentrates the power of world building in an unprecedented dynamism. The ideological virulence of fundamentalists, the initial noncompromising stance that is ultimately revealed as a negotiating posture, the will to power—these emerge not only from a sense of siege but from a conscious imitation of the enemy, secular rationality. So, too, does the progressive, adaptive dynamic of fundamentalists, which places them in tension with primitivists. Fundamentalists create hierarchies, strata, systems; they differentiate; within them, however, is also a paradoxical tendency toward de-differentiation, toward simplification, that proceeds from the primitivist or restorationist impulse that set them on the quest to engage modernity in the first place.

Throughout developing nations, this battle about paths of modernization is fully drawn. In India, for example, *communalism* is the word used to refer to fundamentalist Hindus; and "Universal Harmony" is the slogan of a coalition of liberal and moderate Indians formed to neutralize the influence of Hindu, Sikh, and Muslim communalists. Militant Hindu fundamentalism is "organized Hinduism" with strong canonical and doctrinal overtones. It seeks to redefine India as an explicitly Hindu nation with "Hindu-ness" as the essential requirement for full citizenship in the state. Muslims, Sikhs, and even Christians by this formula are not forced to convert but must practice and behave within the framework of civil laws privileging Hindu customs, rituals, memorial sites, and so on. This Hindu nationalist vision is constructed and presented as a modernizing program for Indian "development."[19]

Conclusion

The appearance of religious movements that imitate and adopt the organizational structures of secular competitors, with a resulting hardening of theology into ideology, is certainly nothing new, as historians of medieval Christianity well know. But the undeniable power and pervasiveness of the modernization process—which seems to grow annually at exponential rates—has posed the dilemma with unprecedented clarity to the believer who seeks to be both religious and politically responsible. The political scientist Glenn Tinder suggests one religiopolitical response that studiously avoids the hegemony-seeking side of many current fundamentalisms while preserving a primitivist-prophetic stance:

> I believe that the primary political requirement of Christianity is not a certain kind of society or a particular program of action but rather an attitude, a way of facing society and of undertaking programs of action. Christianity implies skepticism concerning political ideals and plans. For Christianity to be wedded indissolubly to any of them (as it often has been: "Christian socialism" and Christian celebrations of "the spirit of democratic capitalism" are examples) is idolatrous and thus subversive of Christian faith. Political ideals and plans must vary with times and circumstances. Christianity can indicate only how to stand in the times and circumstances in which—Christians believe—God places us. But that is a great deal. It can enable us to embrace political ideals and plans, which always reduce many people to the status of

means in relations to governmental ends, without betraying individuals exalted through Christ. It can show us how to live in temporal society as citizens of an eternal society.

It is essential to the prophetic stance that it is maintained only by individuals. It is not a standard for group action. A prophetic attitude might for a time be dominant within a group, but it necessarily causes every member to stand off from the group.

The objection may be made that the prophetic stance is therefore a recipe for weakness. I fully agree, if we are speaking of human strength and human weakness. A single, detached individual is nothing against the forces of history. Standing prophetically means being not only without set plans but also without power. The individual is solitary and exposed. Political organization and action are not ways of surmounting this condition, however, for the sense of solidarity and power thus gained is in truth illusory.[20]

Temporal weakness has not been the choice of the new generation of fundamentalist modernizers. The quest for a pristine purity has been a rhetorical and tactical rather than a substantive element in many of the religiopolitical movements known today as fundamentalisms. Primitivist or restorationist movements may well be socially involved and have politically committed members. But the world they seek to restore does not sit easily with the ambition of modern world conquerors.

The consequences of modernity are far more penetrating and transforming than we yet know. By proliferating options in the world, modernity seems, ironically, to have narrowed the choices of the religious revivalists. We see in our time a world-engaging fundamentalism that strays from religious fundamentals, primitive norms, and prophetic stances or reinterprets them in politically utilitarian terms. Yet there are other approaches to the challenges posed by modernity. Primitivism, as one of these, seeks to revive the corporate life, witness, and worship of the believing community while strengthening individual members in their prophetic stance toward the very kingdoms and nation-states that the fundamentalists seek to conquer.

Notes

1. From 1988 to 1994, I served as associate director of the Fundamentalism Project, an interdisciplinary study conducted by the American Academy of Arts and Sciences and based at the University of Chicago.

2. Richard T. Hughes, "Introduction: On Recovering the Theme of Recovery," in Richard T. Hughes, ed., *The American Quest for the Primitive Church* (Urbana: University of Illinois Press, 1988), 3.

3. Ibid., 2.

4. Martin E. Marty and R. Scott Appleby, "An Interim Report on a Hypothetical Family," in Martin E. Marty and R. Scott Appleby, eds., *Fundamentalisms Observed* (Chicago: University of Chicago Press, 1991), 824.

5. Quoted in Hughes, "Introduction," 3.

6. For a discussion of theological modernism in American Christianity, see William R. Hutchison, *The Modernist Impulse in American Protestantism* (Oxford: Oxford University Press, 1976), and R. Scott Appleby, "Church and Age Unite!" in *The Modernist Impulse in American Catholicism* (Notre Dame: University of Notre Dame Press, 1991).

7. See the discussion in Abdulaziz A. Sachedina's "Shi'ite Activism in Iran, Iraq, and Lebanon," in Marty and Appleby, eds., *Fundamentalisms Observed,* 406–20.

8. James Piscatori, "Religion and Realpolitik: Islamic Responses to the Gulf War," in James Piscatori, ed., *Islamic Fundamentalisms and the Gulf Crisis* (Chicago: American Academy of Arts and Sciences, 1991), 1–28.

9. Daniel Gold, "Organized Hinduisms: From Vedic Truth to Hindu Nation," in Marty and Appleby, eds., *Fundamentalisms Observed,* 531–35.

10. Everett Mendelsohn, "Religious Fundamentalism and the Sciences," in Martin E. Marty and R. Scott Appleby, eds., *Fundamentalisms and Society: Reclaiming the Sciences, the Family, and Education* (Chicago: University of Chicago Press, 1993), 23–35.

11. Bruce B. Lawrence, *Defenders of God: The Fundamentalist Revolt against the Modern Age* (San Francisco: Harper and Row, 1989), 25.

12. See Piscatori, "Religion and Realpolitik," xxii.

13. Ibid.

14. While the Tablighi Jamaat is a grass-roots movement with followers from all sections of society, the Jamaat-i-Islami's support base consists mainly of educated, lower middle-class Muslims from both the traditional and modern sectors of society.

15. Mumtaz Ahmad, "Islamic Fundamentalisms in South Asia," in Marty and Appleby, eds., *Fundamentalisms Observed,* 463–64.

16. Barbara D. Metcalf, "Remaking Ourselves: Islamic Self-Fashioning in a Global Movement of Spiritual Renewal," in Martin E. Marty and R. Scott Appleby, eds., *Accounting for Fundamentalisms: The Dynamic Character of Movements* (Chicago: University of Chicago Press, 1994).

17. The radical Sikhs provide another illustrative case. As T. N. Madan points out, historically there have been many sources of Sikhism and several definitions of who is a Sikh. Yet the Singh Sabha movement, led by Sikh cultural elites at the turn of the twentieth century who feared assimilation into a syncretistic Hindu society, narrowed the definitions to one and excluded those who did not conform to it. Prior to this time, "Sikhs and Hindus not only lived together in Punjab but also shared a common cultural life, with common sym-

bols and common cognitive and affective orientations." Sikhs had identified themselves in terms of village, cult, lineage, or caste and did not project a single Sikh identity. But this sense of threat, due to the upsurge of Hindu communalism represented by the Arya Samaj, forced the polarization of the Sikh community and the forging of a new identity. The Arya Samajists denied the autonomy of the Sikhs as a sociocultural community and launched a purificatory movement, aimed first at preventing the conversion of Hindus to Islam and Christianity, later at "reconverting" Sikhs. Inevitably, the Singh Sabhas retaliated and attempted to win latitudinarian Sikhs and Hindu admirers of the faith into the fold of the baptized and the unshorn. Boundaries were set in "the demarcation of Sikh sacred space by clearing holy shrines of Hindu icons and idols, the cultivation of Punjabi as the sacred language of the Sikhs, [and] the foundation of cultural bodies exclusively for youth." Instead of asserting a lost orthodoxy, these early radicals combined elements from diverse and often conflicting Sikh traditions so as to enhance the distinct nature of the religion—a move that resulted in a new and different Sikh identity, complete with ideology and practices commonly associated with Sikhism today. The contemporary heirs of the Singh Sabha movement have adopted the sense of threat and the crisis mentality. They consider themselves "pure Sikhs," defenders of the basic teachings of the Sikh gurus and the economic interests of the community. See Madan, "The Double-Edged Sword: Fundamentalism and the Sikh Religious Tradition," in Marty and Appleby, eds., *Fundamentalisms Observed*, 594–626.

18. Anthony Giddens, *The Consequences of Modernity* (Stanford: Stanford University Press, 1990), 16–17.

19. Robert Frykenberg, "Accounting for Hindu Fundamentalisms," in Marty and Appleby, eds., *Accounting for Fundamentalisms*, 591–614.

20. Glenn Tinder, *The Political Meaning of Christianity* (San Francisco: Harper, 1989), 8–9.

By Primitivism Possessed: How Useful Is the Concept "Primitivism" for Understanding American Fundamentalism?

GEORGE MARSDEN

In the pristine days of the study of American Christianity, i.e., when I was in graduate school, there were giants in the land. Among the greatest of these Nephilim was Sidney E. Mead. His book *The Lively Experiment* was, in my opinion, breathtakingly illuminating.

Among Mead's primal insights was the importance of the theme of primitivism in American Protestantism. This concept depicted an impulse that, once one thought of it that way, could be noticed all over the place in American religion. What Mead pointed out was that Protestant biblicism in America often tended toward historylessness. That is, it accentuated the authority of the original biblical faith and practice of the primitive church and asserted the irrelevance of historical traditions for discovering God's truth revealed in the Bible.[1]

I continue to have a high regard for the insights of Sidney Mead and for primitivism as an illuminating concept. I long have regarded primitivism as a particularly useful shorthand for a type of biblicism that appeals to the authority of Scripture alone and that therefore disparages the authority of traditions and tends toward historylessness. While this concept is especially influential in American religious groups that have been influenced by the Puritans, it appears also among Anabaptists and finds its most overt expressions in the nineteenth-century movements with Presbyterian backgrounds founded by Alexander Campbell and Barton Stone. Most American revivalist groups have some such primitivist biblicist tendencies.[2] Perhaps it is even legitimate to suggest, as does Winton Solberg, that the American Enlightenment involves a cultural primitivism that substitutes the book of nature for the Bible as the best source for discovering God's truth, uncorrupted by human traditions.[3] Richard T. Hughes and C. Leonard Allen have furnished us with valuable insights by bringing together many such themes and demonstrating the influence of this religiously rooted concept on American life and thought generally.[4]

Two Meanings of *Primitivism*

Despite the importance of the theme of primitivism, the concept can become confusing when applied widely to evangelical groups. The term *primitivism,* when applied to evangelical Protestants without qualification, tends to drift back and forth between at least two major meanings. On the one hand, it designates the strongly biblicist tendencies so prominent in most of American low-church Protestantism. The Bible is to be "the only rule of faith and practice" (as the Westminster Confession of Faith put it), and hence American Protestants often have been preoccupied with following biblical patterns both in their churches and in their lives. No theme is more pervasive in American low-church evangelical Protestantism. Sometimes, the effort to follow New Testament patterns with respect to church practice is explicitly called "restorationist"; but many groups who do not resonate to the "restorationist" label nonetheless share the concern to restore primitive biblical standards. Hence it seems appropriate to talk about primitivism in all of these traditions.

Some scholars, however, often give primitivism an even stronger meaning. Here, it refers not only to imitating biblical practices but also to entering into another time, into a lost primordium, first time, or great time. This dramatic entering into a new time may be so strong that it involves not only a sense of historylessness but a sense of timelessness as well.[5] Such practices are also appropriately designated as primitivist.

These two meanings of *primitivism* are seldom distinguished from each other. When describing evangelical Protestants as primitivists, therefore, the degree or intensity of primitivism is seldom clear. Biblicist primitivism, or the simple emphasis on following primitive, biblical rules and models, is, indeed, widespread among low-church Protestants. Since, however, primitivism also suggests an intense experiential recapturing of the primordial spirit of a normative epoch, one might easily imagine that experiential primitivism is widespread and dominant.

Probably every religious group has its experientially primitivist moments. High-church liturgical groups enter primitive times in the Eucharist. Ascetic Christians look for a primitive intensity of earlier saints. Even modernists may see themselves as living by the pure spirit of the Sermon on the Mount, uncorrupted by intervening theological traditions, and may occasionally experience a primitive sense of oneness with the first disciples in their efforts to follow Jesus. Low-church evangelical Protestants may find primal moments in singing the psalms, in the upper-room intensity of the communion service, in the dramatic sermon narrative (especially in African American traditions), in conversion experiences, and in the many ways one might feel the presence or the leading of the Holy Spirit. Baptism by immersion is a particularly dramatic primitivist moment for vast numbers of evangelicals. Or singing the hymns or following the practices of the earlier generations of one's own group may provide a time-dispelling intensity of a sort of second-level primitivism.

Despite the many instances of such practices that are candidates for experiential entries into an earlier first time, such experiences in almost all such groups are occasional. They are not typical of the everyday Christian practice of most of the sincere adherents to these groups and are not even characteristic of most of the worship of many low-church groups. Rather, their efforts to follow the Bible belong to a much more ordinary type. Most of the time, in both their worship and their lives, they simply look for biblical rules to guide them.

So if we use the term *primitivism,* therefore, without any qualifications and apply the term to any group that attempts to follow original biblical models, we are in danger of seeming to suggest that what is pervasive is an intense reliving or recapturing of the power of an earlier primal age. To take an extreme case, it is sometimes argued that early Unitarianism was a primitivist movement.[6] An important part of the rationale for Unitarianism was to get back to the pure teachings of Jesus and the New Testament church, uncorrupted by human theological invention. This is a worthwhile point and it adds something to our understanding of nineteenth-century Unitarianism to see it sharing an impulse with many of its contemporaries, such as the Campbellites and the followers of Barton Stone. Conversely, one gains some insight into the Christian movement by seeing its affinities with Unitarianism. Nonetheless, I wonder if we might not lose more than we gain by designating the Unitarians with a word such as *primitivist* that carries intimations of somehow dramatically reliving a primal great time. No doubt those who comprised the urbane and well-to-do eastern Massachusetts aristocracy had their spiritual moments; yet the primitivist designation seems to mislead.

A particularly notable example of falling victim to the ambiguity of the category is found in Theodore Dwight Bozeman's impressive and often insightful study of American Puritans, *To Live Ancient Lives*. For all his insight, Bozeman gets misled particularly when he talks about Puritanism and modernity. He begins by contrasting his approach to those historians who have emphasized the modernizing aspects of Puritanism. On the face of it, this is a worthwhile balancing of the picture. Puritans should be understood on their own terms and it needs to be emphasized that their outlook included a concern for restoring a primitive biblical order.[7] Yet Bozeman sees Puritan restorationism not only as faithfulness to biblical rules but also as a mysterious primitivist impulse to dramatically enter into a primordium. He makes this point so strongly that he concludes that any Puritan contributions to modernization must have been incidental to the movement. He writes, "If the Puritan standpoint, subversive as it was of the sense of connected tradition, contributed anything to a more modern outlook, it is important to see that it did so by the sheer fortuity of its emergence in the time of transition."[8]

This conclusion, it seems to me, vastly underestimates the essential congeniality to modernization that one finds in Puritan and Protestant antitraditionalism. The firm hand of tradition had governed Western civilization as it had almost every civilization throughout history. Protestantism became a remarkable reform movement by successfully breaking the hold of such authoritarian traditionalism. As Bozeman correctly points out, it introduced the principle of challenging human inventions, a principle that Puritans particularly accentuated. True, they challenged traditionalism by asserting a claim to an even more ancient and reliable traditional authority, that of Scripture. But the point of this emphasis on the past was to reform the church and civilization for the future. Puritans were not, of course, trying to build a modern world such as the one that actually arose. They were not planning a Los Angeles, for instance. Nonetheless they were trying to build a better seventeenth-century world and were forward-looking reformers. A preoccupation with an authority drawn from the past was in no way incompatible with a hope for a reformed and purer future.

Further, although Puritans looked back to the Bible because of the crisis in authority raised by Protestantism, they also sought to develop modern rational methods for best interpreting the Bible. They are justly credited, it seems to me, with contributing to modernization not only by challenging past authority but also by rationalizing present and future authority. Accordingly, they argued that authority must be based on universally accessible principles rather than on norms erected by particular human persons or offices. That idea, the authority of principles over persons, although not entirely new, is one of the major features of modernity to which Puritanism contributed.

Bozeman writes all this off as incidental, apparently because of his fascination with Puritan primitivism in the strong sense of restoring the primordium. Because of their pervasive biblicism it is natural to argue that primitivism was a central concern of Puritans. Furthermore, Puritans often spoke as though they were dramatically reliving biblical times. Hence it is plausible for him to argue both that primitivism was central to Puritans and that their primitivism was of the strong experiential sort. If so, it then seems to follow that *modernizers* is an inappropriate term to apply to them, since they were so preoccupied with dramatically reconstructing a past primal era.[9]

Bozeman's denial of the future orientation of the Puritan reformers is, it seems to me, related to his violation of what I think should be one of the fundamental laws of historical interpretation. That law is that something more familiar is seldom better understood by viewing it as primarily a subtype of something with which we are less familiar (unless, of course, the two are actually related). The field of the history of religions has been especially prone to violate this rule. One can, of course, learn something by seeing commonalities between modern and ancient religious practices. We all talk about "rites of passage" and the like. Yet, if we get preoccupied with our ancient category, we can miss the complexity in what is before us. Thus, Bozeman, in correctly seeing the fascinating analogy between the pervasive and sometimes intensely dramatic Puritan biblicism and other religious quests to recapture a dramatic great time, attributes to the Puritans a pervasive backward-looking character that misses the subtlety of the modern, forward-looking dimensions of the Puritan movement.

Primitivism and Biblicism

To avoid such confusion when discussing low-church Protestants, we should carefully distinguish between the experiential primitivism that we find occasionally in all such movements (some more and some less occasionally) and their biblicist primitivism, or simple efforts to restore biblical patterns, which is much more pervasive and more often a definitive characteristic of these movements. In this way, one might demystify much of that which is classified as primitivist.

One could clarify the picture still more if one recognized that much of what passes for primitivism is virtually synonymous with a simple biblicism, or an effort to follow biblical rules as the highest rule for church practice and for life. Hence, although it may be helpful occasionally to describe such tendencies as primitivism—for instance, in pointing out their ahistorical tendencies—most of the time our concepts would be clearer if we simply referred to evangelical Protestants as biblicists.

When describing most of these groups, *biblicism* would be a less confusing term than *primitivism* (or even *biblicist primitivism*) since *biblicism* was the primary operative category for the people we are discussing. As Christians, their object was to know, trust, and obey God, and for that they considered the Bible to be the most direct source for knowing God's will. Though they might acknowledge that God revealed himself in additional ways, they were convinced that the Bible was simply the highest authority on any subject about which it spoke. Given that premise, their problem was how most consistently to follow the Bible. They might disagree on the extent of the application of the biblicist principle. Lutherans applied it to central doctrines, while Calvinists saw the Bible as providing precedents for church practice as well. Biblicists might also disagree on what should be the operative canon. Was the Old Testament as authoritative as the New? Were the Gospels or the Epistles more central? What was the place of reason in relation to biblical authority? How was tradition to be regarded in the light of the primacy of biblical authority? Was it worthless or a sometimes useful, though subordinate, guide? Such questions are relatively straightforward if we see them in the participants' own terms of consciously wrestling with the implications of their biblicism. If we talk of primitivism, we shift the conversation from a relatively straightforward category to a more mysterious one.

The category of biblicism is also somewhat less mysterious than that of primitivism for explaining the endless varieties of differences among groups who claim the sole authority of Scripture. When we talk of primitivism it is not precisely clear what the variables might be. When we talk of being biblicist, on the other hand, at least we immediately see the problems. Following the Bible consistently is a notoriously difficult thing to do. Rules of interpretation, underlying assumptions, and operative canons vary. Even when people think they understand the Bible, nobody succeeds entirely in following its guidance. Everyone must compromise and be to some degree a pragmatist. The problems are obvious.

Biblicism and Modernization

Biblicism is less confusing especially when talking about our subject of primitivism and modernization. If we use the word *biblicism* it becomes apparent that we are simply talking about a variation on the question of Protestantism and modernization about which we have roughly a century of helpful scholarly discussion. If we say "primitivism and progress," it sounds as though we are dealing with a paradox, and we might be led into assuming these are opposed. If we say "biblicism and progress," we still have something of a paradox, but I think it is pretty straightforward how it might be resolved.

In our straightforward, simpleminded account, the Reformation was, as our English word suggests, trying to reform or restore. What were the reformers trying to restore? The great time? Well, sometimes, and in a sense. But more clearly, they were looking for the truth about God. They were convinced that the church had corrupted that truth and so they sought to restore the truth in its purity. Truth and purity were therefore among their major operative categories. These objectives led directly to the question of authority and hence to their preoccupation with the Bible as the highest authority they knew. Particularly the Anabaptists and the Reformed, though in different ways, attempted systematically to follow the authority of the Bible as the rule for all of life.

Especially via the Reformed heritage this biblicist resolution of the question of authority became influential among the British settlers of North America. One of its concomitants was a strong opposition to the authority of human tradition, especially in church affairs. Such outlooks, together with an ahistorical perspective, flourished especially as the United States emerged as a nation. Practical men and women who had a task of constructing a new civilization seemed particularly attracted to such antitraditional attitudes. Some explicitly rejected all intervening traditions, others simply subjected them to the refining test of their conformity to biblical standards and precedents.

Enlightenment science, of course, was a response to this same crisis in authority and reinforced similar antitraditionalist and ahistorical attitudes. As is often said, Enlightenment thinkers turned to the book of nature as the definitive authority for finding the pure truth, uncorrupted by human traditions.

In America these two traditions of biblicism and Enlightenment science developed in political circumstances that allowed them to merge so that their congenial elements could be accentuated. For instance, many persons have noted the congeniality between biblicism and Baconianism that characterized American evangelicalism of the first half of the nineteenth century. Competing claims of biblicism encouraged people to rationalize their outlooks in order to have a basis for adjudicating such claims.

Once we describe the developments in this straightforward and familiar way, we see that there is no essential incompatibility between American biblicism and American modernization. As Richard T. Hughes points out, the two movements shared antitraditionalism and hence tended to reinforce each other.[10] Many American modernizers in the first half of the nineteenth century were professed biblicists. They disagreed with each other about exactly what biblicism implied, about what parts of the Bible provided laws for modern living, about how helpful it was to be guided by earlier interpreters of the Bible, and about how widely biblicism should be applied in modern life. In general, however, they shared an antitraditionalism and an opposition to Roman Catholicism or to any church authority not directly based on biblical claims. Hence these outlooks opened the door to the individualism and the pragmatism that were so conspicuous both in American Protestant religious life and in the building of a modern industrial society. Strict biblicism might inhibit Christians' participation in isolated features of modernization here or there (they might, for instance, oppose transportation of the mail on the Sabbath), but biblicism was not uncongenial to the enterprise of modernization as a whole.

Since the objective of Reformation biblicism was reform, the degree to which biblicist movements directly fostered modernization depended in part on what was supposed to be reformed. If it was just the church that was to be reformed (or, for later generations, kept reformed), then strict biblicist groups might largely withdraw from society, either figuratively or literally. If the whole of society was to be reformed, as often was true of the Reformed traditions descended from the Puritans, then biblicism and modernization might go hand in hand. If biblicists applied the standards of Scripture to contemporary society, they often discovered that society was in drastic need of change. By the time of the Enlightenment this habit of demanding changes in social and moral standards in the light of God's law was extended to include a scientific as well as a biblical basis for discovering such laws. Biblicists, of course, approved only some of the proposed modern changes; but their critical attitudes made them quite open to looking for systematic techniques for improving the social order.

While some biblicists might have fostered an openness to social change, or at least a dissatisfaction with the social status quo, probably more often biblicists from both the Reformed and Pietist traditions resolved potential conflicts between their biblicism and modern social and economic realities by adopting the compartmentalization that is such a conspicuous part of modern life. So, for instance, pious businessmen during their noon-time prayer meetings in the revival of 1857-

58 might have felt the outpouring of the Holy Spirit that in a sense connected them with primitive apostolic times. But when the meeting ended it was back to business as usual, financing the railroad, keeping wages low enough to ensure a fair profit, and so forth. Maybe they would contribute to a reform movement, but even if they did, there would still be major aspects of their lives that the spiritual experience would hardly touch in any measurable way. Americans learned on their parents' knees to compartmentalize their lives between the biblical (the primitive if you will) and the modern.

Primitivism and Fundamentalism

This background prepares us, then, to address the apparent incongruity between primitivism and congeniality to modernization within fundamentalism. Fundamentalists, of course, have leveled the sharpest attacks against aspects of modernity. Antimodernism is, in fact, essential to the definition of fundamentalism. The most obvious question that arises about fundamentalism is why this antimodernist movement is sometimes so modern. Some fundamentalists, for instance, may argue that the Social Security system or credit cards are the Mark of the Beast. They have at one time or other condemned almost every development of modernity as born of the Devil. Yet, at the same time, every observer notices that there are too many high-tech fundamentalists for this critique of modernity to be truly thoroughgoing. How do we explain this paradox? I think describing fundamentalism as biblicist rather than primitivist solves the riddle.

First of all, the case of fundamentalism illustrates particularly well why our account will become confusing if primitivism is one of our primary analytical categories. Although primitivism works nicely for describing a few features of fundamentalism, for others it does not fit very well at all. Joel Carpenter has pointed out some of these anomalies. Essentially the problems have to do with the implication, if we use the term *primitivism,* that our subjects are consistently preoccupied with replicating New Testament patterns. Fundamentalists, however, show little concern for consistency on such points. Rather than consistently denying the relevance of history, for instance, they often claim to stand for "the historic Christian faith" and claim the traditions of nineteenth-century evangelicals, of Whitefield, of Wesley, and of the Reformation.[11] Such apparent anomalies, I would add, are more easily explained if we see fundamentalists as biblicists. Although they do not take tradition as a primary authority, they do welcome historical precedents that meet their tests for being consistent with biblical standards.

Another crucial aspect of fundamentalism and similar traditions that are not strictly primitivist is the concept of the new birth. On the one hand, the experience of the new birth may be intensely primitivist in the strongest experiential sense. Moreover, the suggestion of a new *birth* has primitivist overtones and is sometimes described as a return to the right relationship with God that was lost at Eden. On the other hand, much of the emphasis on the new birth is on its newness and its unprecedented quality. The experience is seldom described as orienting one to a past age, but rather to giving one a new start for the present and the future. In that sense it is largely a modern, progressivist doctrine. It is clearly biblicist in claiming New Testament precedent and authority; but it is only ambiguously primitivist.

Moreover, in the most distinctive feature of classic fundamentalism, its dispensationalism, the category of primitivism misleads as much as it clarifies. True, there was a primal New Testament strong time that has been lost through a steady decline of the church. New Testament precedents should therefore be the models for one's practice. On the other hand, the even more primitive dispensations of the Old Testament are superseded and carry little authority. Moreover, the church today does not ultimately look forward to a restoration of New Testament times but to the introduction of a new millennial age that will be completely different. Likewise, in the Bible itself, what ultimately is restored is not particularly Edenic. We began in a garden but look forward to a city. I once heard a 1950s recording called *Flight F-I-N-A-L*,[12] which was a narrated arrival of a modern airliner to the New Jerusalem. The pilot, Jesus Christ, comes on the intercom to tell the people to look out the left side to get a glimpse of the streets of gold, the saints casting down their crowns before the throne, and so forth, all of which is described literally from the book of Revelation. That, I think, captures the mix of outlooks and the essentially forward-looking mentality of much of classic fundamentalism. All things will be made new.

Part of the problem with making primitivism a major interpretative category is that the Bible itself is not consistently a primitivist book, if we use *primitivist* in any strict sense. While the Bible consistently emphasizes returning to a right relationship with God, this may or may not involve a return to patterns of an earlier age. History and tradition are also important in the Bible, and history is heading toward something new. As many have observed, the Bible with its noncyclical view of history contains one of the seeds of the modern idea of progress.

Once we recognize that for interpreting fundamentalism biblicism is a much less confusing interpretative category than is primitivism, then we can also see that the category of fundamentalism fits the patterns already described in relating fundamentalists' biblicism to modernization. Biblicism, as it develops in American evangelical Protestantism, fosters attitudes that show little regard for human traditions. Individuals are freed from conventional authority. A rationalized approach to modern life fits well with a rationalized approach to the Bible. In structuring the modern church, therefore, fundamentalists are not only biblicists; they also are rampant pragmatists. Their whole worldview is permeated with rationalized elements. Hence we should not be surprised at the notorious fundamentalist tendency to outdo even the modernists in applying the latest techniques to promoting the ancient gospel.

They themselves would explain the paradox of their antimodernism and their obvious modernity in simple terms that I think are quite helpful. They reject those aspects of modernity that they see used by the Devil to mislead humanity. They themselves attempt to follow biblical principles and commands and are happy to use any modern device that helps them to do so more effectively. As in most of these traditions, the Bible is first of all a rule book. Many of its rules are general ones ("Go ye into all the world and preach the Gospel") and may be implemented by any means available. Most of the time, therefore, fundamentalists are not simply going back to the Bible; they are also applying it to modern times.

We outsiders, of course, may see many inconsistencies in their attempts to apply biblical principles to modern life. Such inconsistencies are not unique to fundamentalists. In practice fundamentalists often resolve potential conflicts between their professed biblicism and their everyday businesses or lives in much the same way as their nineteenth-century predecessors did, by compartmentalizing their lives. In some areas of both public and private life they are extremely zealous in applying biblical principles, while in others they ignore them and behave just like good moderns.

Conclusions

Finally, I want to emphasize that I am not suggesting that primitivism is a useless concept. Rather, I want to suggest that in many instances, *biblicism* is really what we are talking about and will be a less confusing, less mysterious category. In other instances, *primitivism* is a perfectly appropriate term. When we use it, however, we would do well to qualify it or carefully define our meaning. On the one hand we might be talking about a simple biblicist primitivism or biblicism with strong ahistorical or antitraditionalist tendencies. Perhaps *restorationist* might be the more precise term, since that does not carry with it all the same ambiguities.[13] In any case, it is helpful to have available some such term to suggest the ahistorical tendencies sometimes found in groups that emphasize going back to the Bible. On the other hand, if we have primarily experiential primitivism in mind, we should make that clear as well.

In general I think it would be wise to limit the use of *primitivism* as a primary designation to groups that have a strong emphasis on experiential primitivism. Early Quakers, for instance, though not biblicists, were primitivists in recreating the spirit of the New Testament age. The early Mormons provide perhaps the most striking example. They were so primitivist that they went beyond biblicism and had living prophets who received direct revelations and reopened the canon.[14] Pentecostals do something similar, although within a much more traditional biblicist framework. Grant Wacker, I think, is correct in arguing that experiential primitivism is a helpful category for explaining some of the differences between pentecostals and their fundamentalist cousins.[15]

Even in such cases, however, primitivism can become a misleading concept if it is raised from being one dimension of a movement to being a mysterious cosmic force around which everything else is supposed to revolve. Early pentecostals, for instance, despite their strong, experiential primitivist impulse, had more similarities with fundamentalists than they had differences. Both shared most of the commonplaces of the American revivalist tradition, which were drawn from a variety of heritages.

When talking about evangelical Protestantism, *primitivism* will sometimes be the appropriate word. It is a graphic shorthand that highlights some revealing attitudes. When we need greater precision of analysis, however, we might ask whether we can substitute the word *biblicism*. If we can, we may make a small contribution to clarity. Particularly with regard to our topic of modernization, many of the apparent paradoxes will largely disappear.

Notes

1. Sidney E. Mead, *The Lively Experiment: The Shaping of Christianity in America* (New York: Harper and Row, 1963), esp. 108–13.

2. See the valuable essays in Richard T. Hughes, ed., *The American Quest for the Primitive Church* (Urbana: University of Illinois Press, 1988).

3. Winton U. Solberg, "Primitivism in the American Enlightenment," in Hughes, ed., *American Quest,* 63. Cf. Sidney Mead's helpful comment that God's truth rather than the primitive book itself is still the object of the quest.

4. Richard T. Hughes and C. Leonard Allen, *Illusions of Innocence: Protestant Primitivism in America, 1630–1875* (Chicago: University of Chicago Press, 1988).

5. See Grant Wacker's chapter on pentecostalism in this volume.

6. I am indebted to Roger Robins for a graduate paper on this point. Mark Noll, in "Primitivism in Fundamentalism and American Biblical Scholarship: A Response," in Hughes, ed., *American Quest,* 124, makes a similar suggestion.

7. Cf. my own version of this point in "Perry Miller's Rehabilitation of the Puritans: A Critique," *Church History* 39 (Mar. 1970): 91–105.

8. Theodore Dwight Bozeman, *To Live Ancient Lives: The Primitivist Dimension in Puritanism* (Chapel Hill: University of North Carolina Press for the Institute of Early American History and Culture, 1988), 346–47.

9. Cf. Bozeman's broader conclusion that "specifically primitivist opinion" shows that "modernization, understood to include a shift in perspective toward the future, is not the all-encompassing story of historical American thought." Though it is surely correct that modernization is not the whole story, the specific point seems to assume that primitivists cannot be oriented toward present reform, i.e., toward improving the future. See ibid., 351.

10. Richard T. Hughes, "Introduction: On Recovering the Theme of Recovery," in Hughes, ed., *American Quest,* 10.

11. Joel A. Carpenter, "Contending for the Faith Once Delivered: Primitivist Impulses in American Fundamentalism," in Hughes, ed., *American Quest,* 99–119. Cf. Noll, "Primitivism," 120–28.

12. This recording is found in Richard Mouw's private collection of fundamentalist art. See also Mouw's *Texas Sketchbook* (Waco, Tex.: Artists' Press, 1967) for comparable themes.

13. The problems with using *restorationism* are that it has been so often used as synonymous with primitivism that it will be difficult to enforce the distinction; that it, too, suggests a preoccupation with the past that might hide the essential progressivism of most such movements; and that it suggests the particular agendas of self-consciously restorationist groups. Nonetheless, I do think it would be a gain if *restorationism* were used to designate what I am calling biblicist primitivism and *primitivism* were used only to designate experiential primitivism. Furthermore, it would have to be recognized that most restorationists and primitivists are also biblicist in other senses as well, for instance, in ordinary efforts to apply biblical rules to everyday life.

14. Jan Shipps makes a good case for this in Mormonism. See *Mormonism: The Story of a New Religious Tradition* (Urbana: University of Illinois Press, 1985).

15. See Grant Wacker's essay in this volume. See also Wacker, "Playing for Keeps: The Primitivist Impulse in Early Pentecostalism," in Hughes, ed., *American Quest,* 196–219.

PART 2

Perspectives on
the Meaning of the
Restoration Vision

3

The Power of the Restoration Vision and Its Decline in Modern America

FRANKLIN H. LITTELL

From the fourth century when the emperor first created a state-sponsored church, the Constantinian model has dominated European Christianity. Though no formal state church exists in the United States, the Constantinian model has profoundly shaped American Christianity as well.[1]

Shortly after the beginning of the twentieth century in Christian history, the leading American Protestant denominations adopted the "Social Creed of the Churches." With the same optimism that had marked their spirit during the nineteenth century, "the Great Century" of the expansion of Christianity on the world map, one of their largest sectors launched a semipopular religious journal and called it the *Christian Century*. Today, after two confrontations with powerful anti-Christian systems of being—Marxism and Nazism—after participation in two world wars, and after two epochal events—the Holocaust and the establishment of a restored Israel—the magazine is still modestly successful and still carries the same name.

The name—the *Christian Century*—signals that exquisite conflation of Christian beliefs and republican principles that major sectors of "mainline" Protestantism achieved during the nineteenth century. Was that blending of the religious and the political a logical emergence from the conditions in America or was it the kind of "realized eschatology" that earned for the nineteenth-century Protestantism of many countries the summary dismissal: *Kulturreligion?*

Conservative European critics such as the Lutheran theologian Karl Holl long have scorned free churches in a free society as typically Anglo-Saxon. For Holl, the temporal expression of the divine immanence could only be "Christendom" and its concretion in an entity such as the Holy Roman Empire of the German Nation, that precious concept against which all other options were *Schwärmerei* and *Sektiererei*. For him, the patron saint of the Radical Reformation could only be Thomas Müntzer, for whom faith was "the courage and the power [to accomplish] the impossible."[2] Like most champions of the establishments, Holl made no effort to acquaint himself with the primary sources of the sixteenth-century restitutionists.

Unhappily, from that perspective, the French Revolution and the Enlightenment had cast their wretched shadows over the beneficent German model. The end of the empire and the flight of the German emperor, followed by a republic that loosened the ties of church and state, increased the sense of disorientation. And the rebellious Americans persisted in going their own way, a way that he scorned as at best purely marginal to the main thrust of the Reformation.

Holl, like most of his German peers, felt that the critical issue was the importance of *Volk* as a theological concept: *Volk*—which Martin Luther had installed as one of the "orders of creation"—*Volk*—that slippery word that may be translated as "nation" or "people" or "race" and that from 1933 to 1945 certainly carried all three connotations. Holl, in fact, was one of the fathers of *Volkstheologie*: "Therein our German conception is sharply different from the sect-influenced English-American. For us the cohesion in the State, the promoting and deepening of the national/populist/racial community, comprise a value that stands higher than the individual's freedom of movement."[3]

Dying in 1926, Holl did not live to see how a German Christendom that had been in decline for a century and a half might choose a migrant Austrian—a Roman Catholic at that—to defend itself against the perils of republican principles and modernization. Neither did he perceive how an extraordinarily successful left-wing Protestantism in America might attain the status—and the problems—of a religious establishment.

Philip Schaff, a transplanted scholar with classical European training, saw very clearly the potential of voluntary religion in America, with its religious liberty, free churches, and lay initiatives. Schaff was very critical of the situation in European Christendom, where the people in the cities went unshepherded and unschooled in the faith.

Schaff noted that "in large cities on the Continent there are parishes of fifty thousand souls with a single pastor; while in the United States of America there is on an average one pastor to every thousand members."[4] But in Europe itself very few theologians or church historians noticed that attention to religious obligations of the most basic kind, such as attendance at the public worship of God, had been declining all across the continent since the 1840s, decade by decade.

Although Johan Hinrich Wichern had given fair warning at the Leipzig *Kirchentag* of 1848, the year of the Communist Manifesto, church leaders generations later were taken by surprise when the two most important elements in modern, advanced, industrialized societies—the laborers (*Proletariat*) and the university-trained, professional people (*Intellektuellen*)—showed themselves in the times of testing to be anything but seasoned and well-disciplined soldiers in the army of the Lord.

Only once before in the history of the faith have there been defections of such magnitude and that was when—challenged by the simple monotheism of an insurgent Islam and tired to death of the brawlings of the hair-splitting theologians—the baptized defected in droves. With the solitary exceptions of Constantinople and Rome, all the great cities of Christian civilization—Alexandria, Caesarea, Lydda, Damascus, Antioch, Ephesus, Jerusalem—with their great academies and museums and cultural artifacts apostatized to the new faith, leaving only the barbarous, half-baptized tribes of Western Europe to carry on.

Looking back upon this disastrous event in church history, the most calamitous in Christendom until the inroads made by alternative systems of being (*Ersatzreligionen*) in the twentieth century, the fathers gathered at the great missionary and ecumenical conference at Edinburgh in 1910 and summarized their conclusions as follows: "It remains tragically true that had the Church of Syria been faithful to its Master the reproach of Islam had never lain upon Christendom. The thought has sombre consequences. It may be that in the Africa, the China, and the India of to-day new religions are maturing which in like manner will be 'anti-Christian,' and stand in future centuries as a barrier in the way of winning the world."[5] Most of the delegates at Edinburgh were European or American, and they thought they knew where the problem areas were to be found. Today, in retrospect, we see that the "new religions" did indeed emerge. They were, in fact, already emerging in the heart of European Christendom itself.

The "new religions," of which the most powerful were Marxism and Nazism, reached their cataclysmic consummations at the end of the twentieth century.

We do not know whether a post-Christian Western Europe will find a new path and a second reformation. Since the collapse of the Third Reich, the churches in Germany have followed the path of restoration in spite of sometimes vigorous renewal impulses such as the Evangelical Academies and the Kirchentag. A glassine overlay of the German

Landeskirchen today matches the state-church boundaries of 1817 almost exactly. From "Roman Catholic" Italy—where only one out of ten men goes to one confession and one mass a year—to "Lutheran" Sweden—where only 3.4 percent of the total population has any effective relationship with the established church—the facades remain but there is little behind them. Nevertheless, right-wing movements such as Opus Dei are strategizing a refurbished and triumphant Christendom, and much of the politics of the Curia seems to be pointing that way in both Western and Eastern Europe.

In the East, the darkest nightmare is symbolized by a movement such as the "Russian Christian Orthodox People's Movement," which counted some of the bravest and brightest of Stalinism's opponents and now proposes a restored "Holy Russia." With no model of a pluralistic society energized by voluntary religion and blessed by an initiative economy and federalist politics, few seem to remember what the Russian style of Christendom meant for Baptists, Stundists, Jews, Mennonites, Hutterites, Dukhobortsi, Old Believers, and many others who didn't fit. Other countries in the former Soviet Union face similar problems. Even a liberated Poland, where a Polish pope is even now trying to call his people back to their old traditions, every day proves a more stoney ground for authoritarian religion.

This summary of the brute facts about Christendom seems to me a useful preliminary exercise, and not diversionary from the theme of this volume, lest we unthinkingly assume that the difference between the Constantinian model and the restitutionist model of Christian history be a simple confrontation between myths that can be proven "true" or "false" by "facts" or indeed by exercise of the mind alone.

Let it be stated bluntly: the Christendom of ecclesiastical power and triumphalist theology was a terrible place for women, a terrible place for "heretics," and a terrible place for Jews. The latter point struck me forcibly, long after I had spent years on the tribulations of those called "heretics," when I read in Jules Isaac's work the statement, "After very deep historical research, I say and maintain that the fate of Israel [i.e., of the Jewish people] did not take on a truly inhuman character until the 4th century A.D. with the coming of the Christian Empire."[6]

We are not dealing with purely rational and theoretical matters. Most are familiar with the technical use of the term *myth,* and most also are aware that neither "apostolic succession" nor the restorationist view of "apostolicity" can be proven by documents from the distant past. We have grown beyond "proofs" at the level of the "Donation of Constantine." The truth of a myth—and its power—derives from the extent to which it fulfills the needs and informs the identity and oral tradition of a carrier community. If the word *myth* carries too many negative undertones because of its street use, let me plead the case for "root metaphors," of which we have today a dangerous shortage.

Does the continuity model provide a true reading of European Christendom today? Does a discontinuity model afford a true report on Protestantism in America?

America and the Radical Reformation

What is the picture when we turn to religious life in America, where—as William Warren Sweet and Kenneth Scott Latourette, among others, pointed out a half century ago—motifs from the the left wing of the Reformation dominated the scene throughout the seventeenth, eighteenth, and nineteenth centuries?

There are two powerful discontinuity models to which we need to give attention today, models that pose quite different views of the course of salvation history even though many preachers and lay people seem to be able to live with the major contradictions unresolved. We shall take up the older model first.

Take New England, which until recently supplied many of the myths and tales used in the common schools to educate the rising generation in its heritage. Richard T. Hughes and C. Leonard Allen call the New England venture—correctly, I think—"a restorationist crusade."[7] For the conservative John Cotton, the "old," the "first," the "original," the "ancient" provided the norm. Cotton's view of church history was "a reversion, undercutting both Catholic and Anglican appeals to a continuity of tradition, to the first, or primitive, order of things narrated in the Protestant Scriptures."[8] For the radical John Owen, Christ set the normative pattern for both congregational and civic order:

> The church is a *voluntary society*. Persons otherwise absolutely free, as unto all the rules, laws and ends of such a society, do of their own wills and free choice coalesce into it. This is the original of churches. . . .
>
> . . . All *lawful societies*, constituted such by voluntary confederation . . . have a right and power, by the light of nature, to receive into their society those that are willing to meet, engaging themselves to observe the rules, laws, and ends of the society, and to expel them out of it who willfully deviate from those rules. This is the life and form of every lawful society or community of men in the world, without which they can neither coalesce nor submit. . . . This is the foundation of all political societies.[9]

The primitivisms of the Puritan and Pietist movements have been fully documented during the last forty years: all of them divide church history into Golden Age, Fall, and Restitution. From New Lebanon (New York) to Amana (Iowa) to Aurora (Oregon), the periodization of history is the same. Even the Utopian Socialists of the early nineteenth century, such as the followers of Charles Fourier and Etienne Cabet, who founded many colonies in North America, often called their communal life "True Christianity."

Neither can there be doubt that Anglicanism, at the time of the founding of the English settlements in North America, was effectively infiltrated by primitivist views. By the time of Edward VI, even the Prayer Book institution of the Lord's Supper was validated by an appeal to "ancient purity and simplicity."[10] Although Anglicanism was eventually able to fight off submission to the normative use of the primitive church by accenting Bede's *History* and an apostolic period that thereby blended into the Constantinian settlement, the extent of primitivist penetration of the establishment in the pre-Tractarian generations may be illustrated by a passage from Henry Jacobs's 1599 defense of the English state-church. Jacobs was clearly standing at the last barricade, resisting the charge that a fallen church could not be a true church:

> Surely this grosse and wicked absurditie, I could not open better then by this similitude: This man hath a wodden legge, an eye of glasse, his nose deformed, adde if you will, both his armes not naturall, but framed to him of wood or what you will: Ergo this is no true man. Yes Sir, for all this he is a true man. For as much as all this concernes not the verie life and being of a man, though there be most unnaturall additions, and very manie, the like doe I affirme of these externall corruptions in the Church.[11]

Jacobs hoped to save the core by admitting freely the corruptions that had accrued across the centuries. In Holland, Switzerland, Scandinavia, and the German states, religious primitivism in its Pietist mode had a similar effect within Reformed and Lutheran state-churches.

Mennonites, Brethren, Quakers, Baptists, Congregationalists—we can tick off those movements that, with the Anglicans, dominated the English-language church scene during the colonial period and first century of the republic. They were all firmly primitivist, restitutionist, restorationist.

There are two movements, now grown large, that were once solidly in the restitutionist camp, where close attention may reveal some of the problems and ambiguities of churches and church leaders whose program for the future is the recovery of a pattern far in the past but whose "separation" in teaching and practice declines as their eschatology flags. These two movements are the Methodists and the Disciples or Christians.

John Wesley and the Methodists: From Early Church to Assimilation

Let me first address the case of the Methodists, who at the middle of the last century were the largest Christian movement in the United States (including Roman Catholicism), counting one of every five church members in their ranks.

John Wesley was a convinced primitivist, basing his periodization of church history upon a careful reading of Johann Lorentz von Mosheim's ecclesiastical histories. Students of the Radical Reformation and its spiritual progeny will come alert immediately to the notice that von Mosheim, the greatest Lutheran theologian of his generation, published among his many books two major works of *unparteiischen Ketzergeschichte*. From Sebastian Franck through Gottfried Arnold, the historians of the Radical Reformation were fascinated by the idea that during the "fallen" period of the great church the truly Christian style of life was kept alive by those persecuted as "heretics." Wesley urged von Mosheim on his preachers.

Wesley was also a primitivist in his accent on the Scriptures. The Bible was the standard of faith and the early church was the model. He argued that the minister should be proficient in Hebrew and Greek—a position that United Methodist church seminaries might today profitably note. When charged with a certain freedom toward the church's order, he replied, "Permit me to speak plainly. If by catholic principles you mean any other than scriptural, they weigh nothing with me. I allow no other rule, whether of faith or practice, than the Holy Scriptures."[12] No experience was authentically Christian if it contradicted the Bible, and no teaching was legitimate—however fervent the claim of inspiration—if it did not have the support of Scripture. Again, "I would inquire, What is the end of all ecclesiastical order? Is it not to bring souls from the power of Satan to God, and to build them up in His fear and love? Order, then, is so far valuable as it answers these ends; and if it answers them not, it is nothing worth."[13] When he was questioned on his spiritual counseling, with the Oxford Club accused of excessive zeal, Wesley responded that the members' fasting, confessions, attendance on the means of grace, and other practices were all after the custom of the primitive church.

Richard Heitzenrater is certainly correct in stressing the way that the lifestyle of "the Holy Club" at Oxford set Wesley and his friends apart from the university and that it was a lifestyle patterned upon the early church.[14] Moreover, when Wesley much later heralded the disentanglement of religion from the state in the new American republic, he wrote that the American Methodists were "now at full liberty, simply to follow the scriptures and the primitive church."[15]

Wesley was constrained by unity as a primary mark of the apostolic church, and he resisted every temptation to break away from the Anglican communion personally. Using appeal to the early church as his warrant, he admitted "irregular" forms of the ministry, such as lay preaching, field preaching, preaching in a diocese without the bishop's permission, and leading by women. The Anglican discipline was so lax that his conduct went unpunished and he was able to maintain a fiction—that he was a good Anglican priest. In fact, in both practice and theory of church history Wesley was in the line of the Radical Reformation. In Wesley's lifetime, in both England and America, his preachers had to move outside the establishment, a move that he had personally avoided.

Consider what Wesley wrote from within the portals of the established church:

> Our twentieth Article defines a true Church, "a congregation of faithful people, wherein the true word of God is preached and the sacraments duly administered." According to this account the Church of England is that body of faithful people (or holy believers) in England among whom the pure word of God is preached and the sacraments duly administered. Who, then, are the worst Dissenters from this Church? (1) Unholy men of all kinds: swearers, Sabbath-breakers, drunkards, fighters, whoremongers, liars, revilers, evil-speakers; the passionate, the gay, the lovers of money, the lovers of dress or of praise, the lovers of pleasure more than the lovers of God: all these are Dissenters of the highest sort, continually striking at the root of the Church, and themselves in truth belonging to no Church, but to the synagogue of Satan. (2) Men unsound in the faith; those who deny the Scriptures of truth, those who deny the Lord that has bought them, those who deny justification by faith alone, or the present salvation which is by faith: these also are Dissenters of a very high kind; for they likewise strike at the foundation, and, were their principles universally to obtain, there would be no true Church upon earth. Lastly, those who unduly administer the sacraments; who (to instance but in one point) administer the Lord's Supper to such

as have neither the power nor the form of godliness. These, too, are gross Dissenters from the Church of England, and should not cast the first stone at others.[16]

A century after Wesley's death, the Methodist movement stumbled and fell on the issue of church discipline. Perhaps in reaction to the lassitude he perceived and experienced in the Church of England, but more likely in faithfulness to the example of primitive Christianity, Wesley introduced strong disciplinary practices as part of the general priesthood of believers.

In verbal affirmation of church discipline, both magisterial reformers and radical reformers had anticipated Wesley. By the time the Federal Theology was fully developed at Herborn, church discipline had become the *tertior nota* of the True Church among Calvinists—those in establishments as well as those in free churches. In Lutheran circles it was featured as part of the parish visitation programs, and in Anglicanism it became a commonplace even in anti-Puritan centers. Like the ritual of confirmation, church discipline was an Anabaptist contribution to the life of the established churches.[17] Wesley, who once said of himself that he was "but a hair's breadth from Calvinism," was a strict disciplinarian and invented several structures—including the well-known class meeting device—to implement the pastoral office of the members for each other.

Amidst modernity, the thought of church discipline immediately raises the specter of negative controls. In the modern period *freedom* is a positive word and *discipline* is a negative word, whereas in truth voluntary discipline is the essential partner of Christian liberty. But the training program of the spiritual athletes of the remnant was not centered on handling the special cases of those who—so to speak—broke training. Neither was the practiced skill of the warriors of the spirit—to use a medieval metaphor that was very popular among sixteenth-century restitutionists—primarily the result of warnings to individuals to avoid failure and defection from their pledges as true knights in the army of the Lord.

No, among those who survived savage persecution by the Roman Catholic and Protestant state-churches in Europe a culture was developed that stressed those virtues thought to make a person fit for discipleship in the re-pristinated band of disciples that was the True Church (*rechte Kirche*). "Putting on the New Man" was the heart of the matter. Affirming one's conviction by believers' baptism, the "gate to the sheepstall" that might well be the portal to martyrdom, opened the door to the goodwill, mutual aid, and group care that filled out the positive expression of the priesthood of all believers in church discipline.

Indeed, during the first generations of a restorationist movement, when persecution and/or social opprobrium is general, the incidents of negative discipline are few. The pressures of spiritual warfare are constant and intense. As the movement acquires a measure of social acceptability and political security, the practice of loving support and caring attention tends to yield to a calculated and routinized moralism and pietism. The negative, less attractive, and less inspiring aspects of church discipline come to the fore. A preoccupation with self may cast its shadow over the people and splinter the community of renewed discipleship that no longer confronts outside hostility.

One scholar has noted the signs of a Puritanism declining into individualism, coupled with a loss of its sense of participation in the great drama of salvation history, as an "elaborate practice of piety" along these lines: "preparation for conversion; conversion; the great warfare with flesh, world and devil; the watch upon behavior; a marked degree of religious insecurity coupled to a quest for the assurance of salvation; introspection; a close attention to psychological dynamics that amounted virtually to a Puritan psychoanalysis; cases of conscience; discipline of prayer and meditation; spiritual diaries; holy soliloquies; and sabbatarianism."[18] Three hundred years later the "mainline" free churches in America, lacking the chastening control of outside persecution, followed the same declining path.

Smaller and more deliberately intense churches may also experience the same transmutation when their eschatology flags and fails. The present crisis of discipline within the *Bruderhof* movement may be taken as a contemporary illustration of the spiritual problems that arise when martyrdom is far distant and a seductive general culture is very near. The church discipline that once provided loving support and compassionate mutual aid may slide into a negative self-righteousness.

Perhaps it might be illustrative to make a short detour here. In my family's possession is a book of minutes of a little Baptist church in Wayne County, Pennsylvania, minutes covering more than a century of monthly meetings for discipline. It was a congregation that never suffered persecution and bore little social opprobrium from its beginnings until it finally fractured for the last time and went out of existence. There are two recurring topics: drunkenness and fornication.

By contrast to this shift in disciplinary agenda under the economy of religious liberty, in the *Täuferakten* of the sixteenth-century restitutionists there appear only a few cases involving negative discipline: the compelling claim on time and energy came from persecution, martyrdom, care of widows and orphans, and mutual aid.

If it was continuance in an undisciplined Anglican establishment that blurred John Wesley's image as a thoroughgoing restitutionist, it was the decline and abandonment of discipline that marked the watershed in the history of American Methodism. Until the General Conference of 1906, the Methodist Episcopal church still retained the requirement that before being recommended for full standing, applicants for membership should spend six months in training in class. The classes were also to continue as support groups. In that year, with the classes in decline and the requirement widely disregarded, on motion of Daniel Dorchester Jr., the last disciplinary requirement was removed. American Methodism had made the crossing from New Testament restitutionism to culture-religion.

I have presumed your indulgence in paying special attention to the case of Wesley and the Methodists in part for personal reasons, for this is the Christian sector within which I was licensed to preach some sixty years ago. More to the point, it is worth noting that John Wesley has been gravely maligned by persons who would prefer him to be reckoned a slightly irregular Anglican, or even an Anglo-Catholic.

Moreover, one of our late leading scholars and churchmen eagerly put forward and defended in ecumenical circles what has come to be called in the denomination a "Quadrilateral" of authority: experience, reason, tradition, and Scripture.[19] This is a modern invention. For Wesley and his preachers, the Bible was the cornerstone. The centrality of the Bible in the preaching and teaching and pastoral supervision of the founder and the movement in the years before it began to decline, losing more than a million members in a single decade, is beyond dispute.

When a movement that once grew rapidly—propelled by the vision of a restored New Testament church—falls away, its theologians and administrators fall with it. Or, to put the matter in restitutionist language, the misconduct of the professionals is central to the fall. This is precisely the source of the present painful loss of trust between the functionaries and the people in the local churches.

There is no point in indulging in further painful ruminations, painful at least to me, in connection with the present debate over whether the highest judicatory is to be repeatedly pressured with the recommendation that the rules of the church be changed to permit the ordination of declared, practicing homosexuals. Brutal statistics and moral accommodations are but indexes of the way in which a great restitutionist movement, once committed to "separation from the world," once on fire with anticipation of the breaking in of the kingdom of God, can settle down and permit its ideas and its style of life (*Torah*) to be provided by the spirit of the dying age (*Zeitgeist*) rather than the Spirit known and named in the Acts of Apostles.

It is but fair to say, however, that Methodism is only one of the former mainline Protestant movements that has passed from an ardent pursuit of primitive Christian religion to acceptance of minority status in a self-satisfied American culture, its repose only enlivened from time to time by fleeting fads and titillating trends injected from the outside.

The Case of the Disciples or Christians

In the history of the congregations that trace their beginnings to Alexander Campbell, Barton Stone, and Walter Scott, another set of problems has been evident. Richard T. Hughes and his colleagues have provided us with a number of splendid books and articles that show the perils to restitution or restoration when its preachers enjoy religious liberty rather than suffer persecution, when they enjoy citizenship in a vital republic rather than strive to survive under the "divine right of kings."

Alexander Campbell fits the large mold of what we call a "Renaissance man"—eminent as a preacher and church leader, eminent as an educator, eminent as a civic spokesman. He was a child of the Enlightenment as well as a son of the Reformation, which he embraced in its most radical—restorationist—form. This meant, among other things, that under his leadership Bethany College in West Virginia pioneered in physical education as well as instruction in Christian moral philosophy.

The issue of church discipline played little part in his thinking, and "separation" was scarcely a source of trouble for Alexander Campbell. The tension arose in finding the center of "the new order of the ages" in relating the primitivist program of a restitution church and a restored creation to the American historical mission to restore humanity to its primitive glory. In short, as Hughes has written, the question became, What was being restored?

America was an ideological state from its foundation, its identity given by its original covenant. In this regard, America was unlike most nations whose people have had to grope after an identity, more or less successfully, across many generations. In his prime years, Alexander Campbell became one of the most influential and representative of American citizens. As he moved from small beginnings into eminence, the focus of his restitutionism became more American civil religion and less primitive Christian.[20] Or, to put it another way, in the primordium "the Second Adam" blended in with the state of nature, and the millennium—the other bracket enclosing history—became a Christian republic with churches singing in harmony. Millennialism and restorationism, the "opposite and congruent ends of the same historical continuum,"[21] came to rest in a Christian nation of churches uniting.

The sometime millennial goal of a separated pilgrim people passing through to another age and another city was overpowered by the manifest blessings and vital appeal of life in America.

As an out-grouper, I think that the bone that stuck in the throat, methodologically, was the insistence that the religious program qualify by the norms set by Scottish Common Sense philosophy. The secure ground of a powerful myth or root metaphor was left behind, and vigorous minds entered into the intellectual controversies of the age as modernity defined them. To "stick to the facts," to proclaim Bible "facts," to authenticate religious "truth" by grafting it onto "the scientific method"—these are rules more readily related to vital civil life in nineteenth-century America than they are to what could be known and reclaimed from the life of early Christians at Corinth and Antioch and Ephesus. The stance of primitivism, which looks backward for its norms, was replaced by the spirit of modernity, looking blithely toward a future of progressive and orderly change.

For many Disciples and Methodists, Protestant America replaced the primitive church as the midwife of the millennium.[22] Both Alexander Campbell and Matthew Simpson, the Methodist bishop who preached the burial sermon of President Lincoln, were men of extraordinary gifts and influence in both church and body politic, and for both of them the vision of a restored golden age imploded. When the dust settled, they were standing squarely as free citizens in a Christian republic looking toward a Christian century.

As late as 1950, the first president of the National Council of Churches felt able to announce the council's formation as an expression of the "great determination that the American way will be increasingly the Christian way. . . . Together the churches can move forward to the goal—a Christian America in a Christian world."[23] By then, of course, the Roman Catholic church was the largest American denomination and the American Jewish community was the largest and strongest sector of world Jewry. But none of the great liberal Protestant denominations had as yet abandoned "the liberal alliance" and fled New York City for the provinces, and few out-groupers had noticed as yet the growing strength of another radical discontinuity movement.

The Restoration Vision in the Modern World

To be sure, there was not until the end of the twentieth century any conscious friendliness toward the religious and political patterns of the Constantinian model. The primordium, the state of nature, was "ante-civilization, ante-ecclesiasticism, ante-monarchies and dignities and privileges and pomp."[24] But when Christ and nature were progressively "collapsed into a single, common primordium,"[25] the millennium was collapsed into a fulfillment of the American destiny. William McKinley, a Methodist, justified our conquest of the formally Roman Catholic Philippines, for example, in the name of enlightening Filipinos with civilization and Christianity. American Protestantism long retained an energetic condemnation of emperor (fallen civilization) and pope (fallen Christendom) and their later imitators. Emperor Constantine and Pope Sylvester, the "two monstrous whales" that tore the net of the church, remained until 1928 for many American Protestants the twin signs of a fallen religious, social, and political order.

Hope Is Central, the Loss of Eschatology Is Fatal

Without a strong eschatological note, however, "separation" from the world takes on a false face. The "world" from which Christians are called to be separated is not the created order (*kosmos*) but this dying age (*Aeon*). The case for discontinuity is lost when restorationists are seduced into bondage to temporal institutions; but it is equally lost when Christians anchor the case for discontinuity to *hostility* to temporal institutions. Restitutionist "separation" is a kind of "permanent revolution" in which the things of this world are neither despised nor valued too highly.

Walter Klaassen has an interesting but I fear misleading article in an issue of the *Conrad Grebel Review* in which he compares the separation or detachment of earlier mystics to the stance of the Anabaptists, the sixteenth-century pioneers of *restitutio ecclesiae*. Klaassen, a Mennonite scholar, finds a link in the passing down of the term *Gelassenheit* from the Dominican mystics to certain *Täufer* testimonies. With a subtitle on "reinterpretation for today" he concludes, "We need to become detached from created things because we tend to put them in the place of God. . . . [This includes] not merely trees and birds and animals, *but everything that constitutes human life in this world.*"[26]

Is it not somehow strange to think of the Anabaptists/Mennonites, who traditionally are exemplary for their relationships to animals and to the land, as "detached from created things"? One might think that "love" would be a better description of the relationship than "detachment."

No, we are to set no great store by the things of this world, not because we cultivate a posture of distance but because we know that these things, too, must pass away. The Christian stance is not one of indifference toward the good life, but one that cultivates a yet greater love of the time to come. We shall all be changed.

This may be the time to lay to rest another familiar calumny against

the restitutionists, labeled "sectarians" with no interest in general social and political issues. Even otherwise friendly interpreters sometimes
fall into the trap of praising the "churches" because they sustain culture, science, and political structures, while the "sects" only look in-
ward. Albrecht Ritschl was perhaps the most vehement in pursuing this
line of attack, but he has had many successors.

Picking and choosing from today's religious map, it is easy to point
out that the Mennonites shun violent change. It would seem fair, however, to point out that the state-churches of Poland and Bavaria and
Spain have also resisted change—resisted it so violently that they have
been willing to bless those who killed to prevent change. *Stasis* has
been, in fact, the chief characteristic of the Constantinian model.

Because the Radical Reformation has rarely had the chance to shape
social and political structures, observers have generally failed to note
that the restoration theme has always carried a strong note of social
and political redemption. Put very simply, the restitution of the True
Church is to afford the bridge over which the people pass into a restored creation. In the Radical Reformation, the *apokatastasis* of the
New Testament is again proclaimed after the silence of centuries. The
theme *"die Wiederherstellung aller Dingen"* (restoration of all things)
is heard again. This portion of the gospel has been so neglected in contemporary culture-religion that some of us in the churches have grown
more familiar with the Hebrew equivalent: *Tikkun*.

In this respect the Church of Jesus Christ of Latter-day Saints has
given a better account of itself during the twentieth century than many
others who began with a restitution of the church at Jerusalem. The
members of the LDS Church take *this* world and *this* history seriously; for them "the restoration of all things" began at Kirtland, Ohio, on
April 3, 1836.[27]

No true restitutionists should lose the vision of the coming restoration of all things.

Scholarly Misinterpretation of "Church" and "Sect"

Unless we accept the role of myth as a positive force in human existence, unless we live affirmatively an oral tradition as well as make appropriate use of documents, unless we master a hermeneutical spiral
dialectically alternating between critical thinking and glad-hearted affirmation, both primordium and millennium lose their messages for us.
They fall prey to the scavengers who lurk in the back alleys where dis-
sertation topics are chosen and young minds with sharp scalpels and
no memories expose the imperfections and misapprehensions in teachings and beliefs they may depreciate but could never create.

In some educated circles, the restitutionist concept of church history has lost ground to the theme of continuity because seminaries, divinity schools, and graduate faculties in religion persist in misusing the Troeltschian typology in a way that Troeltsch himself warned against. In the last fifty years we have had a solid flow of dissertations demonstrating how sundry small religious groups, starting as "sects," have achieved social and economic upward mobility with their members and are now to be called "churches."

Ernst Troeltsch wrote that his famous church-sect typology could not be applied to the Anglo-American scene and that even in the German states it no longer functioned well after the changes in Protestantism during the nineteenth century. But apart from the question of methodology and critical analysis, is there not something strange in a scheme of definition in which the early church was a "sect" and Christianity attained the status of a "church" by putting itself under the control of more or less "Christian" Roman emperors in exchange for the privilege of persecuting dissenting Christians ("heretics") and Jews?

Of course, Troeltsch did not mean it that way. A dialectician, he thought to hold in tension two vital centers of Christian initiative and invention by scientifically objective use of the terms *church* and *sect*. There is no way, however, that the word *sect* can be anything but defamatory, and there is no Christian group in America—however small and "separated"—that willingly defines itself as a "sect," let alone as a "cult."

The misuse of the typology has confused counsel, corrupted substantive theological discussion, and guided the uncritical into a profound misreading of the American religious scene. The story of Protestant religion in America is not the story of how little sects became great churches, with others nosing their way to the surface following them. Rather, it is the story of how both "church" type and "sect" type have collapsed into Troeltsch's *third type:* the individual, generic Christian who acknowledges neither the obligations of a sacramental order nor the disciplines of a society of brethren. "Its champions [of the 'third type'] desire the spiritual interpretation of the Gospel, and the universality of a Christianity of the people, without the compromises of the Church. . . . Its champions desire the radicalism of a Society which is built upon the ideal of the Gospel, without the narrowness and pettiness of the sect."[28]

A recent Gallup Poll of religion shows something that has missed most of the professors who have guided young scholars into misreading and misusing the Troeltschian typology. According to the pollster, less than 10 percent of Americans are deeply committed and informed

Christians. Most who say they are Christians don't know the basic teachings of the faith, don't have a style of life much different from non-Christians, and in growing numbers say they can sustain their faith without participating in common worship.

George Gallup Jr. has warned that these generic Christians show themselves "open for anything that comes along" and seems to be "spiritual."[29] New Age "spirituality" is his illustration, but anyone who has studied the powerful spirituality (*Geistigkeit*) of the German Nazi movement cannot read that summary statement without a shudder of apprehension.

In sum, assimilation and accommodation have brought the free churches in America to a condition of social establishment not unlike that of the legally established churches of European Christendom today. As Rufus Jones (Quaker, author of the little book *The Remnant*) wrote, seeing in his own time the tendency to settle in and to forget the excitement of the coming kingdom of God, "The fields are so wide and the fences so low that the goats inside are as wild as the goats outside!"

Reformers and Radical Reformers Today

The religious fault line that existed in the sixteenth century between the reformers committed to *reformatio ecclesiae* and the Radical Reformers committed to *restitutio ecclesiae* is still present, but the confrontation is worldwide. In Latin America, there are significant new house church movements based on a recovery of the spirit and life of the early church. In Africa, where Christianity is growing most rapidly, the most vigorous churches are restitutionist. As John Howard Yoder put it fifteen years ago in a fine article, restitutionism points like an arrow toward radical discipleship.[30]

In America, where restitutionist churches once dominated the scene, Roman Catholicism is the largest sector of organized Christianity. Although some American Catholics show the Christian liberty and excitement of sixteenth-century reformers, the eyes of the Curia are obviously fixed on the glorious former times of a triumphant European Christendom. In America, "late bloomers" like the Lutherans and the Orthodox are of growing influence outside their once linguistic compounds. Continuity has displaced discontinuity as a major motif of ecumenical theology and cross-denominational conversations. Committees on church union abound, but conferences on biblical separation are rare.

Some prosperous movements, once restitutionist and hopeful, until now called "mainline" with increasingly dubious justification, have settled down to acceptability as denominations. But a strong wind is arising in another point on the compass. Dean Kelley, in his great book *Why Conservative Churches Are Growing,* has shown very clearly that there is another path from accommodation and decline, one that offers hope, "separation," discipline, and the power of the Word of God.[31] Powerful new movements of restorationist orientation are growing rapidly in both North and South America. And in the United States restitutionism is alive and well. Only, like so many millions of Americans during the last half century, a multitude of those looking for a recovery of New Testament Christianity have changed their ecclesiastical place of residence.

Restoration and Dispensationalism

In large sections of vital Protestantism, the restitution theme has also changed venue. Unnoticed by most outsiders until the critical year of 1967, and little understood since then,[32] a powerful movement has emerged within several denominations that puts the restitution of the early church in a quite different context from traditional restorationist thought. The father of this line of thought, usually called "Dispensationalism," is the most important underestimated person in American church history: John Nelson Darby (1800–1882).

Darby, who began his Christian ministry as an Anglican curate in Ireland, in midcareer developed strong views about the fallen condition of the establishment. With strong views about apostolic austerity of life, simplicity in gatherings for worship, intensive mutual discipline, and expectation of the Second Coming of Christ, he was a founding father of the Plymouth Brethren. When they splintered, he was the leader of the most rigorous branch.

Darby made several trips to the United States, where his strong Calvinist line found its echo among Presbyterians, Baptists, and a few Methodists. He profoundly influenced the preaching and teaching of American premillennialists with his clear reading of Bible prophecy. Integral to his teaching about the times to come were the return of the people of Israel to the land of their fathers, the "rapture" of the Christian remnant, Armageddon, and the coming again of the Messiah.

The life and work of conservative Protestant giants like Dwight L. Moody (1837–99) and Reuben A. Torrey (1856–1928) show the influence of Darby, as do also the ministries of Nathaniel West, William J. Erdman, James H. Brookes, Henry M. Parsons, Arthur T. Pierson, and many others. Across the generations, a most powerful means of spreading the technique for "getting the news in advance" was the International Bible Prophecy Conference founded at Niagara, New York, in 1876. Institutions such as the Moody Bible Institute, the Bible Institute of Los Angeles (BIOLA), the Philadelphia College of the Bible, and Dallas Theological Seminary are well known, but hundreds of Bible colleges in Canada and the United States have also played their part in popularizing the message.

Perhaps the most influential single force in millions of homes has been the Reference Bible prepared by one of Moody's young followers: C. I. Scofield (1843–1921). By red-lettered passages and footnoted commentaries, the Reference Bible explains how the various texts appertain to the several periods ("dispensations") of holy history. The Scofield Bible was published by Oxford University Press in 1909 and has been a best-seller ever since.

Scofield was also instrumental in the formulation of the "five points of Fundamentalism" (1895), and in 1909 two wealthy laymen financed the publication of twelve small volumes entitled *The Fundamentals: A Testimony to the Truth*. At this point the older orthodox teaching of the literal inerrancy of the text was welded to the "prophetic" interpretation of history, providing the powerful double impact of the authority of the Bible and a chiliastic emotional appeal. This was radical Puritanism reborn.[33]

In the beginning dispensationalism was strongly restorationist. Certainly Darby patterned his "gatherings" as closely as possible upon the New Testament and early church. The imitation of Jesus and the life of the apostles who knew him personally lay close at hand. Where it was blended with Wesleyan and Holiness accents—for instance, in the Northfield Conferences and in the Keswick Movement—the movement was blessed with "power for service," and social welfare work became one of the marks of the Christian.

It would seem, however, that an individualistic and heavily rationalistic orthodoxy has been a more characteristic product of dispensationalism. William E. Blackstone appeared with his charts at the 1886 International Prophecy Conference. Reuben Torrey's *What the Bible Teaches* (1898) professed the exactitude of science: the text is plain, with no hidden meanings, and the literal rendition is always to be preferred. With the natural scientist as the model carrier of the word, the message tends to become a dry package of propositions and "facts."[34]

The popular influence of dispensationalism, which cuts across denominational lines, can be judged by the fact that Hal Lindsey's *The Late Great Planet Earth*[35] has sold over twenty million copies since 1970 and is still going strong. Every crisis event in the Middle East launches a new flood of popular books of Bible prophecy. Although there is still friendly obeisance to the early church model, much more exciting are such exercises as "the seven-year countdown" and the attempt to discern and proclaim the signs of the end time. Along the scale of holy history, the attention directed to the final events far outweighs the passing attention to the primordial model.

This is a different sidetrack from that on which restorationism was shunted when the millennium became a blend of Americanism and "spiritual renewal." Nevertheless, it too is a sidetrack away from a strong emphasis upon the restitution of the True Church. The very precise dogmas and charts about the coming stages of history simply erase any basic significance of the pattern of restitution, as well as the importance of the church as a counterculture in this intermediate age between the fall of the church and the end time.

In dispensationalism, Israel and Jerusalem are returned to the center both geographically and salvifically. The restoration of the state in 1948 was greeted with joy in the congregations, but it was the signal victory of Israel in the Six Day War (1967) that brought the dispensationalists out from behind their walls into the political arena.

Incidentally, North and South America are not mentioned in the Bible, and hence—unlike the periodization found in Mormon writings—in pure dispensationalism there is no authentic, special place for America in the realization of God's sovereign, inexorable plan of salvation.[36] Where Americanism (of sorts) takes center stage among dispensationalists, as during a Southern Baptist assembly in Atlanta during the 1990s, it enters through the back door.

Even in Darby's writings, there is not a clear program for restoration of the New Testament and early church: in each dispensation the seeds of people's disobedience and the disintegration of their programs are already present. Only when Christ comes again in glory will the model be actualized and the way be made straight.

Restorationism Today

The restitution of the early church is still a very powerful model, especially in Latin America and Africa, and wherever else the oral tradition ("story") is cultivated and believers have managed to maintain the creative tension between the affirmative and the critical ("the hermeneutical spiral"). The understanding of apostolicity that restoration involves is at least as credible scientifically as "apostolic succession." In my view, biblical restorationism is vastly to be preferred to the restoration of another model—"Christendom"—which has been so much a brutal perversion of Christian belief and a miserable site for Jews and "heretics."

Latin Christendom has given verbal approval to slow change, while Greek and Russian Christendom froze Christian doctrine with the last of the great Fathers of the Church: St. John of Damascus (?700–754?). In his mummy, which can be viewed today at Mar Saba in the Kidron valley east of Bethlehem, we have a perfect symbol of the *stasis* that has afflicted Christendom and brought Christianity into disrepute among so-called "Christian" peoples as well as across the world map.

Indeed, John Howard Yoder's "arrow" can be blunted or deflected in several ways. In this essay, the two most vivid deflections have been revealed in North America in the collapse of sectors of the Disciples and the Methodists into *Kulturreligion* and in a parallel undermining of the joy and surprise of the restoration of all things through the propositional rigidity shown by many dispensationalists.

Whether Immanuel Velikovsky's model of catastrophic changes and reversals[37] can win over the modern mind, it should be clear that the evolutionary model is profoundly dysfunctional when applied to holy history and the works of the Holy Spirit. Marshall Berman, in *All That Is Solid Melts into Air,* finds the essence of modernity in gradual change, change that avoids the agony of transition, change like the passage of armies on parade—"glittering hardware, gaudy colors, flowing lines, fast and graceful movements, modernity without tears."[38]

Closing Observations

Where does this leave us?

There are several paradigms affecting change in Christian teaching and practice. Honoring the mummy at Mar Saba symbolizes resistance to change. Spotlighting the church as the body of Christ, with the image reinforced by a series of encyclicals about the *Corpus Mysticum* issued by reactionary popes, makes criticism of the Curia virtually impossible and slows change to a glacial pace. Accent on the third person of the Holy Trinity, the Holy Spirit, was congenial to many if not most of the Radical Reformers. ("It seemed good to the Holy Spirit and to us." *Acts* 15:28.)

The exercise of a lively dialogue among the living, in a setting that also affords to those who have died in the faith their appropriate hearing, opens the door to rapid change when necessary and radical change when imperative. The present state of Christian culture-religion in Europe and America demands radical departures.

Meanwhile, in the accommodation and assimilation that characterize the "fallen" churches of Christendom and seem to corrupt, as well, much of the restitutionist/restorationist sector of Protestantism, we risk being deafened by the clamor and crash of collapsing primordia and millennia. The Southern Baptists, meeting under a huge American flag in Atlanta, salute a millennium that elegantly blends a reasserted innocence—or at least a state of nature—with Americanism (of one sort or another). The "progressive" and "modern" sectors of "mainline" Protestantism, such as the Methodists and Disciples, are ambling (to avoid the forbidden imagery evoked by the word *marching*) forward into the next "Christian century," rather restlessly indigenized. They congeal in groupings (to avoid a word like *columns*) of American *Kulturreligion*, under banners of pacifism and churches uniting, liberalism and liberation, freedom and feminism, resistance and righteousness.

Marching in columns may be eliminated, but the lockstep and unison chant are ever with us—perhaps *especially* with us in the new modes of civil religion.

The "gay rights" sector, thoroughly ecumenical in respect to traditional denominational lines and conventional disciplines, is screaming its enthusiasm for a freedom euphemistically called "sexual preference." They have not noticed, evidently, that in the primordium the disturbing tension between the sexes—which in this life produces both anxiety and bliss—is resolved not by "sexual preference" but by androgynous primordial Man. And in the millennium, in so far as the Christian Bible is the final canon, there is no giving or taking in marriage. Presumably we shall also be relieved to discover that in time to come there will be no wrangling about gay ordination "rights" or "same sex" liaisons.

Where is the dialectical tension still retained and affirmed? Where in this eon—this present history with its conditional liberties, its tenuous freedoms, and its transitory engines of power—are there to be found communities of discipleship? Where are those who practice the dialogue with the past generations of this dispensation, but are not immobilized by that dialogue? Where are those who have put their hope in things unseen, but do not disdain the travel orders presently issued to us?

Where, in sum, are there Christians able to think and to act as communities of ministry, knowing that our times are in God's hands—our *primordial* histories, before humanity rebelled and the church betrayed; our *present* fallen history, in a world poisoned by sinful abuse and misuse of power, with religious establishments that serve and worship the "high places" (Lev. 26:30, Num. 33:52, Ezek. 6:3); our *future* history, when a church being redeemed and restituted shall be the bridge to the restoration of all things?

When we are brought alive by faith, we know that our dying age—with its wars and exploitation and dehumanization, with its dictators and despots, with its popes and spiritual potentates—shall pass away; indeed, the judgment of God has already been passed upon it.

We know that the gospel is not the bad news that things must stay the way they are. The gospel is the good news that we shall all be changed.

We know that in the covenant of fathers and sons, of mothers and daughters, and in the dialogue with those who share or have shared our habitat in this intermediate age, we may look with eagerness to the fulfillment of the promises. Unlike those who have telescoped the generations and elided the primordium and the millennium, and distinct from all those who defend some form of realized eschatology, we have the lively hope—in the end—to be surprised by joy.

Notes

1. A personal Prolegomenon: More than forty years ago I was able to adapt from the classical literature studies of Arthur O. Lovejoy and his circle a typology that has proven very useful in interpreting the course of church history. In applying the typology, I discovered, in sum, that there was a "grand canyon" between those churches that benefited from and provided the apologetic for the Constantinian model of church-state relations and those churches that idealized and pursued the Early Church norm. The state-church Reformers followed, with the Eastern Orthodox and the Roman Catholic church, the continuity model of the Ascension to the Second Coming with little earth shaking in between; the Radical Reformers followed the primitivist periodization scheme of Golden Age, Fall, and Restitution.

See Franklin H. Littell, *The Anabaptist View of the Church* (Chicago: American Society of Church History, 1952); revised edition published as *The Origins of Sectarian Protestantism* (New York: Macmillan, 1964). See also *Landgraf Philipp und die Toleranz* (Bad Nauheim, Germany: Christian Verlag, 1957), 15ff.

2. Karl Holl, *Gesammelte Aufsätze zur Kirchengeschichte,* vol. 1 (Tübingen: J. C. B. Mohr, 1928), 429.

3. Ibid., 466.

4. Philip Schaff, *Church and State in the United States* (New York: G. P. Putnam's Sons, 1888), 81.

5. *The Missionary Message in Relation to Non-Christian Religions* (New York: Fleming H. Revell, 1910), 244.

6. Jules Isaac, *Has Anti-Semitism Roots in Christianity?* (New York: National Conference of Christians and Jews, 1961), 45.

7. Richard T. Hughes and C. Leonard Allen, *Illusions of Innocence: Protestant Primitivism in America, 1630–1875* (Chicago: University of Chicago Press, 1988), 50.

8. Theodore Dwight Bozeman, *To Live Ancient Lives: The Primitivist Dimension in Puritanism* (Chapel Hill: University of North Carolina Press for the Institute of Early American History and Culture, 1988), 11.

9. John Owen, *The True Nature of a Gospel Church and Its Government* (1689; London: James Clarke, 1947), 61, 107.

10. James C. Spalding, "Restitution as a Normative Factor for Puritan Dissent," *Journal of the American Academy of Religion* (Mar. 1976): 44, 47–64, quotation from 57.

11. Henry Jacob, *A Defence of the Churches and Ministry of Englande* (Middelburg, England: Richard Schilders, 1599), 24.

12. *The Letters of John Wesley,* ed. John Telford (London: Epworth Press, 1931), letter to James Hervey, May 20, 1739, 1:286.

13. Ibid., letter to John Smith, 1746, 2:77–78.

14. Richard P. Heitzenrater, *Mirror and Memory: Reflections on Early Methodism* (Nashville: Kingswood Books and Abingdon Press, 1989), 15.

15. Ibid., 193.

16. Journal entry of February 6, 1740, published in Richard M. Cameron, ed., *The Rise of Methodism: A Source Book* (New York: Philosophical Library, 1954), 291.

17. See Littell, *Origins,* 36.

18. Bozeman, *To Live Ancient Lives,* 9–10.

19. See Albert Outler, "The Wesleyan Quadrilateral in John Wesley," *Wesleyan Theological Journal* 20 (Spring 1985): 7–18.

20. Richard T. Hughes, "From Primitive Church to Civil Religion: The Millennial Odyssey of Alexander Campbell," *Journal of the American Academy of Religion* 44 (Mar. 1976): 87–104.

21. Ibid., 92.

22. Hughes and Allen, *Illusions of Innocence,* 171–72.

23. Mark A. Noll, "The Public Church in the Years of Conflict," *Christian Century,* May 15–22, 1991, 553.

24. Edwin S. Gaustad, "Restitution, Revolution, and the American Dream," *Journal of the American Academy of Religion* 44 (Mar. 1976): 77–86, quotation from 80–81.

25. Hughes and Allen, *Illusions of Innocence,* 19.

26. Walter Klaassen, "'Gelassenheit' and Creation," *Conrad Grebel Review* 9 (Winter 1991): 23–35, quotation from 34.

27. Richard T. Hughes, "Introduction: On Recovering the Theme of Recovery," in Hughes, ed., *American Quest,* 6; see also Hughes and Allen, *Illusions of Innocence,* 137–38.

28. Ernst Troeltsch, *Gesammelte Schriften, 1: Die Soziallehren der christlichen Kirchen und Gruppen* (Tübingen: J. C. B. Mohr, 1919), 425n197.

29. *National and International Religion Report* 11 (May 20, 1991): 1.

30. John H. Yoder, "Anabaptism and History: 'Restitution' and the Possibility of Renewal," in Hans-Jürgen Goertz, ed., *Umstrittenes Täufertum, 1525–1975: Neue Forschungen* (Göttingen: Vandenhoeck and Ruprecht, 1975), 244–58.

31. Dean Kelley, *Why Conservative Churches Are Growing* (New York: Harper and Row, 1972).

32. See Franklin H. Littell, *American Protestantism and Antisemitism* (Jerusalem: Hebrew University, 1985), 18, 25.

33. See Peter Toon, ed., *Puritans, the Millennium, and the Future of Israel: Puritan Eschatology, 1600 to 1660* (Cambridge: James Clarke, 1970).

34. George Marsden, *Fundamentalism and American Culture: the Shaping of Twentieth-Century Evangelicalism, 1870–1925* (New York: Oxford University Press, 1980), 60–61.

35. Hal Lindsey, *The Late Great Planet Earth* (Grand Rapids, Mich.: Zondervan, 1970).

36. I want especially to thank Erich Geldbach of Marburg (Philipps-Universität) and Bensheim (Konfessionskundliche Institut) for sharing with me—prepublication—his paper "Jerusalem and the Plymouth Brethren," presented at the 1990 Jerusalem Conference on Holy Land Studies. See also his *Christliche Versammlung und Heilsgeschichte bei John Nelson Darby* (Wuppertal, Germany: Verlag Rolf Brockhaus, 1975), 3d ed.

37. Immanuel Velikovsky, *Worlds in Collision* (New York: Macmillan, 1950), *Ages in Chaos* (Garden City, N.Y.: Doubleday, 1952), and *Earth in Upheaval* (Garden City, N.Y.: Doubleday, 1955). See also *Velikovsky Reconsidered* (New York: Doubleday, 1976).

38. Marshall Berman, *All That Is Solid Melts into Air* (New York: Simon and Schuster, 1982), 137.

4

Primitivism in the Radical Reformation: Strengths and Weaknesses

JOHN HOWARD YODER

The phrasing of my title, which was assigned to me, seems to rest upon four assumptions that are not easy for me to appropriate sufficiently to build upon them. Naming them will be the best way to get started.

The first assumption is that "Radical Reformation"[1] labels an entity that could be described easily, a community whose members would all have thought basically the same thoughts. Nobody in the sixteenth century assumed that.

Any historian can distill, from among the multiplicity of movements to the left of John Calvin, what is considered most worthy of attention, most representative of the outworking of this or that axiom, or most likely to survive over the centuries, but the criterion of that unity is in the mind of the historian.

I also have attempted such a distillation, taking as my standard the presence of certain arguments in recorded debates between Reformed reformers and their Anabaptist contemporaries.[2] Other historians did such selective syntheses before me and others have done so since.[3] Such a distillation is not necessarily circular or arbitrary; one can justify one's principles of selection. But what one cannot do is represent, in such a selective synthesis, the whole scope of variability gathered, for example, in the encyclopedic narrative by George Williams, which gave to the phrase *Radical Reformation* its currency. Whatever *primitivism* means, it is not a univocal category for all "Anabaptists."

Thereby I have come upon the second difficult assumption; it is the label *primitivism* itself. No sixteenth-century radical said, "I am a primitivist." No sixteenth-century nonradical said, "Primitivism is wrong." The term is the construct of historians, probably first used pejoratively (as were the terms *Lutheran, Anabaptist,* and others). It designates *some kind* of orientation toward beginnings; but what beginnings? What kind of orientation?

For some "radicals" the beginning was Eden; the Levellers rejected class separations in society because there had been none in Genesis 2. Some accused Flemish Anabaptists of taking off their clothes in their meetings as a memorial of Adamic innocence. For other radicals, the beginning was the church of Acts, perennial point of beginning and of beginning again. For Luther, the beginning was the gospel as articulated by Paul.[4] There was no one in the sixteenth century who did not *in some way* claim first-century validation. Even the so-called "spiritualists" like Sebastian Franck and Kaspar Schwenckfeld, who on profound theological grounds downplayed the importance of literal conformity to the *words* of Scripture, were concerned to validate that view as having been that of the apostle, who said that "the letter kills and the Spirit gives life" (2 Cor. 3). Likewise, the papalists arguing the authority of Petrine succession or the appropriateness of doctrinal development beyond the New Testament proved their case by the New Testament.

"Primitivism" is not a position; it is a "fuzzy set" of notions concerning the contribution that remembering the origins of God's work makes to believers' participation in that work at some later time. I could suggest a spectrum of six or a dozen ways to make that appeal *ad fontes;* I would have to, if it needed to be clear what that spectrum would be expected to do for us.[5]

In thus doubting the univocality of the label, I am continuing a gentle debate with Richard T. Hughes that reaches back into the history of the critical communities we are reading about. In the 1970s Hughes described something of the difference between the restoration motif of the Campbellites and that of the Anabaptists.[6]

A comparable difference existed within the nineteenth century itself. The Churches of Christ, with their British and Puritan backgrounds, and the Churches of God, more Germanic and Pietist, used the same words and themes in nineteenth-century Indiana, but they were not doing quite the same thing. They seem not even to have contemplated working together.[7] The Campbellites made "restoration" a program; they wore it as a badge, and church order was the priority focus. For the Pietists it was a mentality, with experience the focus. For the Swiss Brethren it had been a tacit assumption,[8] but there was no abiding predilection among the later Doopsgezinde to continue arguing in those terms.

So instead of framing my assignment thus: The Anabaptists (and they alone in their time) were primitivist; what strengths and weaknesses did that stance have? my question must rather be, Everybody in the sixteenth century wanted to renew original Christianity; what problems were inherent in that vision?

The third ambivalent assumption stands in an odd way in tension with the second; it is that Mennonites and Hutterites in the eighteenth century or the twentieth ought to consider themselves called not simply to restoring first-century Christianity but also to perpetuating or restoring the sixteenth-century restoration, so that while we reject the Romans' or the Lutherans' obeisance to their respective precursors, we should properly measure Mennonite fidelity to Schleitheim or Dordrecht. This phenomenon takes on an especially paradoxical quality when a once "radical" group has been numerically successful for several generations, so that for their descendants the "old-time religion" they want to go back to means honoring as an established tradition the innovations introduced by the earlier radicals. One generation's innovators beget the next generation's conservatives.

This last-noted paradox is, however, not peculiar to the Baptists and their like. The majority of the people who characterize themselves as "catholic" (Roman or otherwise) hold no less to components of tradition as if these practices had always been the same, which, however, were in fact novel when they first were adopted. Christian anti-Judaism and Hellenistic apologetics were innovations in the second century. Celebrating Constantine and imposing dogmas by imperial "ecumenical" councils were brand new in the fourth. Clerical intervention in the decisions of civil rulers was new in the High Middle Ages, as civil rulers governing the institutional church had been new in the fourth century.[9]

The fourth assumption to test is that there is an easy way to discern "strengths and weaknesses." It is as if there might be some standpoint above the melee from where we could measure against each other what we, as historians, with or without empathy, might consider to be such pros or cons, without being ourselves stuck in the same circularity. Circularity dogs the contemporary historian just as it rendered petitionary the claim of Conrad Grebel or Johannes Denck, Carlstadt or Melchior Hofmann, Erasmus or Martin Bucer, to be beginning again with the apostles. If the confidence that one can find a place to stand from which to stand in judgment on the past had not been fully relativized by our standard skills as historians, it would in any case have been wiped away by "modernity." There is no way past these difficulties; I must therefore build them into my review. Instead of knowing, by measuring with some criterion from beyond the mix, what is a "strength" and what is a "weakness," I shall seek simply to identify the agenda, the questions that need to be dealt with, *if* a community within history is committed both to living in its own age and to deriving its identity from a finite set of definitional events in first-century Palestine.

What Were the Swiss Brethren Restoring?

Toward this end there is no reason to rehearse all we know about the ways in which in the 1520s infant baptism, war, the oath, usury, civil control of the church, "images," and indulgences were condemned by appealing to the New Testament and the usage of the earliest centuries. Two specimens must suffice; one where the Swiss Brethren diverged from Huldrych Zwingli and one where they did not.

The Cross and the Sword

Richard T. Hughes has suggested that what sets the sixteenth-century radicals apart from other "restorations" was the object of the restoration, namely, "discipleship."[10] Only at one particular point does that seem to me to be true, of just one strand of Anabaptists,[11] on just one subject. Article 6 of the Schleitheim "Brotherly Understanding" answers challenges to the rejection of the sword by pointing to the responses of the Jesus of the Gospels to those same questions. Jesus refused to participate in inflicting the death penalty, refused to pass judgment in a conflict between brothers, refused the office of king when it was offered him. These three cases are prefaced by "Christ teaches and commands us to learn from him, for he is meek." They are followed by "as Christ our head is minded, so must be minded[12] the members of the body . . . so that his body may remain whole."

Thus the notion that sharing the mind of Christ empowers and obligates us to act as the earthly Jesus did is powerfully present. This is the strong sense of the modern term *discipleship*, although it was not the usage in the sixteenth century.[13] Yet this kind of "identification" is much narrower than what many mean by "discipleship," and the only issue to which it applies in this way is the sword. It was not original to the Swiss Brethren; they had received the core of it from Zwingli, and he from Erasmus.

The Lord's Supper and the Last Supper

Rather than look further for someone using the word *discipleship* or for the kind of argument for which *discipleship* is our modern cipher, I suggest that we ask at what point the notion of appealing to original

Christianity to judge and renew present patterns was first operational in the Zurich beginnings. That had to do with the reformation not of ethics but of worship; namely with purging the canon of the mass. This was a topic that Zwingli and the left wing of his followers agreed upon. Following through on the doctrinal direction stated in article 18 of the Sixty-seven Theses he had proposed for debate in January,[14] on August 29 Zwingli published a first draft (in Latin) of his program for revising the mass;[15] it provoked criticism by his friends and he accepted their criticism, publishing an *apologia* on October 9.[16]

At the end of that month, the transformation of the mass into an evangelical Lord's Supper was the first item on the agenda for the second reformation disputation.[17] Regularly throughout the argument, the appeal was to the New Testament words of institution and the practice of the early church, to demonstrate that the Eucharist is not a "sacrifice." After the doctrinal basis had been abundantly argued, mostly by Zwingli himself, the conversation turned to "abuses."[18] Balthasar Hubmaier spoke first. To celebrate the Eucharist without proclamation of the Word, whereas Jesus had said, "Do this in my memory," and Paul had said, "You proclaim his death," is an abuse. Another is to read Latin to German-speaking listeners, whereas Jesus certainly spoke "loud and understandably," or for the celebrant to "communicate" alone without serving the congregation, whereas Jesus had said, "All of you drink of it."

Then Zwingli continued: there should not be songs that even most of the clergy do not understand, when Paul wrote that he would rather speak five words that edify than ten thousand in tongues (1 Cor. 12:19). The supper should not be bound to one particular time. The celebrant should not wear a special robe (although Zwingli had been willing to condone that in August) because it supports a wrong association with the sacrificial cult of the Old Testament.

Conrad Grebel then took the floor: it is wrong to require unleavened wafers when Jesus used ordinary bread. Water should not be poured into the wine. The priest should not put the host in the communicant's mouth. Celebration should not be limited to the forenoon, and the communicant should not need to be fasting, since Jesus broke bread to his disciples in the evening in the midst of a meal. Nor should a priest's officiating be limited to the days prescribed by his prebend.

Zwingli began to preside, answering Grebel point by point. On most points he agreed with Grebel, though with some concern not to be too prescriptive (we should not have to wear the same clothes Jesus and his disciples did or wash each others' feet), and with concern to leave maximum freedom to the local congregation. Grebel said he was satisfied.

Neither Zwingli nor Grebel was seeking to imitate woodenly what they took the early Christian practice to have been, although this misinterpretation has been common.[19] They rather appealed to the New Testament *against* the prescriptive claims made by medieval tradition for nonbiblical forms in favor of congregational freedom. They wanted to be able to celebrate at any time of the day, whereas the tradition insisted on breaking a fast. They cited the gospel accounts of the Last Supper not to validate a rule but to loosen one. The same was the case for the use of ordinary bread taken from the table, for the communicant's taking the bread in the hand, and for all communicants' sharing the cup. The general principle was local congregational responsibility, a principle that Zwingli supported in theory from January 1523 to October 1523 but not really later.

There are good arguments, in the long run, for linking Anabaptist "restitution" with the issues of church and state, war, and the oath. But that is the narrowing imposed upon the debate by the way Zwingli (different only in detail from Luther at about the same time) later turned away from the radical implications of his own early program. From the beginning it was not so; the first Zwinglian agenda was purging Christian worship of superstition and sacerdotalism. The appeal to the New Testament posited neither golden age nor literalism. It merely took seriously the historical character of the faith, placing the burden of proof with the nonbiblical innovations. When Catholics claimed that celebrations like the Eucharist had been instituted in the first century, that claim made them vulnerable to the canonical appeal as some other doctrines and practices might not have.

Historiography for Christ's Sake

Somebody writing a letter *to the Hebrews* nineteen centuries ago admonished his or her readers to "remember your leaders, those who spoke to you the word of God" (Heb. 13:7–8). That appeal is founded in the fact that Jesus Christ is "the same yesterday, today, and forever." Already by the time of writing (according to chapter 6 of the epistle) some people were falling away from the faith once confessed, and some (chapter 10) were neglecting their common meetings. The fact that the author looked forward to "that Day drawing near" at some yet future time did not make identity maintenance less important, even though today some make the odd claim that apocalypticism is uninterested in history.

The need to recall a faith community to fidelity in the face of threats to identity arises necessarily from the historical particularity of their founding events. That need becomes conscious as soon as the community becomes aware of the passing of time. It is not a sign of weakness or failure. It is multiplied in direct proportion to the community's missionary aggressiveness, which provides new occasions for change. It is multiplied in proportion to the clarity with which it claims normativity, as Hebrews so pointedly does, for the founding events.

In order to specify when in the experience of the church the appeal to normative origins becomes important, we need to ask in what situation it might arise that the normative quality of the origins would be set aside. We could take a wider view of all the possible arguments in favor of some norm *other* than the appeal to beginnings, but it will suffice for now to watch the mainstream of "catholic" theology as it in fact evolved. One early landmark along this path is the development, toward the middle of the second century, of the kind of argument we call "apologetics," whereby Christians sought to restate their testimony in terms borrowed from the elite unbelieving culture around them. This included closing the door between Christianity and its Jewish mother culture. In the real life of neighborhoods, synagogues, and churches, this door did not really close; there continued for generations to be a Jewish Christianity fraternizing both with the nonmessianic synagogues (what we later call "Judaism") and with the Gentile communities believing in the Jew Jesus (which we call "Christian"). But for the "apologetes," the Jewishness of Jesus was unimportant or was even a handicap to be overcome. Particularity is no advantage for the Hellenistic mind to which the "apologetes" wanted to commend their faith. The truest truth is commended by its timelessness, placelessness.[20]

This opened the door in turn for an additional set of priorities to begin to change. Some of these changes centered on speculative theology and some on the escalation of ceremonial religiosity, with its implications for priesthood and sacramentology. Arendt Theodoor van Leeuwen projected, a generation ago, in his *Christianity in World History*,[21] the characterization of pagan thought as "ontocratic," i.e., as nonhistorical, with "the way things are" being its own ultimate norm. Like any ambitious synthesis, van Leeuwen's work oversimplifies, but it is not false. It enables us to characterize what it was that was forsaken when (one school of) apologetes bought into Neoplatonism.

The beginning of historical consciousness is represented in our story by the figure of Abraham, forsaking the heart of Babylonian imperial culture in order to live—and to migrate— toward another yet unbuilt city. It might be that there could be such a thing as a moral monotheism that would not be historical. At least the outward form of monotheism and the outward shape of morality can be affirmed in a dehistoricized, de-Semiticized Christian theology. But at the beginning, the separated sociology of Abraham and his descendents was an indispensable vehicle for the intervention in human affairs of a God whose identity (as distinct from that of the other gods) can best be described as personlike and moral.

If that narrative particularity, in which the God of the heavens elects one thread through the world to save the rest of the world, is the correct way to characterize the stream of grace from Abraham to Jesus and his apostles, then the reversion to antiparticular pagan generality, whether it be (earlier) Canaanite with a focus on fertility or Hellenistic with a focus on gnosis or Roman with a devotion to empire or (later) Germanic with yet another focus, will characterize the beginning dilution of the Abrahamic vision.

It is important to note above that the normativity of the foundational events was not challenged by the very fact of missionary aggressiveness. As long as conversion is given substance by strong catechesis, and as long as the moral quality of the life of discipleship is assured by the messianic equivalent of Torah, missionary success reinforces rather than relativizes the normativity of Jesus and his gospel. Entering new cultures and incorporating new members heightens rather than weakens particular identity, *if and when* conversion is given serious content. It was neither numerical growth as such, nor entering other cultures as such, that led to apostasy.

It is also important to note that the beginning dilution of messianic specificity began at the very beginning of Christianity and began to be spelled out intellectually in the second century. This should protect us from the oversimple notion that the big turn did not come until the fourth century. Yet, it is clear that the largest portion of the later case for primitivism arose then. Between the third century and the fifth, the relationship between the church and the world was profoundly redefined, in ways that raised the notion of restoration to a qualitatively new level. We look to that change, then, as representative, prototypical, but not as the whole of the reason renewal would be needed.

It is a mistake to think that the change associated in legend with the name of Constantine has to do principally with the relationship of church and state. For the sake of my present assignment, I shall be pursuing the church-state theme, but that is only one facet, and perhaps not the most important, of what was transformed.

It is also a mistake to focus our interpretation of the change, as legend has done, on the man Constantine, as if he were the only major actor. Constantine was in fact a larger-than-life figure; the orders he gave did in fact reverse the course of history with regard to the place of Christianity in the empire. Yet his coming to be seen as a savior figure, as an inaugurator of the millennium, was not his work alone. He was decisively abetted by the mythmaking capacities both of popular culture and of Eusebius of Caesarea. Some of the systemic changes that Constantine as a mythic figure symbolizes for the historian (such as Christians' believing that God favored the empire against its enemies) had begun before he came along, and some (like the legal prohibition of the pagan cult or the prosecution of Christian dissent) took a century after him to be worked through. So when his name is used as mythic cipher it would be a mistake to concentrate on his biography.

From Christianity to Christendom

Before pursuing my assigned concentration on the social ethic, let me briefly summarize the other kinds of changes that separate the Christian life patterns of the fifth century from those of the second. Neither time nor my competence permits arguing at length which changes were causes and which effects.

The dominantly Hebraic world vision within which the church was born, with a personlike God calling creatures into covenant, was replaced by a Greco-Roman mix of Platonism and Stoicism. Jahweh of hosts was replaced by the Prime Mover. Pagan religiosity was baptized rather than renounced. The solstice festival became Christmas, spring fertility rites became Easter, local pre-Roman deities became village patron saints. The relation between the visible church and the Christian hope was turned around;[22] whereas in the first century God's ultimate victory had to be believed but the believing community was empirically known; in the fifth the reverse was the case. A monarchical sacerdotal class was reintroduced in a community that had begun with the affirmation that Jesus had put an end to the priesthood. The Lord's Supper became a rigid ritual.

Christianitas became the word for the people under Caesar's rule. People outside the empire were heretics (Arians to the north, Eutychians to the south, Nestorians to the east). Farther out were the infidels. Only the rare European imagined that any of those people might possibly become Christian, and if they did it could only be as vassals to Rome.

The Social Axioms of Establishment

Once before when I described the way in which the new sociology had changed the logic of ethics,[23] I identified four aspects of the change;

that was quite incomplete. A more adequate account would list at least the following aspects of how medieval and modern assumptions differ from those of the early centuries.

1. Ethics was not for "saints," i.e., not for a convinced and converted moral elite, but for ordinary people, "everyman" or the "common person," whose baptism did not signify a profound conversion and who may in fact have been coerced. This is at the origin of the split between "counsels of perfection" for religious people and an ethic of precepts for *hoi polloi.*

2. Ethics was not for "saints" but for "sinners." Augustine built into his normative anthropology an incorrigible sinfulness to which ethical idealism had to adjust. In this setting, justification is more representative of what the gospel is about than is sanctification. It would be wrong to think about God's holy will as something that can be done.

3. Ethics became consequentialist. Since Christians held power, they became accustomed to explaining decisions in terms of their predictable effects, subject to evaluation in cost-benefit terms. Only people accustomed to power can thus juxtapose their decisions with results.

4. Ethical reasoning assumed generalizability. As all agents were assumed to be of the same kind, since everyone was baptized, it was evident that moral logic should be guided by the formal definition of the categorical imperative; what can be a rule for me must be a rule for everyone.

5. Constantine was the prototypical actor for whom ethics must be tailored. Rather than asking Constantine to be converted to follow Jesus, Christian ethics was transformed to fit ("pastorally") the task of running an empire.

6. Constantine was the unique, elect instrument of God in history. What the empire did was not merely morally *licit* (as in axiom 5) but redemptive. The vehicle of salvation history was seen ("prophetically") to be not the faith community but the empire. It was not enough to say that Constantine was a mover of salvation history; kingship as such became sacral. This moved beyond ethics in that Caesar governed ("saved") the church as well.

7. Rather than by particular revelation, ethics in society was directed by "common sense" in the sense of consensus. *Jus gentium* was what everyone believed. Under this heading medieval thought retrieved the heritage of Plato and Aristotle for talking about the nature of things, that of Cicero for talking about justice.

8. Rather than by particular revelation, ethics in society was directed by "common sense" in the sense of an intuitive immediacy, a special skill for knowing (as in "horse sense" or "sixth sense") what "anyone can plainly see."

I turn now to itemize what all of these axioms have in common:

1. In situations where there has not been a Constantinian shift (whether Judaism since Jeremiah, Christianity before A.D. 200, or later Christianity outside Christendom), none of these axioms would be self-evident.

2. In the Constantinian situation they were so self-evident that without philosophical sophistication ordinary people could not even imagine that one could reason otherwise.

3. They seem all to combine to make a case for legitimate violence, whereas each of the alternative components of the pre-Constantinian system was congenial to pacifism. Thus Richard T. Hughes's assigning me the task of accentuating the social ethic of the Swiss Brethren is fitting, although that narrowing leaves out much that would matter no less.[24]

4. In a similar way, the new axioms of Christendom are compatible with human slavery, with patriarchalism, with racial or ethnic discrimination, and with empire. One of the ways that the appeal to "the way things are" (axiom 7 above) was baptized was that the previously pagan cosmological positivism was made into a doctrine of creation. Empire, patriarchy, slavery, and racism are not contingent arrangements that might be challenged, but the nature of things.

If our concern is with the presuppositions of social ethics, *then* the form of "restitution" will be whatever it takes to call into question the above Constantinian axioms, especially wherever they contradict the ethical import of the gospel, and to reverse the sociological changes that made them self-evident. This was the case for the Czech Brethren of the style of Peter Cheltschitski or for the Swiss Brethren of the style of the Schleitheim Confession. For them, and for others of their type, the challenge they addressed to war and to social privilege, for instance, was derived from an intrinsic logic based on their challenge to infant baptism, which followed in turn from their appealing to the New Testament, but also from their Erasmian-Zwinglian programmatic *ad fontes* appeal and from Zwingli's telescoping of "sacrament" into "significance."

If, on the other hand, our concern is (like Luther's) for retrieving the Pauline proclamation of justification or (like Thomas Müntzer, Johannes Denck, and Kaspar Schwenckfeld, all in different ways) the recovery of authentic inner piety, then the criteria for renewal will be accordingly different, and so will the means. Differences of diagnosis yield differences of treatment. Since Luther's key was the loss of the Pauline message of justification, that key not only dictated positively the changes that he thought needed to be made in preaching and catechesis; it also explained why certain other concerns, which mattered

to others, were for him *adiaphora*. Martin Bucer and his pupil John
Calvin did not agree with Luther that those matters of order (e.g., episcopacy or the presbyters' independence of the magistrate) did not matter; they wanted to restore proper *forms* (i.e., forms prescribed by the
New Testament) of ministry and discipline. Not for nothing do we call
that tradition "*reformed.*"

To those critiques addressed to piety and church order, one must
add critiques of the civil order (to which I shall soon turn) and wealth.
The ground had been prepared for Francis of Assisi and Waldo of Lyons by the scandal of simony. Cheltschitski in the fifteenth century began by condemning the class structure of society; the Hutterites of the
sixteenth began their renewal with the economy of *Gelassenheit*. This
is where John Wesley focused his doctrine of the Constantinian fall.[25]

The difference of style to which Franklin Littell has pointed, between moderate "reformation" that seeks to make corrections organically and radical "restitution" that wants to start over, helps to illumine
particular debates but it does not put everybody into just two neat pi-
geonholes. People tended to be patient "reformers" when they were
being listened to by those in power and impatient "radicals" when
turned away; "radical" on what they cared about the most and "reformers" on less important issues.

I have simplified thus far by asking only, What went wrong and how
should we therefore fix it? in order to spread out the spectrum of different visions of renewal. There were, however, other differences of
vision as well, which would spread out different spectrums. For some
"radicals" the villain was "Constantine," the mythic figure created by
Eusebius whom they stood on his head; for others it was "the pope."
For Thomas Müntzer it was the venal priesthood. For the most critical Quakers it seems to have been the first postapostolic generation.
For some visions the ideal cure would be a historyless return to "go,"
as if the centuries had not happened. For others, from Joachim of Fiori
to Müntzer, John Hut, and Melchior Hofmann, the corrective move
would be not backward but forward, and the scriptural appeal that
empowers us to denounce apostasy would be in itself powerless to heal
without a new divine intervention. I do not read this variety as either
a "strength" or a "weakness" of the notion of canonically governed renewal, but only as a reminder that the debate must be more detailed.

We Cannot Go Home Again

Something we have been taught to call "historical consciousness" comes
between us and the sixteenth century (to say nothing of our more dis-

tant past). Historians of ideas differ on just when to date it and just how to describe it, and it does not exhaust the meaning of "modernity," but there is no doubt about its being there as a great divide. We cannot divest ourselves of our awareness of historical change and relativity. It teaches us that there is no univocal interpretation of fidelity to ancient models.

Yet this does not free us from the duty to seek to be empathetically fair to historical actors for whom our version of this relativizing awareness was not possible. The responsibility for the intellectual stretching that it takes to make sense of what moved an actor in a bygone age belongs to the historian, not to the actor.[26] That *we* know that the Scriptures are not univocal is not pertinent to our interpreting the inner consistency of the position of any sixteenth-century figure.

For some, "historical consciousness" is a product of the unbelieving enlightenment, and it relativizes everything that went before. In the face of its doubts, anything older than the eighteenth-century's discovery of "Reason" can be only of archaeological interest. "Enlightenment" has thus become its own new and final *Heilsgeschichte,* a new and saving sect. (Its critical acids apply less to Reformation biblicism, be it noted, than to later Protestant scholastic doctrines of infallibility.)

For others, who seem to me to be wiser, the ability to relativize one's own identity-giving recent and local past, in the interest of a longer history and a wider world, is a part of the Christian's missionary cosmology[27] and a most congruent extrapolation of the appeal to Abraham and Jesus as leverage against apostasy. It may preserve us from absolutizing our present as well as free us to honor other epochs than our own. Then "modernity" is a child and ally of "restitution," not its enemy.[28] Modernity in this sense is the enemy of that mode of establishment that claims to be self-evidently "catholic," rather than the enemy of the critical historical appeal.

Trial Balance

What can we now identify as "strengths and weaknesses" accompanying the versions of restitution that were operative from the fifteenth century to the eighteenth? As explained before, I prefer to ask, What are the questions they raise? They all have been touched on above.

1. How do we interpret the variety of initial questions that the several kinds of "renewers" took to their reading of church history and their scriptural appeal? Does the priority belong to proper church order, to the message of salvation, to the life of discipleship, to correct doctrine . . . ? Can these different focuses be assigned relative priority

on the grounds of criteria derived either from the critique of Christendom or from the Bible? Might the priorities vary depending on the particular kind of trough the church is in just now? Or is there a proper *ordo salutis* that demands taking first things first? The assumptions underlying this volume would seem to be that all primitivisms are equal, just so long as one restores something; yet all of the founder figures would have agreed to reject that.[29]

2. How do we evaluate the points at which Christians intentionally and consciously "corrected" or "completed" the biblical heritage by borrowing from ancient philosophers or from pagan religions? The "catholic" traditions claim for those adjustments the authority of the Holy Spirit and of an authorized episcopal magisterium. Enlightenment Christianity claims the authority of progress. Some such appropriation of non-Hebraic materials may be justified as redemptive missionary creativity; yet, some such cases must also certainly be denounced as betrayal. With what criteria do we sort out the differences? Those for whom someone else's notion of "restitution" is too simple do not resolve the question by that judgment.

3. How do we reinterpret after "modernity" the possibility of basing any normative argument on an appeal to the Bible? The several waves of changing critical methodologies have not made people stop reading their Bibles; how does a "canon" now serve, when readers are relativistic about reading ancient texts?[30]

In the normal continuity whereby each generation has to climb to eminence over the corpses of its parents, the currently prominent style of critical historiography is to be critical especially of anyone whose critique appeals to any particular vision of normative origins. A critical dialogue with this currently "politically correct" line of argument is an important missing component of this volume. This question does not belong to my assignment as initially phrased, but it is important that I identify it in order to challenge the notion that it has somehow ended the discussion. Examples would be Robert Wilken's *Myth of Christian Beginnings* in patristic studies, Burton Mack's *The Myth of Innocence* in New Testament studies, and Jonathan Z. Smith's *Drudgery Divine* in the history of religions.[31] The needed dialogue would be complicated, since the argument of the debunkers is unavoidably paradoxical as they undertake to undercut one kind of (often naive) normative claim with another whose biases are less clearly avowed, yet which also goes on tracing past becoming, as if it mattered.[32] Such a dialogue would clarify the difference between the naive appeal to the apostles that Wilken traces from Hegesippus to Ernst Käsemann, on the one hand, and the Radical Reformers' appeal to the New Testament on the other.

Jonathan Z. Smith has reviewed with his customary thickness and verve a number of the most current ways in which the contrast between "original" and "degenerate" religious expressions has served to hide value biases under the cover of what pretends to be simple historical description. The historian reports how Jesus was replaced by Paul, Hebraic thought patterns were replaced by Greek, historic modes of perception were overruled by "cyclical" timelessness, biblical religion was replaced by "paganism," and so the story goes on, usually downhill. The invidious comparisons can be shown generally to be petitionary, usually anti-Catholic in the modern Protestant world, and usually anti-Jewish.

Smith has made his case well, for those cases that he has selected to pursue. He watched closely one chosen concept, that of "mystery," and one mythic narrative, that of the dying and rising god. What Smith does not do at all is to round out the picture by identifying an alternative. Would it be possible for historical communities to get along without facing the question of normative identity? Could one avoid it by recourse to a monolinear historical evolution validating itself by the power of its univocality? Would the wholesome alternative be a mode of appeal to prior history or present community that would be less naive than the specimens Smith shows to be too simple? Would it be a "map" not subject to invalidation by its failing to fit the world?

Once we have set aside the notion that this historical critique refutes a priori the concept of a canonical appeal, it has much to teach us. Let me lift one example from Smith's account. Reading straightforwardly the texts as they stand, we assume that the apostle Paul is, so to speak, the pinnacle of the New Testament. We read from the Gospels on into Acts, and Paul is three-fifths of Acts. Then Paul is three-fourths of the Epistles, which he dominates not only in quantity but also in quality. His message, nothing but Christ crucified, and its implication of justification by faith alone must therefore be the heart of the gospel.

Yet Christians in the second century did not know that. Most churches were not founded by Paul. It took a century for the corpus of his writings to be collected and still longer for them to be appealed to as authoritative; this may have been done first by Marcion. Graydon Snyder has shown that the art in Christian cemeteries gives no evidence of the crucifixion of Jesus.[33] A generation earlier Thomas Torrance showed that the concept of grace in the early fathers was strikingly un-Pauline.[34] Does this prove that Paul is not at the center of the canon or that the cross is not central for Christians? Not at all. What it does show us is something more important for our purposes, namely, that origins only take on their definition and their authority later, when they are appealed to in order to throw light on conflicting definitions of present faithfulness. This kind of appeal began on one level in the origins of the gospel as literature,[35] on another in the gathering of the New Testament as corpus, and on yet another in the origins of church history. The fact that the textual baseline to which the later argument appeals was not there at the outset, but is the product of the appeal, does not make that "myth" false; that is the only way it could have come to be. That fact does not accredit as somehow more true, or true on other grounds, truth claims that avoid vulnerability in the arena of history. The paradox is that we need the canon, with Paul at its heart, *not* because the witness of Paul was at the heart of the life of all the churches of the first century, but because it was not. The "golden age" metaphor turns out to be the opposite of how the canonical appeal works.

4. What can be done to overcome the widespread notion that these questions apply only to the free churches? They are equally pertinent in seeking to understand Francis of Assisi or Trent. They are raised no less by Martin Luther or by the Anglican case for episcopacy.[36]

If we seek to understand the search for Christian faithfulness in all of pre-Enlightenment Christendom, and in popular pre-Enlightenment Christendom that is still alive today, the argument against the appeal to the apostles, based primarily on the diversity of historical data and the relativity of historical knowledge, is not an argument against the "primitivists" in particular. Everyone in that earlier history was claiming to be biblical, in some way or other;[37] historical seriousness must honor that intent, naive though it was, rather than mock it, and must not attribute it only to someone else.

5. The debate between criticism that challenges the transformations imposed by the Constantinian millennium, on the one hand, and the appeal to "catholic" "continuity," on the other, is made narrow and petty when it is understood to be primarily an internal debate within the world Constantine made, about matters of pastoral practice and social ethics. As long as those matters do have to be debated, I am not granting that there is any reason to yield on the issues of sacerdotalism,[38] pedobaptism,[39] and violence,[40] just because they are internal and narrow. But more is needed; the original stake, as I said above, was Christological. "Restitution" is a cipher, although (as we have seen) a misleading one, for the claim that Jesus Christ is God's authoritative Word, tomorrow as well as yesterday. The opposite of "restitution" is then also a Christological claim, namely, that there are norms above Jesus Christ, sometimes clothed in the notion that there is a "Christ" above Jesus, or another Jesus above the one in the Gospels. Sometimes these other

norms are called "nature," sometimes "reason," sometimes "creation." They tended for centuries to concretize their imperatives more through the state than through the church.

What originally was at stake was the missionary nature of the church. The world Constantine made put an end to authentic proclamation of the gospel beyond the limits of the empire except in the form of the expansion of empire.[41] Those who expanded the empire, whether Charlemagne, the Crusaders, or Columbus, told themselves and their victims that they were extending the church and glorifying God; but what they propagated at the edge of the sword was not the gospel of Christ crucified.[42] This was the case not only because of the linking of "mission" with violence and empire; it was the case also because of ethnocentrism and cultural genocide, which we had occasion to remember especially in 1992 as we thought of Columbus. In the "catholic" synthesis, "mission" tends to collapse into the mandate to Christianize (and usually to homogenize) one's own culture, to the neglect of a message of reconciliation capable by its very nature of addressing all the nations.

Where Are We If We Can't Go Home Again?

If it were my assignment here to project what might be a theologically "normative" vision of the appeal to origins, it might be that the above-cited book by my old friend and former colleague Robert Wilken could serve as a useful background review of the history of the use of history. His title, *The Myth of Christian Beginnings*, would seem at first to suggest that in the appeal to origins something false or deceptive is going on, but that is not the argument Wilken provides. He does not define "myth" in a clear way, nor does he argue that it is something one could do without. He rather demonstrates how it could not be otherwise, since, with the passage of time, Christians had to tell, with normative weight, the story of the link between the story of Jesus and their own.

Hegesippus, not yet the father of church history but the greatest early Christian collector of anecdotes and lists, already used the image of the early church as a virgin, who in a bare century had been corrupted by various false teachers. That metaphor serves Wilken as the threading theme; it posits a point in real history where there had been a pure beginning, whose value has since been lost.

When Eusebius initiated the retelling of history as a theological genre, he took over from Hegesippus the metaphor and with it the inability to deal with real change as anything but betrayal. He compiled legends about the apostles that played along with that vision. Yet two considerations within that story count against that interpretation, more than Wilken acknowledges. In the apologetic encounter with pagan scoffers, Eusebius appealed not to the first century but farther back (to Abraham) and infinitely farther forward (to eternity). Instead of inviting unbelievers into the experience of redemptive community as the churches of the earlier generations had done, he made a nonhistorical intellectual claim. That was the beginning of the Hellenistic relativizing of the historical appeal.

More important, however, was Eusebius' proclaiming that the reign of Constantine was a major shift in salvation history, a radical irruption of the divine to destroy the pattern of declension. Wilken does not (in this 1971 volume) take account of how the savior status ascribed to Constantine dulls the edge of the older metaphor. There is no point in asking Eusebius to sort out for us some principle of consistency to hold together his proclaiming a new age and his mourning lost virginity. Both are present; each governs one part of Eusebius' account. Each makes ripples in later Christian thought. What is problematic about Wilken's retelling is that he follows only one set of ripples. For the purposes of this volume it is important that Wilken does not make the mistake that I warned against above, namely, to ascribe naivete about origins only to Baptists and Disciples. He properly recognizes that the argument from the virgin metaphor has marked mainstream theological discourse in all of the Christian families. Since his field is the early centuries, he attends little to the post-Reformation free churches.

What Wilken does that I must challenge is to associate change only with improvement, bypassing the issue of betrayal, which moved all of the reformers. Certainly not all change is betrayal; in that Wilken is right, although he seems to me to overesteem the novelty of his making the point. But some change is betrayal; that is a topic which he simply ignores. Facing the phenomenon of Christian anti-Semitism Wilken says, "The only Christianity there is is the Christianity of our historical experience." This is certainly too simple; there are several Christianities in our experience, not just one.[43] There are also various ways to appropriate one's own history: sometimes repentance is more needful, sometimes perseverance, sometimes doxology. The reason for the appeal to origins is precisely that there are several contesting normative claims, all of them within historical experience. Sometimes they can be reconciled with one another pluralistically; but in crucial cases, which the churches of the Reformation sometimes call *status confessionis*, a choice is imperative. The inadequacy of Wilken's picture is well

illustrated by his effort to stretch the metaphor. "Perhaps we can rescue the metaphor for our day by suggesting that virginity implies in-
completeness. Eusebius thought it was better to be a virgin, and la-
mented the church's loss; we might say it is better not to be a virgin:
losing one's virginity is a stage in life's way."[44]

There are several ways to lose one's virginity. Marriage and mother-
hood fit Wilken's favorable vision of "completeness," although less nor-
matively so in the Catholic traditions than in Wilken's Lutheranism. But
what Hegesippus was talking about was seduction or rape or prostitution. Those are not ways in which it is "better not to be a virgin." To
make the case for change without identifying criteria to discriminate
between good and bad change is to take history as jeopardy less seriously than God does. Wilken never directly denies that there is a mystery of evil, that there can be heresy or apostasy; he merely looks past
it, telling his part of the story as if the other part were not there, and
thereby is unfair to the wholeness of Hegesippus' moral story.

The Burden of Proof

To go back to Robert Wilken's transformation of the image from Hegesippus: change must in principle be possible, since God's intentions
are to move within history. Any notion of the "primitive" that posits
as possible the rejection of all change is impossible. Yet not all movements in history move forward. Sometimes virginity yields to matri-
mony, sometimes to rape or adultery. In order to know the difference,
the changes must all be evaluated, rather than all being rejected or
all being accepted. There are kinds of conservatism that reject all
change (or at least that think they do so, although often the very rep-
etition of the old words or gestures in a new setting is a change).
There are kinds of openness to change that are uncritical or that let
decisions be made by the power of numbers or of the state. If the
criteria for evaluating the change are drawn from within the change
they are not really criteria. For criteria to judge accurately and well,
they must be drawn from within the historicity we call incarnation.
It is a mistake if terms like *restitution* lead people to think that the
basis for the canonical claim is the quality of some community's
achievement in the first centuries. What the apostolic community affords us is not the quality of its achievement but the proximity of its
witness to Jesus and to Pentecost. The change to which it calls us
looks not to the past but to the future, since that is the direction in
which Pentecost looked.

Notes

1. At the conference "Christian Primitivism and Modernization: Coming to Terms with Our Age" at Pepperdine University in 1991, this term was assumed to apply only to the sixteenth century. I prefer to use it for a pattern that surfaces in many centuries: see my "The Free Church Syndrome" in Terry L. Brensinger and E. Morris Sider, eds., *Within the Perfection of Christ* (Nappanee, Ind.: Evangel Press, 1990), 169–76.

2. I sought to do this in my book *Täufertum und Reformation* (Zurich: EVZ-Verlag, 1968). Here only the Reformed (i.e., Zwinglian) reformation was the interlocutor; conversation with Lutherans was a different story. Earlier I had written "The Prophetic Dissent of the Anabaptists" in Guy F. Hershberger, ed., *The Recovery of the Anabaptist Vision: A Sixtieth Anniversary Tribute to Harold S. Bender* (Scottdale, Pa.: Herald Press, 1957), 93–104.

3. Only Robert Friedmann tackled theology at length in *Theology of Anabaptism* (Scottdale, Pa.: Herald Press, 1973). Most efforts to characterize "Anabaptism" theologically have been briefer. See, e.g., numerous articles in the *Mennonite Quarterly Review* for January 1950. Such efforts have generally been quite selective (as was Friedmann) as to which kind of Anabaptism they sought to describe. Seldom was an interpretation as glowing as Donovan Smucker's in "The Theological Triumph of the Anabaptist-Mennonites," *Mennonite Quarterly Review* 19 (Jan. 1945): 5–26.

4. As a guest of a Reformation history research institute in Germany in 1976, I heard a strong claim that Luther was more radical than the Anabaptists because the Pauline gospel that he retrieved was both older and more centrally Christian than the themes from the Gospels that the Anabaptists pursued.

5. Sometimes the lost form is a Platonic ideal, sometimes a prehistoric Eden, sometimes a historic beginning. Sometimes the loss is a "fall," someone's fault. For others it is a normal effect of growth or fatigue. For some the "restoration" must happen repeatedly; for others it is unique, even apocalyptic. For some it rather simply begins again at "go"; for others the event of renewal is itself a forward movement.

6. Richard T. Hughes, "A Comparison of the Restoration Motifs of the Campbells (1809–1830) and the Anabaptists (1524–1560)," *Mennonite Quarterly Review* 45 (Oct. 1971): 312–30.

7. In fact, for a brief time D. S. Warner, primary founder figure of the Church of God (Anderson), formally investigated the possibility of joining forces with the Wesleyanized Mennonite group that was to become the Mennonite Brethren in Christ. See A. L. Byers, *The Birth of a Reformation* (Guthrie, Okla.: Faith, 1966), 206–8; John W. V. Smith, "The Church of God at Eighty-six," *School of Theology Bulletin* (Anderson College) (Spring 1967): 5–6.

8. Another of the variations within "primitivism" has to do with whether one thinks that a full beginning "according to the New Testament pattern" has now been achieved or must remain the object of perennial search and con-

troversy. Such differences seem to be standard themes internal to the communities of radical critique.

9. The oddity is especially evident in the definition attributed to Vincent of Lérins: "catholic" is "what has been believed always and everywhere by everyone." Obviously none of the three defining terms can be taken straight. The primary themes of "catholic" identity that "primitivists" challenge were absent for the first two Christian centuries.

10. The word *discipleship* has different meanings; our concern here is not with the term (see note 13) but with the thought pattern whereby Christ's life is a pattern for ours. Historians have made much of Hans Denck's unique use of the verb *nachvolgen*. This text by Denck is an apologetic contribution to the debate about human nature with no treatment of the substance of ethics. It may even have been written before Denck's baptism. When Denck does come to specifically Anabaptist themes, his argument on the sword does not duplicate the focus of the Schleitheim Confession on the example of the earthly Jesus. See Clarence Bauman, *The Spiritual Legacy of Hans Denck* (Leiden: Brill, 1991), 112, 198–201.

11. Even the group called Swiss Brethren was not fully agreed about the nonresistant position described here until years later.

12. Probably an allusion to Phil. 2:5; the notion of Christlikeness here points not to the Jesus of the Gospels but to the self-emptying of the divine Son. The Schleitheim text is available in my book *The Legacy of Michael Sattler* (Scottdale, Pa.: Herald Press, 1973), 34–43.

13. There is no general use in the sixteenth century of the equivalent of *discipleship*, namely *Jüngerschaft*. The rough equivalent, *Nachfolge*, did not then have the specialized meaning of modeling one's ethics after Jesus'. The word *discipleship* came to be used by historians as a key to Anabaptist identity only in this century.

14. Huldrych Zwingli, *Sämmtliche Schriften*, vol. 2 of *Corpus Reformatorum 89*, ed. Emil Egli and Georg Finsler (Leipzig: Heinsius, 1908), 111: "That Christ offered himself once for all, being eternally an abidingly valid sacrifice for the sins of all believers; whereby is discerned that the mass is not a sacrifice, but a memorial of his sacrifice and an assurance of the redemption which Christ has proven to us." It is remarkable that only one article among the sixty-seven dealt with this issue, which would later be regarded as the most characteristic mark of Zwingli's distinctive theology.

15. Ibid., 551–608.

16. Ibid., 617–25. The substance of the conversation is reported in my book *Die Gespräche zwischen Täufern und Reformatoren* (Karlsruhe, Germany: Mennonitischer Geschichtsverein, 1962), 18.

17. Yoder, *Gespräche*, 20–25. The entire section of the debate is available in English in Leland Harder, ed., *The Sources of Swiss Anabaptism* (Scottdale, Pa.: Herald Press, 1985), 238–50. The fullest interpretation of the event is in my articles "The Turning Point in the Zwinglian Reformation," *Mennonite Quarterly Review* 32 (Apr. 1959): 128–40, and "The Evolution of the Zwinglian Reformation," *Mennonite Quarterly Review* 43 (Jan. 1969): 95–122.

18. Zwingli, *Sämmtliche Schriften*, 783–84; Harder, *Sources*, 244–48.

19. See Harold S. Bender, *Conrad Grebel* (Scottdale, Pa.: Herald Press, 1950); Bender's narration of the October 1523 events is not chronological and thus hard to follow. On 101 he ascribes to Conrad Grebel "a tendency to legalism." He ignores that Hubmaier, Zwingli, and Grebel were all concerned with the same kinds of details.

20. What I challenge here is not "apologetics" as such, which designates the effort to make sense to some particular "public." The apostle Paul already did that, and the free church generally does that more than the "established" church. The error of the wrong *kind* of "apologetics" is that it compromises the content of the witness in order to meet alien criteria of credibility.

21. Arendt Theodoor van Leeuwen, *Christianity in World History* (London: Edinburgh House Press, 1964).

22. I capsule here observations I already made in *The Priestly Kingdom: Social Ethics as Gospel* (Notre Dame: University of Notre Dame Press, 1984), 135–47.

23. Ibid.

24. Other dimensions of the "fall" of the church, in the eyes of those who see the change in an unfavorable light, include changed attitudes to wealth, superstition, empire, patriarchalism, fertility religion, local cults, cults of the dead, and the ritual sanctification of the cycles of the year and of life.

25. "Persecution never did, never could give any lasting wound to genuine Christianity. But the greatest it ever received, the grand blow which was struck at the very root of that humble, gentle, patient love, which is the fulfilling of the Christian law, the whole essence of true religion, was struck in the fourth century by Constantine the Great, when he called himself a Christian, and poured in a flood of riches, honours, and power upon the Christians, more especially upon the clergy." *The Works of John Wesley*, ed. Albert Outler (Nashville: Abingdon, 1985), "The Mystery of Iniquity," sermon 61, 2:463.

26. Paradoxically, to impose the lenses of our historical relativity on actors of premodern ages, suggesting that it was a mental or moral flaw on their part to think more simply about "letting the Word of God work to reform the church," is itself a failure of historical imagination.

27. As I noted above, this "mission" may be said to have begun with Abraham.

28. I argued this in *Priestly Kingdom*, 59–61.

29. If I had to argue that one facet is more strategic than the others, it probably should be the procedural "rule of Christ" rather than one issue of polity (as with Campbell) or of soteriology (as with Luther) or mood (as with spiritualizers and Pietists) or ethics (as with Puritans and second-generation Anabaptists). But my prima facie preference would be to doubt that there can be or that there would need to be any such one right place to step into the circle.

30. Part of the answer, of course, is that authentic modernity will also make us relativistic about ourselves and about our debt to the enlightenment.

31. Robert L. Wilken, *The Myth of Christian Beginnings* (Garden City, N.Y.: Doubleday, 1971; rpt., Notre Dame: University of Notre Dame Press, 1980).

Burton Mack, *The Myth of Innocence* (Philadelphia: Fortress, 1988). Jonathan Z. Smith, *Drudgery Divine* (Chicago: University of Chicago Press, 1990)

32. There is an analogy here to the spiritualism of Franck and Schwenckfeld. They cited texts literally to prove the superiority of the spirit over the letter. These agents of suspicion read ancient texts with great thoroughness in order to undercut the axiom that they have a core message.

33. Graydon Snyder, *Ante Pacem: Archaeological Evidence of Church Life before Constantine* (Macon, Ga.: Mercer University Press, 1985). While accepting the point made by Snyder and Smith for the purpose of this argument, I should point out that there might be good reasons not to expect that all "church life," to say nothing of all of Christian thought, would be represented in cemetery art.

34. Thomas F. Torrance, *The Doctrine of Grace in the Apostolic Fathers* (Edinburgh: Oliver and Boyd, 1948), 137: "The most astonishing feature was *the failure to grasp the significance of the death of Christ.*" Thus Torrance saw as an early falling-away from what the historian would call a pre-Pauline position.

35. Cf. the analogous argument of Mack.

36. Jonathan Z. Smith's primary attack is not against believers' church restitutionists; they are not in his field of vision. He is critiquing mainstream Protestants whose use of the normative past is anti-Catholic and anti-Jewish. Robert Wilken similarly ignores the free church restitutionists (unless we should count the Pietist Gottfried Arnold) and finds mainline theologians of all schools—John Henry Cardinal Newman, Adolf von Harnack, Käsemann—guilty of the mistake that Eusebius took over from Hegesippus.

37. Cf. these two verses from Charles Wesley's hymn "Jesus, from Whom All Blessings Flow:"

> The few that truly call thee Lord,
> And wait thy sanctifying word,
> And thee their utmost Savior own,
> Unite, and perfect them in one;
> *In them let all mankind behold*
> *How Christians lived in days of old,*
> Mighty their envious foes to move,
> A proverb of reproach—and love.
>   (emphasis added)

Wesley wrote two poems totalling twenty verses from which these were drawn, together entitled "Primitive Christianity." Albert C. Outler describes Methodism as primitivist but not restorationist; see "'Biblical Primitivism' in Early American Methodism," in Richard T. Hughes, ed., *The American Quest for the Primitive Church* (Urbana: University of Illinois Press, 1988), esp. 136–37; or *The Wesleyan Theological Heritage* (Grand Rapids, Mich.: Zondervan, 1991), 145–57.

38. See my works *The Fullness of Christ* (Elgin, Ill.: Brethren Press, 1987) and "The One and the Many" in David Eller, ed., *Servants of the Word* (Elgin, Ill.: Brethren Press, 1991), 51–64.

39. See my article "Adjusting to the Changing Shape of the Debate on Infant Baptism" in Arie Lambo, ed., *Oecumennisme* (Amsterdam: ADS, 1989), 201–14. It is most noteworthy that within the "mainstream" churches, considerations of pastoral realism and new research in the history of worship have led to a new questioning of the general obligation of infant baptism. The primary cause has not been that the majority churches have paid any attention to the ecumenical witness of the Baptist churches, or that they have paid much attention to biblically based arguments for revision. That is, they are using a Constantinian epistemology to come around toward a restitutionist polity.

40. Roman Catholic moral thought has recently been changing strikingly with regard to war. For the first time, *The Challenge of Peace* (Washington, D.C.: United States Catholic Conference, 1983) affirmed the legitimacy of pacifism as a Christian position. Since Hiroshima, even more since Vietnam, and even more since the U.S. war with Iraq, growing doubt has arisen among Catholic moral theologians as to the adequacy of the Just War tradition.

41. See my article "Reformation and Missions: A Literature Review," *Occasional Bulletin of the Missionary Research Library* 30 (June 1971): 1–9. Radical Reformation movements are in principle missionary, both in their theoretical ecclesiology and in their actual social shape, as "established" churches are not.

42. See my article "The Disavowal of Constantine: An Alternative Perspective on Interfaith Dialogue," in W. Wegener and W. Harrelson, eds., *Annals 1975–76* (Tantur, Palestine: Ecumenical Institute for Advanced Theological Studies, 1979), 47–68.

43. Wilken, *Myth,* 198. There were philo-Judaic strands within eastern Christianity at least as late as Chrysostom, as Wilken's later publications demonstrate.

44. Ibid., 159.

5

Primitive, Present, Future: A Vision for the Church in the Modern World

JAMES WM. MCCLENDON JR.

In this volume, there are certain recurring themes and questions. One is the explicit question, Is primitivism antimodern? That is Richard T. Hughes's question,[1] and in some way it engages all of us who care about our origins. Is there something about our beginnings that will keep us from going where we need to go? Or (to turn the question around) do our reclaimed beginnings (and they alone) *enable* us to go where we must? Hughes's question pervades our conversation here, but there are others. Is primitivism ahistorical, historyless? Do we lose our own place in history when we try to restore the ancient landmarks? Does our actual location vanish whenever we look back to primitive times or look forward to the last times? This leads to another, which is less explicit but still central for many: Does primitivism defeat unity? If we are primitivists, can we be ecumenists? Is the church apostolic capable of being the church universal, the church catholic?

Let me call your attention to a curious fact. Here are scholars from, and students of, six faith communities. They are in varied degrees insiders to those traditions, but none is a mere outsider. And those communities honor the primitive. Yet as they address these central questions—Can primitivism modernize? Can primitivism acknowledge real history? Can primitivism be ecumenical?—it is *not* modernity or historicism or ecumenism that has been on trial for its life here: it is primitivism. It is the recovery of the first times that must justify itself at the bar of modernity, appear in the courtroom of historicism, stand at the judgment gate of ecumenism. These latter are in the saddle, and if the primitive is to have a place it must be by their fiat or at least with their permission.

A second curious fact must be noted. Six sorts of Christian community are singled out for examination here; their primitivism is on trial and must justify itself. Yet scholar after scholar points out that it is the entire Christian community, the whole church of God, that is fascinated by its origins. So this could well have been a full ecumenical gathering; the problems would seem the same though the names would change. Not pentecostals and Holiness followers and small-*b* baptists, but Catholics and Magisterial Protestants and Episcopalians would gather. They would not discuss primitivism, but they would discuss apostolicity; they would not discuss modernization, but they would discuss development. Traditionalism and primitivism generate similar, yet not identical, problems.[2] Such similarity should make us glad for two reasons: one, if we are in trouble, we are glad others are (misery, they say, loves company); and two, any solutions we may find here are for the good of the whole church, for all who take the name of Jesus with them. Those who would *believe in one holy, catholic, and apostolic church*[3] are very near those who would be pentecostal and primitive and one in the Spirit. Here we seek pentecostal *holiness,* we seek *apostolic* primitivity, we seek *catholic* unity (where *catholicity* means exactly "oneness"). The trouble with primitivists may be not that we are so different from others, but so much like all the rest. Common problems, common wants.

Return yet again to this troublesome concept "primitivism." What can it possibly mean to "restore" the past? There are several possibilities; it can mean to revere the past, to imitate the past, to acknowledge a particular past as one's heritage or roots, to confuse one's identity with that of some character from the past (if I believe I am not James McClendon but instead am the Russian czar, I am likely to be locked up). Primitivism ranges from the *crazy* (there is no czar; Cleopatra really is dead) to the merely *misinformed* (since the first century A.D. more has changed than I realize) to the *inconsequential* (suppose I do revere Plato or Jesus of Nazareth or Leonardo; how does that matter to the here and now?). Is there any Christian sense of restoration primitivism that is not crazy or absurd, not simply historylessness or trivial antiquarianism; is there a sense that matters in the way the deep, central convictions of the faith must matter to Christian believers?

Note what we are asking for: a sense of restitution that (1) will help us to see the Bible as basic to Christian faith in our modern world, (2) will strengthen, not weaken, the reality of the present moment in our journey, and (3) will not be divisive but ecumenical, yet will not wash out the distinct contribution of this portion of God's peculiar people, either.

Start with the Bible. It is well known that Scripture has its own method of reclaiming previous Scripture. A key cluster of terms gathers around the Greek *typos,* "pattern." In Romans 6:17, apostolic teaching provides a pattern for believers' lives; in 1 Peter 2:21 Christ who suffered for us left us an example (here the term is *hypogrammos,* "master copy"); Paul's conduct is a pattern (*typos*) for the Philippian church (3:17), and the Thessalonian church, having followed (*mimetai*) the example set by Paul and by the Lord, has itself become a pattern (*typos*) for believers throughout that whole country (1:6–7). Yet this same vocabulary is used by the apostle to declare that Adam was a pattern (again *typos*) for Christ (Rom. 5:14); in this case the earlier can only foreshadow the one who came after; Christ fulfilled the divine pattern; Adam did not. And in Paul's use the pattern can serve as a negative warning as well. Thus in 1 Corinthians he advises church members not to presume upon their baptism or upon their "supernatural food and drink" (the Lord's Supper); Israel, too, was "baptized" in the Red Sea and in the numinous cloud of the Lord; Israel also received supernatural food, manna, and water from the rock in the wilderness, yet those very Israelites perished for their sins. Those events, says Paul, are *typoi,* patterns, that the Corinthian believers must keep in mind. "If you think you are standing firm, take care, or you may fall" (1 Cor. 10:1–12 REB).

Here, then, we see a biblical way, a way that would make no sense without Scripture, for a believing community to reach beyond its present experience. This way finds in Jesus (and in others also) a model for living; it finds in the apostolic *didache* a pattern for its teaching; it finds significant events by which to construe its own significant happenings (e.g., baptism construed as crossing the Red Sea); it finds personal identities made out in terms of others' identities (Christ as a new Adam). What should interest us in particular is that this was not *a* way to read Scripture; it was for them *the* way. To us, this way may seem strained or trivial or a mere literary device. For them, it was the very key to the book. Thus Leonhard Goppelt in *Theological Dictionary of the New Testament* writes, "This way of relating OT phenomena to the present situation of the community is *the central and distinctive NT way of understanding Scripture.* . . . It is the decisive interpretation of Jesus, the Gospel, and the Church."[4]

Doubtless this reading strategy can be abused. (What strategy cannot?) We will shortly see one sort of distortion to which it is open. One may first think, though, of a proper name for this primitive reading strategy. We can call it *typology* (after *typos,* "pattern" or "type") but for many that term has been trivialized beyond usefulness. Anyway, the strategy is more than typology, and it is more than "promise and fulfillment," though that, too, is part of the picture.[5] I call it a *vision,* a way of seeing. Because it appears first in the prophets of Israel, I call it *the prophetic vision;* because it appears in modern times among the so-called Anabaptists, I call it (omitting the pejorative "Ana") the *baptist vision* and write that with a small *b,* analogous to small-*c* catholic and small-*p* protestant. I believe this prophetic-baptist vision has been at work again not only among present-day Mennonites and Brethren, pentecostals and Holiness people, Baptists and Methodists, indeed among experience-saturated Bible believers of many sorts, but also here and there among those partisans of "one holy, catholic, apostolic church," the Roman Catholics— thinking now of charismatics and house-churches and Latin American "basic communities."

Illustration will aid our understanding. First, from Scripture, Luke 9. "Who do the people say I am?" If Jesus had wanted information, the disciples were full of it. "They answered, 'Some say John the Baptist, others Elijah, others that one of the prophets of old has come back to life'" (18–19). Now those mistaken identifications were indeed accurate reportings of what people were saying. If we look a few lines above we see that Herod, who had beheaded John the Baptist to satisfy a mistress's whim, was hearing similar rumors and half believed them. Superstition and guilt converged in Herod's hollow head. Herod yearned to see for himself: Was Jesus Elijah? Was he another prophet? Was it possible that a murdered prophet would not stay dead? That meddlesome John, here again? (7–10). But such fantastic recalling of the past was a misreading of reality, and it was far from Jesus' focus. "'And you,' he said, 'who do you say I am?'" Peter answered not with a fantastic reversal of time but with a great scriptural image, "the anointed one," "God's Messiah" (20). That was a better shot; Jesus does not dismiss it, but he does not rest with it; he gives his own scriptural image, "the Son of Man," *huios tou anthropou,* the Truly Human One—and with that he goes on to speak of suffering and death and resurrection.[6]

Now notice that in this brief exchange the kind of vision possessed is the key to understanding the entire passage, both its misses and its hits. Jesus' life is not a replay of the past; he is not John the Baptist. That is bad vision; it is Herod's superstition, it is history-*denying.* But Jesus was in the business not of denying but of making history, and in order to do that he had to create a new sense of history. The Gospels show us Jesus did this by drawing upon the great formative scriptural *images,* applying them to himself to define his role in the unfolding story.[7] He was the Anointed One, the Son of David whose kingdom would have no end. Yes, but he was also the coming Child of Humani-

ty, the Truly Human One, Adam's heir, Ezekiel's antitype, who must
"endure great sufferings, and . . . be rejected by the elders, chief priests,
and scribes, to be put to death, and to be raised again on the third day"
(Luke 9:18–22). History that is more than chronology and necrology
appears only when it is viewed with eyes like Jesus' eyes, eyes that can
see how this is that, how storied past and prophetic future converge
upon this present. No wonder this became the apostolic strategy in
reading Scripture. Must it not also have been Jesus' own hermeneutic, passed along to his inner circle, as when according to Luke the risen
Lord opened "in the whole of scripture the things that referred to himself" (24:27)?

Certainly this same reading strategy is at work in Luke's second volume, the Acts of the Apostles. There, at Pentecost, fire falls, tongues
are liberated to speak free, the dumb disciples are transformed into
servants and handmaids of the risen Lord. How are such doings to be
comprehended? Luke's answer in the mouth of Simon Peter is God's
word: "In the last days I will pour out my Spirit on all mankind" (2:17).
The words are drawn from the Septuagint version of Joel (2:28–32);
according to Charles Harold Dodd they are a part of the apostolic *tes-
timonia*, the Scripture passages on which early Christians especially
relied.[8] My focus now is Acts 2:16. In the King James Version, "this is
that," i.e., what Joel the prophet said in the fourth century B.C. The
"that" is required in order to make sense of a present "this," namely,
what is happening on Pentecost in Jerusalem.

Second, out of a thousand available, a single illustration from church
history. I choose one from that old Anabaptist book, Thieleman van
Braght's *Martyrs Mirror.* In 1535, an edict of Charles V, Holy Roman
Emperor, required that those who committed anabaptism be brought
"to the most extreme punishment." There was to be some sensitivity:
while leaders must be burned to death, mere members, if repentant,
could be executed with a sword instead, and the women buried (alive,
of course) in a pit. The year after the edict, the alert bailiff at Zierich-
see in the Netherlands arrested Peter Gerrits, Peter Joris, Peter Ley-
decker, and Johanna Mels. These four, interrogated, answered from the
Bible, but the Burgomaster said, "We care not for your Word of God,
but hold to the mandate of the emperor," warning that they faced death.
Then they replied, "Lord Burgomaster, by this you prove yourself to
be a protector of the kingdom of Babel and of Bel for which you will
indeed reap some reward here on earth, but hereafter, with antichrist
and the crowned beast, eternal damnation in the lake of fire." I would
like to tell you that after they provided so insightful a scriptural diagnosis of the situation, the Burgomaster set these four young baptists

free. It was not so; I spare you the details of their torture and death. "Thus," concludes *Martyrs Mirror,* "they offered up their sacrifices."[9] Note now that when their crisis came, the three Peters and Johanna were guided by their perception that "this is that"; *their present peril, their place in history, could not be grasped by the modernity of six-teenth-century politics alone; only by reading the story of beginnings and endings they found in Scripture could it be understood.*[10] *They* were Daniels in distress; *their tormentors* were the evil king Astyages and his god Bel.

Here I have not taken up the prophetic vision as it sees ahead to end times, but only as it looks back to first times, though in fact it does both.[11] Nor have I sought out the ways present communities, includ-ing some under study here, are guided by this vision—the various uses they have made of it, including the ways they, like Herod, have some-times gotten the matter wrong, out of self-interest turning the vision of Jesus into crude superstition. Any practice can be abused, but in the kingdom of Christ abuses must be detected and set right, or so we teach others, and we must take our own medicine.

So what do we think of all this? And by "we" I mean those of us, or that part of ourselves, that is neither primitivist nor modernized, nei-ther adheres to these communities of reference nor rejects them; I mean that self or part of a self that wants to know if this reading strat-egy *works.* Can "this is that" cope critically with modernity? Can "then is now" (for that is the other, future side of this vision) enable us to see the present as it really is, not as sleepwalkers, not as the self-deluded, not as a historyless people, but as part of God's own story? But surely there can be no single, once-for-all answer to such a ques-tion. Here we touch the profound. Is the universe friendly? Does life matter? Is the mercy of God great enough to wash away all my sin? Has humanity a future? Anyone who offers snap answers to such ques-tions does not yet know what they mean. How does the past—God's past—impinge upon the present? The historical determinist can offer some sort of cause-and-effect answer. By it, we are the victims of our own past, trapped by a historicist determinism more relentless than any predestinarian theology.

But the historian, and the Christian, need be no determinist. Those who resist the allure of determinism may discern in history a messian-ic people that have been formed not by inexorable causes but by cer-tain living images. The images come from old Israel and beyond: the divine king, the mantic prophet, the sacrificial priest. In Jesus of Naz-areth these images converge and are transformed: he is the King—who dies; he is the Prophet—without honor; he is the Priest—who is the sacrifice.[12] This vision formed a people royal but without princely rank, a people prophetic but without privilege, a priestly people, yet with no priests. The vision persists; it fades again; it flames anew. To detect its flickering, persistent light is the radical historian's task.[13]

Notes

1. Richard T. Hughes, "Introduction: On Recovering the Theme of Recovery," in Richard T. Hughes, ed., *The American Quest for the Primitive Church* (Urbana: University of Illinois Press, 1988), 1–15; Hughes, "Christian Primitivism as Perfectionism: From Anabaptists to Pentecostals," in Stanley M. Burgess, ed., *Reaching Beyond: Chapters in the History of American Pentecostalism* (Peabody, Mass.: Hendrickson, 1986), 213–55; Hughes, chapter 1 and epilogue of Hughes and C. Leonard Allen, *Illusions of Innocence: Protestant Primitivism in America, 1630–1875* (Chicago: University of Chicago Press, 1988), 1–24, 226–32; Hughes, "From Primitive Church to Civil Religion: The Millennial Odyssey of Alexander Campbell," *Journal of the American Academy of Religion* 44 (Mar. 1976): 87–104; and Hughes's preface to this volume. A less hesitant case against one sort of primitivism is found in Robert L. Wilken's *The Myth of Christian Beginnings* (Garden City, N.Y.: Doubleday, 1971; rpt., Notre Dame: University of Notre Dame Press, 1980). See also the point of view presented by Arthur O. Lovejoy and George Boas in *Primitivism and Related Ideas in Antiquity* (Baltimore: Johns Hopkins University Press, 1935).

2. Samuel S. Hill Jr. notes some connection but does not point out the close similarity between traditionalist and primitivist concerns in his "Typology of American Restitutionism: From Frontier Revivalism and Mormonism to the Jesus Movement," *Journal of the American Academy of Religion* 44 (Mar. 1976): 65–76.

3. The phrase appears at least as early as the Niceno-Constantinopolitan Creed of A.D. 381.

4. Leonhard Goppelt, *Typos,* in Gerhard Kittel, ed., and Geoffrey Bromiley, trans., *Theological Dictionary of the New Testament* (Grand Rapids, Mich.: Eerdmans, 1964–76), 8:255–56, emphasis added.

5. See especially E. Earle Ellis, *Paul's Use of the Old Testament* (Grand Rapids, Mich.: Eerdmans, 1957); also G. W. H. Lampe and K. J. Woolcombe, *Essays on Typology,* Studies in Biblical Theology no. 22 (London: SCM Press, 1957); Austin M. Farrer, "Important Hypotheses Reconsidered VIII: Typology," *Expository Times* 67 (1955–56): 228–31; Leonhard Goppelt, *Typos: Die Typologische Deutung des Alten Testaments im Neuen* (Gutersloh, Germany, 1939).

6. A helpful discussion of the narrative structure of Luke 9 appears in Robert Tannehill's *The Narrative Unity of Luke-Acts: A Literary Interpretation* (Philadelphia: Fortress, 1986), 1:147–52.

7. On the central role of images in the making of inspired Scripture and

the conveyance of divine revelation, see Austin M. Farrer, *The Glass of Vision: Bampton Lectures for 1948* (Westminster, England: Dacre Press, 1948); also James Wm. McClendon Jr., *Biography as Theology: How Life Stories Can Remake Today's Theology* (Philadelphia: Trinity Press International, 1990).

8. Charles Harold Dodd, *According to the Scriptures: The Sub-structure of New Testament Theology* (London: Nisbet, 1952).

9. Thieleman J. van Braght, *Martyrs Mirror: The Story of Fifteen Centuries of Christian Martyrdom from the Time of Christ to A.D. 1660,* trans. Joseph F. Sohm (Scottdale, Pa.: Herald Press, 1950), 442–44.

10. The story of Bel and the Dragon and the evil King Astyages is found in the Septuagint version of the book of Daniel and was included in the Bibles many Anabaptists studied. Relegated to the Apocrypha, it can be read as "Daniel, Bel, and the Snake" in recent English versions such as REB.

11. For further discussion of the baptist vision both in its reclamation of the biblical past and its expectation of the biblical future, see James Wm. McClendon Jr., *Ethics: Systematic Theology* (Nashville: Abingdon Press, 1986), vol. 1, esp. chap. 1; and McClendon, *Doctrine: Systematic Theology,* vol. 2 (Nashville: Abingdon Press, 1994), esp. chap. 1.

12. I am influenced in this understanding of the role of biblical images by the work of Austin M. Farrer. See especially his *Glass of Vision* and my *Biography as Theology,* chap. 4.

13. An excellent example of such radical historical work is found in the work of John Howard Yoder: see especially his *Priestly Kingdom: Social Ethics as Gospel* (Notre Dame: University of Notre Dame Press, 1984).

There is a theological task as well. Those under study here are a part, yet only a part, of the whole people of God, the gathering church catholic. We are only a part, but a part for whom the discourse has taken a unique turn. We are vividly aware of our identity as formed by those primal moments in God's story. If others take as their motto "one holy, catholic, apostolic church," we are more likely to take as our motto "one pentecostal, obedient, primitive people of God." Where terms differ, ideas do also, so we address similar problems yet not merely identical ones. How, then, can the people who consciously share such a vision offer their distinctive gift to the whole people of God? This question sets the theological task, and it may be divided into three questions: How can we be faithful though not sectarian?—the question of theological ethics. How can we be truthful though not dogmatic?—the question of theological doctrine. How can we be visionary though not speculative or fantastic?—the question of theological vision. By faith we see that we face such difficult yet not impossible tasks. Faith sets theology this threefold task, and some of us must undertake the task if this particular gift to some of God's children is to become a shared gift for which all may give grateful thanks.

(These three questions correspond to the three parts of the systematic theology "in light of the baptist vision" that is my current project. See note 11.)

PART 3

Primitivism and Modernization:
Five Case Studies

6

Christian Primitivism and Modernization in the Stone-Campbell Movement

DAVID EDWIN HARRELL JR.

Long before the Disciples of Christ movement began in America, restoration rhetoric reverberated through the valleys of Scotland and Ulster. Many of the primitivist assumptions of the early Disciples were no more than restatements of Reformation Calvinism. The Westminster Confession of Faith grandly framed the most basic beliefs of American Disciples long before the birth of Alexander Campbell or Barton Stone: "The whole counsel of god, concerning all things necessary for his own glory, man's salvation, faith, and life, is either expressly set down in Scripture, or by good and necessary consequence may be deduced from Scripture: unto which nothing at any time is to be added, whether by new revelations of the Spirit, or traditions of men."[1] Reformation Calvinists had their own vision of the ancient order, although the Westminster Confession acknowledged that "particular churches" in any age would only be "more or less pure, according as the doctrine of the gospel is taught and embraced, ordinances administered, and public worship performed more or less purely in them."[2]

The American restoration movement shaped by Alexander Campbell and Barton W. Stone owes a more direct debt to such Scottish independents as John Glas, Robert Sandeman, and the brothers James Alexander and Robert Haldane. Glas was expelled from the Church of Scotland in 1728 because he preached that the "Church in the days of the Apostles . . . was *a pattern for all time*." Until his death in 1773 Glas and his followers pressed their search for the "purity of the Apostolic Church."[3] By the time the Disciples movement had begun to take form in America, the Glasites had a well-developed primitivist formula:

1. We think ourselves obliged to regard all the words of Christ and his apostles, in their plain, obvious, and original meaning; looking upon every precept in the New Testament (except such as may relate to what is properly miraculous), to be binding upon us now, as much as upon the first churches.

2. We think ourselves bound to follow the practices of the primitive disciples and churches, as far as we can learn from the New Testament how they walked, while the apostles were with them, beholding their order and steadfastness in the faith.

3. We think ourselves also bound carefully to avoid all the things for which they were reproved, by our Lord or his apostles.[4]

The American restoration movement of the early nineteenth century was as much a product of Scotland as of the United States, a continuation of the search for spiritual purity that pervaded the age of Reformation and reached its argumentative and fastidious pinnacle in the polemics of Scottish Presbyterians. For all of the Americanness of the Disciples of Christ tradition, the names of early leaders of the movement—Alexander Campbell, Walter Scott, James Shannon—exposed cultural roots reaching deeply into Reformed Protestantism.

However, the restoration movement also shared in the democratic, Jeffersonian assumptions of early nineteenth-century America. The word *aristocracy* was unknown in "Republican America," wrote Alexander Campbell; America was a new land without elites. The restored church, Campbell continued, was "a great leveling institution, which brought down and raised up, and made the rich and the poor one, placing them on a common level." Two years before his death, Campbell expressed fears that an "aristocratic malady" was creeping into American society and the church; he regretted that some of the evangelistic reports sent to the *Millennial Harbinger* boasted that "the first citizens of the place, or some of the most wealthy and influential have embraced the gospel."[5] In short, the restoration movement was a product of America, sharing in the democratization of the religions of the republic and of its intellectual inheritance from the Scottish Reformation.

There was nothing essentially antimodern about the thought of the early leaders of the Disciples of Christ/Christian Church movement. Most had been trained as Presbyterian clergymen, and like their Presbyterian contemporaries, they were ambitious school builders, prolific editors and publishers, and careful students of natural and divine philosophy. They believed that modern thought was freeing the world from ignorance, superstition, and Roman Catholicism and making possible the reestablishment of the kingdom of God on earth; they believed themselves to be fully in step with the enlightenment of their age. Disciples shared these assumptions with most other Americans. At the same time, primitivism and optimism pervaded American political, social, and religious thought in the early nineteenth century. The particular forms that primitivism took in the Disciples movement were continuous with the Scotch-Irish heritage of the church's early leaders.

Early Divisions

The institutional history of the Disciples of Christ movement is complicated. It has been a wonderfully individualistic and divisive movement, worthy of its cantankerous Scottish ancestors. No other American religious tradition has so carefully guarded the principle of congregational autonomy, magnifying the Disciples' propensity for innovation, debate, and schism. Local churches have divided over scores of idiosyncratic doctrinal questions, including the number of communion containers and the veiling of women during worship.

More far-reaching were major divisions within the movement in the nineteenth and twentieth centuries. The first splintering began to take shape shortly after the Civil War and reached a symbolic end with the restructure of the Christian Church (Disciples of Christ) in 1968. Those divisions effectively separated the movement into three informal but distinct groupings of churches—the Christian Church (Disciples of Christ), the Christian Churches/Churches of Christ (Independent), and the Churches of Christ (Noninstrumental).[6] In the twentieth century the Churches of Christ repeated this schismatic cycle. A division in the 1950s separated a group of conservative congregations (generally called anti-institutional) from the mainstream of the Churches of Christ. By the 1990s, the mainstream Churches of Christ were separated into two factions—clustered around papers, schools, and personalities—that had diminishing contacts with one another.

Neither the causes nor the parameters of these divisions were neat or easily defined. Generally speaking, the splinter groups within the restoration movement have sociological as well as theological profiles; I have written a good deal about those patterns. Statistical information collected in four federal surveys of religious bodies between 1906 and 1936 makes it clear that the Disciples of Christ was the most urban and middle-class, the Independent Christian Churches were more rural and lower middle class, and the Churches of Christ included the poorest and most rural congregations in the movement.

The three groups also divided along regional lines—as the initial spread of the movement had been regionally determined by its western leadership and the closing of the South to new ideas in the 1830s. The Disciples were strongest in the Upper Midwest, the more prosperous agricultural regions of Kentucky, and in cities; the Independent Christian Churches flourished in the border states and the Unionist areas of the rural South; the Churches of Christ won over a majority of the churches in Tennessee, Alabama, Arkansas, and Texas. Unfortunately, no similar statistical material on the religious bodies of the late twentieth century has been collected. I am certain, however, that the later divisions in the Churches of Christ followed similar sociological patterns.

I think we are past debating the fact that these patterns of division exist. It is time to focus our debates on explaining the patterns. Modernization provides a useful focus for the discussion. In the nineteenth and twentieth centuries Disciples reacted to modernization like other Americans—they embraced it, accommodated it, and rejected it.

In *Quest for a Christian America,* I offered an interpretive framework for Disciples history in an introductory chapter entitled "The Mind of a Movement." While that book was written to highlight the sociological and sectional tensions within the movement, I never imagined that the splintering of the Disciples had no intellectual underpinnings. Rather, I then saw the movement, as I now do, as a collection of disparate thinkers united by the heady euphoria of early nineteenth-century reformism. I wrote, "Disciples were New Testament primitivists and Christian humanitarians; they were temperamentally fanatics and moderates; they were out-group iconoclasts and in-group constructive critics; they were noninterventionists in civil government and they were political activists; they were sectarian and they were denominational."[7] Like other early nineteenth-century religious reforms, the Disciples movement attracted a diverse clientele with varied motives and agendas.

It was difficult to hold together such contradictory personalities and ideas. By 1865, I concluded, there were two clear focuses within the movement. "One group conceived of Christianity in the denominational framework of practical religion, social and political activism, and, often, a nationalistic postmillennialism. A second group emphasized the sectarian tradition of Biblical legalism, a fanatical disposition, and uncompromising separation from the world."[8] While these intellectual tensions became the basis for the first division in the Disciples of Christ movement, the pattern of the division, I argued, was "at least partially, a part of the story of the American nation."[9] The intellectual and social changes accompanying late nineteenth-century modernization placed enormous pressures on Disciples' primitivist assumptions.

Several historians of the Disciples movement, particularly Richard

T. Hughes and C. Leonard Allen, have grappled to find keys in restoration thought that account for the movement's diverse reactions to modernization. I regard some of their ideas as wrongheaded. Hughes's efforts to trace the Disciples of Christ/Churches of Christ division to a historic Stone-Campbell dichotomy is a revision of an old idea that defies verification.[10] I believe that it oversimplifies the thought of the two early leaders, raises more questions about the regional influence of each man than it answers, and underestimates the dispersion of leadership in the amorphous restoration movement. The first generation comprised a loose and experimental era in Disciples history, a time when consistent application of primitivist ideas was rare. As I wrote in *Quest for a Christian America*, "the Disciple of the pre–Civil War period did not simply tolerate diversity—he was diversity."[11]

Even more problematic, it seems to me, is Hughes's suggestion in the same article that the basic tensions in Disciples history were somehow related to changing views on the millennium. While this essay is not the place to address that theory, I believe that it has little value in explaining the meandering of the restoration movement. In the first place, premillennialism never has been a much-discussed theological issue among Disciples (except during two brief periods); the question was rarely examined in the movement's major journals. When asked his views on the millennium in 1895, David Lipscomb replied that he knew "so little about the millennium that I do not feel inclined to attempt to answer this." "It is an untaught question," he wrote, "and therefore no man's salvation depends upon an answer to it, and it aids no man in his soul's salvation to know about it."[12] The atypical division in the Churches of Christ over premillennialism in the 1940s had more to do with power and church politics than with genuine doctrinal diversity. Second, premillennial, postmillennial, and amillennial views never have been neatly identified with a particular segment of the movement. In the late nineteenth century, those most receptive to the rising dispensational prophecy movement were to be found not in the Churches of Christ but among the leaders of the Disciples of Christ.[13]

Having challenged those two ideas, let me say that Hughes has his finger on the pulse of Disciples history when he argues that the movement early harbored people with sharply different worldviews. Some Disciples (Campbell may be a good type) were comfortable with the world and saw the Disciples movement as a part of the modernization of their time; others (Stone may be a good type) were uncomfortable with the world and saw Christians as spiritual pilgrims. Hughes is right, I believe, in linking subsequent divisions in the restoration movement to the incompatibility of these two worldviews.

Primitivism and Modernization

How have these dissimilar worldviews molded religious primitivism in the restoration movement? The critical theological issue in the divisions in the restoration has not been premillennialism—or for that matter the nature of the church or any other specific doctrinal question. It has been the survival of restoration biblicism itself. The underlying assumption of the restoration movement in America, as in Scotland, was that the New Testament "contained the pattern of a one-and-only primitive Christian Church."[14]

In short, primitivism was a part of the spirit of the age in the early nineteenth century, an idea that seemingly had little to fear from modern thinking, but the plea for a commonsense restoration of primitive Christianity encountered increasing difficulties with the modernity of the late nineteenth century. Writing in 1940, Disciples historian Alfred T. DeGroot argued that the repeated schisms in the Disciples of Christ movement had one basic cause: "the principle of restoring a fixed pattern of a primitive Christian church."[15] Modernization has called for repeated reevaluations of the plea on the part of those who felt reasonably comfortable with their society. The degree to which primitivism has been abandoned or moderated by Disciples has been a measure of their adjustment to the modernization of their time.

By the early twentieth century the Disciples movement embraced widely diverging views of modern society and thought. On one extreme was a group of young scholars associated with the University of Chicago, including Herbert L. Willett, Edward Scribner Ames, and Winfred Garrison. They celebrated modernity and contributed in important ways to American religious modernism in the twentieth century. They saw little in their heritage that deserved memorializing save the intellectualism of Alexander Campbell and the themes of liberty and Christian union. Disciples liberals built the Disciples of Christ Historical Society, but they have had little use for it. They contributed to American religion a stable of serious theologians, ecumenical leaders, and mainstream Protestantism's leading journal, the *Christian Century*, but they have never been overly fond of their history.

In short, the price of modernization for liberal Disciples was primitivism. Simple notions about the commonsense restoration of a "once-for-all revealed" primitive church vanished in the complexities of modern thought, as surely as had Jefferson's "self-evident truths." Long before the turn of the twentieth century, liberal Disciples leaders confessed, "we follow the apostolic example whenever we like it; when we do not, we depart from it." They looked forward, not backward, and insisted that modern Disciples must be open to new truth. Two months before the close of the nineteenth century, the editor of the *Christian Oracle,* later the *Christian Century,* wrote, "There are no limitations . . . preventing us to be hospitable to every truth that may be discovered or any that may be rediscovered. So today whatever of truth there may be in the doctrine of sanctification, or faith healing, or Christian Science, or Christian Socialism . . . we are free to accept."[16] Thoroughly comfortable with the thinking of their day, these Disciples leaders, writes DeGroot, discarded "the proof text method" designed to reproduce the "forms and methods of the ancient faith."[17]

Some Disciples at the end of the nineteenth century were less at home with the intellectual changes of the period, but, in their own way, they were quite at home in modern society. Indeed, by 1900 Disciples churches were crowded with Midwestern merchants and farmers who had embraced success, material progress, and the American nation. The chief aim of this group of Disciples was the legitimizing of the restoration movement, the building of a respectable denomination. The election to the presidency of Disciples educator James A. Garfield was the most inspiring single moment in the denomination's ascent toward respectability. Isaac Errett, a Cincinnati editor and personal friend to Garfield, was profoundly orthodox, but at the same time he believed that his church must play a constructive role in American society. "To our mind," Errett wrote in 1866, "there is no more pernicious idea prevailing in religious society, than this of isolating religion from the affairs of every-day life, and imprisoning it in the sanctuary as a thing of doctrine, and rite, and sentiment."[18]

Moderate Disciples' engagement with American society was marked partly by a growing sense of denominational pride. By the end of the century, Disciples' papers were filled with calls for "vim, vigor and victory" and announcements concerning the erection of new church buildings that were an "ornament to the city."[19] While the familiar rhetoric of restoration still resounded from the pulpits of these upwardly mobile churches, this successful new generation was less combative in its claims, less dogmatic in its search for New Testament patterns, and more anxious to be identified as a part of the evangelical community. "It is but a little while since we became orthodox," trumpeted a gratified speaker at the Missouri Christian Lectures in 1884. "Before that we were something like the Mormons, or Sandemanians: a set of crude errorists."[20] In 1875, the editor James H. Garrison summarized this broader vision for the movement. "To aid in family and church culture, to promote greater love and piety among the brethren, in order to encourage individual growth and church co-operation, to keep before the world our great plea of the restoration of primitive Christianity and the union of Christians, and to insist upon a practical demonstration, in our own history, of the unifying power of the ancient gospel—this shall be our line of work."[21]

A third version of restoration primitivism was widely accepted in the South at the turn of the twentieth century. The Texas preacher James L. Thornberry wrote in 1885, "The only way to sustain Christianity and have union, is for all of us to say and believe that all God's statements are facts and truths . . . and that all his commandments are to be believed and obeyed literally."[22] In 1891, David Lipscomb, conservative editor of the *Gospel Advocate,* announced plans for the opening of a Bible school in Nashville under the control of "safe and competent teachers." Religious instruction at the school would focus on "the Bible, excluding all human opinions and philosophy." The Scriptures would be "the only rule of faith and practice."[23]

This commonsense primitivism found its strongest support among those Disciples who were most insulated from the social and intellectual changes of the post–Civil War era. David Lipscomb became the most articulate spokesman for these socially alienated Disciples. Lipscomb believed that Christians should not vote or hold office, a position shared by many, though probably not a majority, of southern Disciples.[24] An overwhelming majority did agree, however, with Lipscomb's conclusion that political and social reform should not be combined with religion: "Bringing this work into the church dwarfs and destroys the spirituality and activity of the church."[25]

In the years after the Civil War, these southern preachers saw clear connections between northern Disciples' compromise of restoration primitivism and their growing social contentment. Partly, they believed, the compromise had been intellectual. "Loose, rationalistic and semi-infidel teachings are prevailing in some churches of Disciples in the Northern states," Lipscomb warned in 1891.[26] But the northern churches had also succumbed to success; "wealth and social respectability" were more important than New Testament purity.[27] In 1897, Lipscomb summarized the "fundamental difference between the Disciples of Christ [Churches of Christ] and the society folks." The southern conservatives wanted people to "come to Christ," while Disciples liberals wanted to build "a strong and respectable denomination" based on "moneyed societies, fine houses, fashionable music, and eloquent speeches."[28]

The Churches of Christ in the early twentieth century, then, embraced commonsense biblical primitivism, combining it with a deep-seated suspicion of modernity. Not only did they reject modern ideas

(Darwin had few friends even among Methodists in the South of the early twentieth century), they felt ill at ease with all of modern culture—urban living, the growth of the professions, and the new business techniques that had brought prosperity to the North. For these early twentieth-century Church of Christ leaders primitivism was not a strategy for progress based on the best of modern thought but rather a conservative bastion against the buffeting of modernization.

As in the nineteenth century, however, feelings of world rejection never spread perfectly evenly throughout the Churches of Christ. Time and success slowly eroded feelings of alienation as the Churches of Christ grew. Since World War II, a generation of thoughtful leaders has been trying to understand the growing diversity within the movement and to reevaluate the relevance of the restoration hermeneutic.

The 1991 conference on primitivism at Pepperdine University, along with others sponsored by Churches of Christ colleges in recent years, exemplifies the presence of a generation of young scholars within the Churches of Christ who are fully conversant with modern thought and reasonably comfortable with it. The leadership of many of the church's institutions has passed into the hands of people with graduate degrees from the nation's most prestigious universities; at these institutions there is a growing willingness to rethink primitivism in the light of modern thought. The 1990 Christian Scholar's Conference at Abilene Christian University featured calls for updating the restoration hermeneutic in the light of postmodern thought and gave a peek at a deconstructionist critique of commonsense primitivism. One speaker warned that old-time restoration thinking might well be as "anachronistic as the flat earth society."[29]

Many other Christians who would consider such suggestions heretical capitulations to modern thought have made their own accommodation with modernization. Hundreds of sermons are preached every Sunday in glitzy Churches of Christ filled with upwardly mobile members of the best country clubs and leaders of the Republican party. The sermons are more likely to feature advice on how to achieve success, have a good marriage, and cope with modern drug problems than disquisitions on biblical primitivism. These congregations make up the worldly church chronicled by C. Leonard Allen, Richard T. Hughes, and Michael R. Weed, a secularized version of the Churches of Christ.[30] These Christians are perfectly at home in modern American society; for them, commonsense primitivism is not a rationale for escape from modernity but the ground of denominational legitimacy.

Finally, historic Disciples primitivism still lingers in the less-successful congregations left behind by their more educated and prosperous brethren. This remnant is clearly discernible in the Churches of Christ. At the end of the twentieth century, hundreds of Churches of Christ were still preoccupied with searching biblical texts to determine whether elders must have more than one child or if the Lord's Supper may be taken in the evening. Primarily, this lively primitivism survives, as it did in the late nineteenth century, among those whose sense of social alienation remains strongest. An issue of a magazine circulated among the anti-institutional Churches of Christ featured the section "Christ versus Culture." The editor wrote, "Few themes in the Bible recur more often than the plaintive plea to 'come out from among them, and be ye separate.' . . . Few things trouble me more than seeing churches filled with good people being sucked into the maelstrom of a decadent culture—listening to the world, reading its books, watching its television and swallowing its values."[31]

Conclusion

In short, the unfolding of Disciples history is primarily a story of changing understandings of the movement's primitivist plea. In the nineteenth and twentieth centuries those Disciples most comfortable with modernization either abandoned or modified Disciples primitivism. Many Disciples, like many other Americans, have continued to be suspicious of the most radical ideas of their day, but at the same time rambunctiously celebratory of their times and of the American nation. Primitivist rhetoric became for them a family treasure, an explanation of their authenticity. Finally, restoration primitivism remained a usable explanatory system for thousands in the twentieth century who were ignorant or distrustful of modern thought and who, for a variety of reasons, felt uncomfortable in the impersonal and confusing world that surrounded them.

Notes

1. Philip Schaff, ed., *The Creeds of Christendom* (New York: Harper and Brothers, 1919), 3:603.

2. Ibid., 658.

3. John Glas, *A Treatise on the Lord's Supper* (Edinburgh: J. Cochran, 1743), 1–13.

4. *An Account of the Christian Practices Observed by the Churches Called Glasites in Scotland and Sandemanians in America* (Galashiels, Scotland: D. Fair, 1832), 4.

5. Alexander Campbell, "Aristocracy," *Millennial Harbinger,* fifth series, vol. 6 (Apr. 1863): 168–70.

6. In this essay I shall refer to the three groups as the Disciples of Christ, the Independent Christian Churches, and the Churches of Christ.

7. David Edwin Harrell Jr., *Quest for a Christian America: The Disciples of Christ and American Society to 1866* (Nashville: Disciples of Christ Historical Society, 1966), 58–59.

8. Ibid., 60.

9. Ibid. Volume 2 of my social history of the Disciples of Christ explores the playing out of those divisive themes. See *The Social Sources of Division in the Disciples of Christ, 1865–1900* (Athens, Ga.: Publishing Systems, 1973).

10. Richard T. Hughes, "The Apocalyptic Origins of Churches of Christ and the Triumph of Modernism," *Religion and American Culture* 2 (Summer 1992): 181–214.

11. Harrell, *Quest,* 59.

12. David Lipscomb, "Queries," *Gospel Advocate* 37 (July 11, 1895): 437. See also Lipscomb, "Queries," *Gospel Advocate* 40 (June 23, 1898): 397.

13. See "Are We Nearing a Great Historic Epoch?" *Christian Evangelist,* Jan. 22, 1891, 50; "Our Budget," *Christian Evangelist,* Nov. 11, 1886, 712.

14. Alfred T. DeGroot, *The Grounds of Division among the Disciples of Christ* (Chicago: privately printed, 1940), 4.

15. Ibid., 8.

16. "The Jubilee Conventions," *Christian Oracle* 16 (Oct. 26, 1899): 4.

17. DeGroot, *Grounds,* 92, 184.

18. Isaac Errett, "Religion and Politics," *Christian Standard* 1 (Sept. 29, 1866): 204.

19. James Small, "A Visit to Iowa," *Christian Standard* 32 (Oct. 23, 1897): 1356. See also Isaac Errett, "Rich Men's Gifts," *Christian Standard* 18 (Mar. 10, 1883): 114; R. M. Yost, "True Greatness," *Christian Standard* 12 (May 12, 1877): 146.

20. D. R. Dungan, "How Shall We Sustain the Gospel in the Cities," in *The Missouri Christian Lectures* (Kansas City, Mo.: J. H. Smart, 1886), 109.

21. James H. Garrison, "The New Year," *Christian Standard* 3 (Jan. 7, 1875): 4.

22. James L. Thornberry, "The American Congress of Churches," *Gospel Advocate* 27 (May 5, 1885): 279.

23. David Lipscomb, "Bible School," *Gospel Advocate* 33 (June 17, 1891): 377.

24. See David Lipscomb, *Civil Government* (Nashville: Gospel Advocate, 1957). Beginning in October 1880, the *Gospel Advocate* published a long debate between David Lipscomb and John F. Rowe on the subject of the Christian's relation to civil government.

25. David Lipscomb, "Politics and Religion," *Gospel Advocate* 29 (Oct. 26, 1887): 678.

26. David Lipscomb, "Should Women Preach Publicly," *Gospel Advocate* 33 (Aug. 5, 1891): 486.

27. David Lipscomb, "Among Our Exchanges," *Apostolic Guide* 3 (Mar. 4, 1887): 1.

28. David Lipscomb, "The Churches across the Mountains," *Gospel Advocate* 39 (Jan. 7, 1897): 4.

29. Darryl Tippens, "Postmodern Theories of Interpretation: What They Say to Restorationists," paper presented at the Christian Scholars Conference, Abilene Christian University, Abilene, Tex., 1990.

30. C. Leonard Allen, Richard T. Hughes, and Michael R. Weed, *The Worldly Church* (Abilene, Tex.: Abilene Christian University Press, 1988).

31. David Edwin Harrell, "Christ versus Culture," *Christianity Magazine,* June 1988, 11.

7

"Bumping" into Modernity: Primitive/Modern Tensions in the Wesleyan/Holiness Movement

SUSIE C. STANLEY

For the Wesleyan/Holiness tradition, coping with modernity is a lot like waltzing. Try as one might, it is often difficult on a crowded floor to avoid bumping against other dancers or even sometimes stepping on other dancers' toes.

Likewise, in the dance of life, many in the Wesleyan/Holiness movement have sought to avoid modernization. The floor, however, is far too crowded for isolation, and most in the Wesleyan/Holiness tradition have bumped up against modernization time and again, in spite of their own best efforts to the contrary. Indeed, many scholars note that the Wesleyan/Holiness movement adopted from an early date an antimodern or countermodern posture.[1]

For the purposes of this essay, *modernity* is a mind-set embodying Enlightenment ideas such as individualism, rationalism, naturalism, skepticism, systematization, bureaucracy, and optimism. *Modernism,* on the other hand, is a theological response to modernity at the turn of the twentieth century.

While it is generally true that the Wesleyan/Holiness movement adopted an antimodern posture, we must be clear on the meaning of the term *antimodern.* In the first place, it is incorrect to conclude that the Wesleyan/Holiness movement is fundamentalist. James Davison Hunter repeats the mistake of others when he forces a large segment of American Protestantism, including the Wesleyan/Holiness movement, into the fundamentalist camp.[2] This movement simply does not correspond to the either/or nature of the fundamentalist/modernist paradigm and has often resisted both these extremes.[3] Fred Bruffett, writing in a Holiness paper in 1924, made the point well:

> We face two extremes. On the one hand are the ultra liberal modernists, denying the miracles of the Bible, the virgin birth, and the resurrection of Jesus. On the other hand are the ultra conservatives, with their cold water brigade, trying to put out the fire that is burning. The first class recklessly throws the fundamental doctrines of the Bible to the winds; the second delights in rigid, stereotyped, doctrinal fixing that raises creed above Christ, leaving only a lifeless, powerless, religious machine. Both extremes kill and destroy faith in Jesus, and result in nothing, but dead formality in religion.[4]

While it therefore would be inaccurate to locate the antimodern dimensions of the Wesleyan/Holiness tradition in "fundamentalism," it would be profoundly accurate to locate that posture in the reversionist outlook scholars often designate as "primitivism." After all, while the modern mind "errs in the direction of idolatry of the new,"[5] primitivists celebrate the past and many seek to reconstruct the past in the present. But here again we must be clear, for the Wesleyan/Holiness tradition has embraced primitivism in a variety of forms. Indeed, one finds in the Wesleyan/Holiness tradition all three categories of primitivism—ecclesiastical, ethical, and experiential—outlined by Richard T. Hughes.[6]

This essay, then, will undertake two tasks. First, it will challenge the fundamentalist/modernist paradigm as a way to understand the antimodern dimensions of the Wesleyan/Holiness tradition. Second, it will seek to examine the variety of "primitivisms" this tradition has employed over the course of its history. Along the way, it will ask how each type of primitivism "bumped" into modernity, using the Church of God (Anderson) as a case study.[7]

Challenging the Fundamentalist/Modernist Paradigm: The Wesleyan/Holiness Movement and Biblical Authority

James Davison Hunter placed the Wesleyan/Holiness movement in the fundamentalist camp by including this movement within evangelicalism, which he then equated with fundamentalism.[8] This is particularly evident in his discussion of inerrancy, in which he consistently claimed that all evangelicals are inerrantists.[9] While this statement holds true for evangelicals who trace their roots to fundamentalism, it does not hold true for all evangelicals.

Wesleyan/Holiness groups initially did not participate in the battle over the Bible. Their view of scriptural authority provided an alternative to fundamentalist and modernist positions on the Bible. H. Orton Wiley, a member of the Church of the Nazarene, articulated this third alternative:

> Spiritual men and women—those filled with the Holy Spirit, are not unduly concerned with either higher or lower criticism. They do not rest merely in the letter which must be defended by argument. They have a broader and more substantial basis for their faith. It rests in their risen Lord, the glorified Christ. They know that the Bible is true, not primarily through the efforts of the apologists, but because they are acquainted with its Author. The Spirit which inspired the Word dwells within them and witnesses to its truth.[10]

The insistence upon the internal witness of the Holy Spirit as a source of biblical authority meant that Wesleyan/Holiness adherents were not as worried as fundamentalists by issues emerging from higher criticism.[11]

The Wesleyan/Holiness emphasis on experience added to the lack of concern about higher criticism. The Free Methodist statement on Scripture states that the Bible "proves itself true in human experience."[12] John W. V. Smith emphasized a major distinction between Church of God pioneers and fundamentalists when he claimed that for the former, the authority of Scripture was validated by religious experience rather than an inerrant text validating Scripture as claimed by fundamentalists.[13]

Early Church of God leaders such as Henry Wickersham and R. R. Byrum emphasized that God inspired the authors rather than the words of Scripture. In 1894, Wickersham defined his understanding of inspiration: "The different writers of the books of the Bible were inspired of God. It is not the words of the Bible that were inspired, it is not the thoughts of the Bible that were inspired; it is the men who wrote the Bible that were inspired. Inspiration acts . . . on the man himself; so that he, . . . under the impulse of the Holy Ghost, conceives certain thoughts and gives utterance to them in certain words."[14] Byrum expressed a lack of concern regarding possible errors in the Bible: "If the critics could actually prove that the original manuscripts of the Bible contain errors, it would not disprove divine inspiration, but would merely require many believers in inspiration to allow a larger place for the human element."[15]

The witness of the Holy Spirit, the importance of experience in authenticating Scripture, and the interaction of the human and divine in biblical authorship all pointed to an understanding of the Bible that was amenable to a higher criticism that still allowed for supernaturalism.[16] The popularity of the inductive method of Bible study at many Wesleyan/Holiness schools is another factor contributing to the movement's openness to higher criticism.[17] Donald Dayton observes that acceptance of biblical criticism, albeit in a restrained form, persists in most Holiness schools.[18]

Despite Wesleyan/Holiness scholars' understanding of biblical authority and a limited acceptance of higher criticism, Wesleyan/Holiness groups have faced an invasion of fundamentalist influences within their ranks. Because of this reality, scholars generally have focused on the movement's accommodation to fundamentalism rather than its relation to modernity.[19]

Paul Bassett credits H. Orton Wiley for preventing fundamentalist "leavening" in the Church of the Nazarene's "Course of Study for Licensed Ministers," which was required for ordination. Wiley successfully thwarted an attempt in 1928 to add a book promoting inerrancy to the reading list for those enrolled in the course.[20] "Inerrancy" was added to the Nazarene Articles of Faith the same year when it was modified thus: "*inerrantly* revealing the will of God concerning us in all things necessary to our salvation."[21] This statement limited inerrancy rather than adopting the fundamentalist position that all Scripture was inerrant. J. Kenneth Grider recognizes that perhaps this addition was an effort "to nudge the denomination toward fundamentalism."[22]

Other Wesleyan/Holiness churches have responded to inerrancy in a variety of ways. The Free Methodist statement on Scripture declares that the Bible "bears unerring witness of Jesus Christ" and "is completely truthful in all it affirms."[23] An attempt to add *inerrancy* to the statement in 1989 was thwarted.[24] The Wesleyan Methodist church (now known as the Wesleyan church since merging with the Pilgrim Holiness church) adopted a position supporting inerrancy in 1951.[25] The Evangelical church, founded in 1968 by Evangelical United Brethren members who did not merge with the Methodist church to become the United Methodist church, also affirms the inerrancy of the Bible.[26]

The Church of God exhibits a high degree of diversity in its understanding of biblical authority. Steve Stall examined eight Church of God teachers of past generations and eighteen who were still teaching to determine their views on biblical inspiration and authority. Stall used four statements of faith ranging from a fundamentalist view of inerrancy to the United Methodist doctrine, a liberal Wesleyan position, to assess views of biblical authority. He determined that only one of the early leaders, Charles Ewing Brown, considered himself an inerrantist.[27] John W. V. Smith agreed with Stall's assessment but added that Brown admitted, in oral conversations, that there were errors in the Bible.[28] Views of the eighteen contemporary teachers and leaders ranged across the entire spectrum with only two maintaining an unequivocally inerrantist position.[29]

The Church of God also tolerates various interpretations of the book of Revelation. Early pioneers such as D. S. Warner and F. G. Smith interpreted Revelation via the church-historical approach, understanding Daniel and Revelation as depicting the restoration of the pure primitive church. In 1930, Otto F. Linn followed in the footsteps of Warner and Smith, depicting paganism, Protestantism, and papalism as the enemies of the restored primitive church. Linn began as a primitivist but his Ph.D. in the New Testament at the University of Chicago transformed him from a primitivist to a higher critic. In 1942, the Gospel Trumpet Company, the publishing arm of the Church of God, refused to print Linn's commentary on Revelation because it departed from the primitivist hermeneutic. Within ten years, Linn had moved from a primitivist to a historical, critical, preterist approach that located the meaning of Revelation, not in the restoration of the primitive church, but in the first century. Linn's book was a watershed, followed quietly in 1943 by the Gospel Trumpet's publication of Adam Miller's *A Brief Introduction to the New Testament*, which outlined four diverse interpretations of Revelation. Whereas Linn was the center of a storm, probably because he repudiated his prior primitivism, the church generally accepted Miller's more irenic approach. The Church of God continues to recognize those who advocate a primitivist interpretation of Revelation as well as those who favor other approaches.[30]

In this section, I have examined the issue of biblical authority to illustrate how the Wesleyan/Holiness movement challenges the fundamentalist/modernist paradigm. It does not comfortably fit in either category. For the most part, Wesleyan/Holiness churches have resisted efforts to incorporate inerrancy into their doctrinal statements on the Bible. Wesleyan/Holiness scholars who have accepted higher criticism have been able to maintain a high view of biblical authority since they also believe that experience and the witness of the Holy Spirit authenticate Scripture.

Ecclesiastical Primitivism

Pioneers in the early years of the Church of God often asked others, "Have you seen the church?" The church they envisioned was "a divine institution in all its aspects—its boundaries, its membership, its structure, its creed, and its work. All these aspects are under the control of 'the personal presence and authority of the Holy Ghost.' Man-rule is to be avoided at *all* these points if the church is really to function as the united instrument of God's work in the world."[31] Christians who had "seen the church" came out of denominations that were mere human constructions and affiliated with other members of God's universal church under the sole leadership of the Holy Spirit.

Charles Ewing Brown, a second-generation leader in the Church of God, affirmed the role of the Holy Ghost in church polity: "It is my belief that the apostolic church was spiritually organized by the Holy Ghost."[32] Early leaders in the Church of God sought to model this understanding of the apostolic church and condemned churches that resorted to human means of organization.[33] This section will focus on the polity of the Church of God and the understanding of unity that resulted from its theology of the universal church.

While Brown opposed human *organization* in the Church of God, he argued that the *work* of the church could be organized.[34] His justification, however, came after the fact since significant organization had already occurred in the Church of God by 1930, when Brown first voiced his rationale supporting organization.[35] Five national agencies were in existence by this time.

Despite Brown's argument, primitivist resistance to organization occurred. The Watchman movement is a prominent example. L. Earl Slacum began the attack in 1944 with the sermon "Watchmen on the Walls," which castigated the "man-made organizations" that had emerged at Anderson, Indiana.[36] Reconciliation efforts failed and several pastors and congregations withdrew from the Church of God, forming the Slacum, or Watchman, movement. Slacum grew disillusioned even with this group and informed his followers in 1951, "We have more organization in less than five years than they [Anderson] had in twenty-five years."[37] He resigned his positions and refellowshipped with the Church of God.

The apparently irresistible urge to bureaucratize reflects a modern mind-set. Marvin Hartman has observed, "The General Ministerial Assembly found it could not do the work of the Lord unorganized in a highly organized society."[38] The Church of God has accommodated to secular methods of institutionalization despite its theological aversion to organization. The organizational chart in the church yearbook attests to movement away from the initial understanding of ecclesiastical primitivism. The 1991 yearbook contains thirty pages of information on the general agencies and committees of the church.[39] But the tension remains. Various study committees (in themselves indications of modernity) have been established to consider the issue, including the Task Force on Governance and Polity, established in 1987. The church's ecclesiastical primitivism, while not preventing organization, has maintained a tension that has continued to challenge or restrain organizational efforts. Some argue that the church has capitulated and organized itself along human lines. Others, admitting that some organization has occurred, contend that primitivist ideas prevail.

While ecclesiastical primitivism determined polity for the Church of God, it also informed an organic concept of unity. The modernist movement at the turn of the twentieth century offered two views of unity—federalist and organic. While federalists, by far the larger of the two groups, proposed ecumenism among denominations, organic unionists "believed that the One Church already exists, and that the problem was to make it visible."[40]

The Church of God rejected federalist options to achieve unity because of its aversion to the denominational system. Early Church of God leaders vehemently opposed the denominational system, which they firmly believed was a human distortion of God's intention. Radically challenging the structure of American Protestantism, their vision of the church disregarded all denominational boundaries. D. S. Warner graphically stated his position when he asked, "O Sectarianism! thou abomination of the earth, thou bane of the cause of God, when will thy corrupt and wicked walls fall to earth and cease to curse men to hell?"[41] *Sectarianism* was a derogatory term used by Warner and his followers to denote all denominations. For Warner, sanctified persons verified the experience of holiness when they recognized that the lines of denominational division were human distortions of God's order and "came out" of their denominations.[42] The Church of God has refused to join organizations such as the National Council of Churches, the National Association of Evangelicals, and even the Christian Holiness Association because to do so would undermine its vision of organic unity.

The faculty and staff of Anderson School of Theology reaffirmed the church's continuing support of organic unity in a "statement of conviction" published in 1979: *"God's church is intended to be a unified community. The dividedness among Christian people today is not just unfortunate; it is inappropriate and wholly unacceptable. Unity is clearly God's will for the Church. . . . The goal is less a contrived peace treaty among deeply divided church organizations and more a radical reconsideration of what is an appropriate network of relationships among brothers and sisters in Christ."*[43] Despite the long-standing opposition to the denominational system, the Church of God has engaged in conversations regarding unity with various groups, most recently with the Christian Churches/Churches of Christ.

Conversion is the only requirement for membership in the Church of God. The practice of open communion reflects the belief that all Christians are members of the Church of God.[44] Any individual who believes she or he is a Christian is welcome at the communion table.

The Church of God is noncreedal. By refusing to formulate a creed for its members to affirm, the Church of God has resisted modernity's compulsion to systematize.[45] Perhaps fearful that the contents of the seminary's statement of conviction would be perceived as a creedal statement, Robert Reardon, then president of the college, stressed in the preface, "While the statement seeks to share some critical convictions, it is not intended to be creedal."[46] Despite the disclaimer, one faculty member refused to sign the statement because of his primitivist opposition to creeds.

Today, the Church of God looks and acts in many ways like a denomination.[47] It has struggled to maintain its ideal of ecclesiastical primitivism despite the reality of increased organization. Continued affirmation of membership based on conversion and continued opposition to a creed signify the ongoing commitment to organic unity.

Experiential Primitivism

Hughes focused primarily on the gift of speaking in tongues in his discussion of experiential primitivism.[48] I would like to expand this category by adding gifts of the Holy Spirit related to leadership and also the charismatic authority derived from the Holy Spirit.

Charles Ewing Brown described leadership in the apostolic church: "The Scriptures teach what might be called charismatic church government, that is, the government of the church by the Holy Spirit through the bestowal of his gifts."[49] The officers of the apostolic church were those who were recognized "as possessors of certain gifts of the Spirit."[50] Ongoing authority of those in office depended upon "the *continuous recognition* of them as possessors of the gifts of the Spirit."[51]

Brown further described the apostolic church as a spiritual democracy, which he defined as the "fundamental doctrine of spiritual equality and the universal priesthood of believers set in the New Testament."[52] Brown was explicit about the consequences of spiritual democracy: "The equality of all Christians before God leaves no place for autocratic and dictatorial rule in God's church."[53] The ordinance of foot washing practiced in the Church of God symbolized the equality and mutual servanthood of the apostolic church. In a spiritual democracy, "there are no grades of order, no superior nor inferior, no higher and lower, no difference in quality and dignity."[54] The priesthood of believers included women since "prejudice and privilege" had no place in spiritual democracy.[55] The Holy Spirit was no respecter of persons and gifted both men and women to preach.[56] Therefore, ordination recognized those gifted to preach, irrespective of gender. Perhaps the category of egalitarian primitivism should be added to Hughes's typology to signify this aspect of spiritual democracy. Egalitarian primitivism was the basis for spiritual democracy, which incorporated the affirmation of women clergy.[57]

Modernity corresponds with the priestly model of authority rather than with the prophetic model described above. As groups shift from prophetic to priestly authority in today's world, they accommodate to modernity in that they rely less and less on the supernatural as the source of authority. The process of institutionalization and routinization of charisma stifles the Holy Spirit. One evidence of modernity's influence in the Church of God is the drastic reduction of women ministers. In 1925, women pastored 32 percent of the congregations but by 1985, the number had dropped to 2 percent.[58]

Acceptance of church growth theories also reflects inroads of modernity in the understanding of church leadership. The church growth model advocates that the pastor or church leader emulate the business model of authority epitomized by the chief executive officer. In some cases, a name change indicates the shift in thinking as when a state coordinator adopts the title executive coordinator. Undermining egalitarian primitivism, church growth programs advocate male pastors since the male represents authority in our culture. The CEO model of leadership squeezes out the role of the Holy Spirit in gifting whom it chooses to lead. Spiritual democracy likewise erodes when church councils elected by congregational vote are replaced by councils appointed by the pastor.

Ethical Primitivism

Since the Church of God is most similar to other Wesleyan/Holiness groups in its ethical primitivism, the general comments in this section apply to the Wesleyan/Holiness movement as a whole.

Ethical primitivism involves more than a war against worldliness; it challenges modernity's emphasis on individualism and self-centeredness. Ethical primitivism promotes the ethic of love based on Luke 10:27 ("You shall love the Lord your God with all your heart, and with all your soul, and with all your strength, and with all your mind; and your neighbor as yourself"). John Wesley repeatedly stressed his conviction that Christian perfection is love for God and love for neighbors.[59]

The ethic of love resulted in social holiness, the Wesleyan/Holiness expression of social Christianity.[60] A biblical text that summarizes the social holiness vision of social transformation is Galatians 3:28 ("There is neither Jew nor Greek, there is neither bond nor free, there is neither male nor female; for you are all one in Christ Jesus"). Holiness workers challenged existing dualistic and hierarchical structures in society and combated racism, classism, and sexism by offering radical egalitarian alternatives to those structures.

The Wesleyan/Holiness movement has challenged racism in various ways. The Wesleyan Methodist Connection sought to actualize the vision of racial unity by its antislavery activities. Though the Church of God has not always lived up to its ideal, its percentage of African American members exceeds the percentage of African Americans in the United States. Renewed efforts to achieve racial unity in the Church of God are evidenced by the fact that the executive secretary and the dean of the seminary are African American.[61]

Urban workers addressed economic slavery or classism as they worked to remove the chains of poverty from its victims. Reform activities stemming from the ethic of love have diminished but efforts to keep it alive are on the increase. For example, the Church of the Nazarene recently has sponsored two conferences on compassionate ministries in an effort to revive its initial emphasis.

The third phrase of Galatians 3:28, "there is neither male nor female," received the most attention from social holiness advocates. They expanded their vision of gender equality beyond the walls of the church by actively promoting suffrage for women. Alma White and the Pillar of Fire church endorsed the Equal Rights Amendment at its inception to eliminate discrimination in the legal arena.[62]

While the Wesleyan/Holiness movement was antiworldly in terms of behavior and appearance, its ethic of love provided a vision of the redemption of the world through activities motivated by love and made possible by the empowerment of the Holy Spirit. Rather than viewing the world with a resigned pessimism, Wesleyan/Holiness believers saw themselves as God's agents in the world, working to transform it.

The Wesleyan/Holiness movement shared the optimism of modernity but differed regarding the source of that optimism. Modernity's optimism stemmed from the belief that science and culture offered unlimited human potential. The Wesleyan/Holiness movement, on the other hand, believed that progress was possible with the help of God through the empowerment of the Holy Spirit. The Wesleyan/Holiness emphasis on the Holy Spirit's immanence, however, paralleled in some ways the views of the modernists at the turn of the twentieth century. A dominant theme of modernism was "God's presence in the world and in human culture."[63] Both traditions stressed God's immanence, but modernists believed God acted through human culture while the Wesleyan/Holiness movement contended that the Holy Spirit empowered individuals to transform culture. Fundamentalists rejected both means of God's involvement in society, emphasizing God's transcendence.

Conclusion

In closing, I return to the metaphor of the dance floor. Initially, Wesleyan/Holiness primitivists refused to dance with fundamentalists or modernists at the turn of the twentieth century. Subsequently, they bumped into both fundamentalists and modernists, who have tried to cut in. Depending on the tune, they experienced some compatibility with each of the new partners. For the most part, though, the Wesleyan/Holiness primitivists tended to go their own way.

Despite conscious efforts to avoid bumping into modernity, members of the Church of God have interacted with modernity at different levels of intensity. In sociological terms, these encounters result in cognitive bargaining, or "interaction between religious world views and the structures and processes of modernity."[64] Individuals often experience different levels of cognitive bargaining depending on the issue under consideration. Some have brushed lightly against modernity, experiencing little cognitive bargaining. Others not only have bumped into modernity; they actually appear to be dancing with it.

Educated persons find themselves in tension with two dance partners—their primitive heritage and their education, which has been shaped by modernity. Some resolve the tension by choosing modernity and leaving the church. Others stay, living with the tension. Several Church of God scholars are pursuing a third option. Bumping into a new dancer on the floor, they are questioning modernity's assumptions from a postmodern perspective.[65]

Despite cognitive bargaining, primitive ideals have persisted in the Church of God. Although her reference was to the Assemblies of God, Margaret Poloma could have been speaking of the Church of God when she summarized: "The religious rhetoric of the ideal remains, but its content is diminished."[66] Primitivism provides a tension that has prevented the Church of God from accommodating completely to modernity. Sociological determinism predicts that modernity ultimately will lead, being the stronger partner. But that perspective does not account for the Holy Spirit who hovers over the dance floor ready to empower dancers to continue the reformation, retaining primitive values in a modern world.

Notes

1. Peter Williams considers the Holiness movement in the chapter "Reactions to Modernity" in *America's Religions: Traditions and Cultures* (New York: Macmillan, 1990), 253–57. Martin Marty mentions the Holiness movement in two paragraphs in "The Carapaces of Reactive Protestantism," a chapter in the section "Countermodernism" in *Modern American Religion: The Irony of It All* (Chicago: University of Chicago Press, 1986), 1:241–42. See also William Warren Sweet, *The Story of Religion in America* (New York: Harper and Brothers, 1950), 352–53.

2. James Davison Hunter, *Evangelicalism: The Coming Generation* (Chicago: University of Chicago Press, 1987). Donald Dayton briefly summarizes this tendency using Bernard Ramm's *The Evangelical Heritage* and Hunter's work as examples in "Yet Another Layer of the Onion; or, Opening the Ecumenical Door to Let the Riffraff In," *Ecumenical Review* 40 (1988): 97–100.

3. Bruce Lawrence's analysis is helpful on this point. He speaks of modernism/fundamentalism as a contrary that has been inflated into a contradiction "because the modernist mind thinks dialectically. It frames and counterposes antinomies. It sets the stage and then compels the choice between incommensurable, hostile, exclusive opposites." Lawrence explains the difference between contraries and contradictories: contraries "pose sharp differences . . . but they never allow the contrast to exclude the possibility of rapprochement and even, from time to time, inversion. Contradictories, however, are incommensurate opposites. They allow no dialectical or sympathetic interaction but only stark juxtaposition. . . . Seeing only contradictions, they posit irresolvable opposites. Though black and white are dominant color tones, we argue that gray also has its value." Bruce B. Lawrence, *Defenders of God: The Fundamentalist Revolt against the Modern Age* (San Francisco: Harper and Row, 1989), 40, 17.

4. Fred Bruffett, "God's Answer to Modernism," *Gospel Trumpet* 44 (Sept. 11, 1924): 12. *Gospel Trumpet* (renamed *Vital Christianity* in 1962) is a Church of God (Anderson) periodical.

5. Christopher Hall, "Back to the Fathers," *Christianity Today*, Sept. 24, 1990, 31.

6. Hughes places the Holiness movement in the ethical primitivist category. See "Christian Primitivism as Perfectionism: From Anabaptists to Pentecostals," in Stanley Burgess, ed., *Reaching Beyond: Chapters in the History of Perfectionism* (Peabody, Mass.: Hendrickson, 1986), 213–55. Margaret Poloma also views the Wesleyan/Holiness movement as a group that promoted ethical primitivism, which she limits to a legalistic system of "don'ts." She fails

to recognize or acknowledge similarities between the Wesleyan/Holiness movement and the Assemblies of God in terms of its experiential emphasis. See *Assemblies of God at the Crossroads: Charisma and Institutional Dilemmas* (Knoxville: University of Tennessee Press, 1989), 15, 145, 177.

7. The Church of God (Anderson) is not typical of the Wesleyan/Holiness movement or of primitivist groups in general. While members of most Wesleyan/Holiness churches initially were ex-Methodists, only about 50 percent of the Church of God "came out" of Methodistic churches. Val Clear, *Where the Saints Have Trod: A Social History of the Church of God Reformation Movement* (Chesterfield, Ind.: Midwest Publications, 1977), 58. Anabaptist influences nudged the Church of God toward a stronger primitivist stance. In terms of primitivism, the Church of God differs from other primitivist groups in that it is not ahistorical. The first comprehensive church history by a Church of God author appeared in 1900. See Henry C. Wickersham, *A History of the Church* (Moundsville, W.Va.: Gospel Trumpet, 1900). For a discussion of the historical roots of the Church of God, see Charles Ewing Brown, *The Apostolic Church* (Anderson, Ind.: Warner Press, 1947), 252–56. References to the Church of God in the remainder of this essay denote the Church of God (Anderson).

8. Hunter, *Evangelicalism*, 3–4, 20. Hunter makes the equation in his early work as well. For example, see "Operationalizing Evangelicalism: A Review, Critique, and Proposal," *Sociological Analysis* 42 (1981): 268, 371. Hunter incorporates Pietistic traditions, which include the Wesleyan/Holiness movement, in his definition of evangelicalism. See *American Evangelicalism: Conservative Religion and the Quandary of Modernity* (New Brunswick, N.J.: Rutgers University Press, 1983), 7. He states that evangelicalism is "not always synonymous with Fundamentalism" (4) but he consistently forgets this distinction and equates the two terms. William J. Abraham points out the "fatal flaw" of Hunter's work: "Hunter fails from the outset to understand the internal diversity of the evangelical tradition" by identifying it with fundamentalism. See William J. Abraham, Review of *Evangelicalism: The Coming Generation* by James Davison Hunter, *Perkins Journal* 41 (Apr. 1988): 33. Wesleyan/Holiness scholars Robert Wall and Frank Spina deal explicitly with Hunter's "category mistake," which is Spina's term. See Robert W. Wall, Review of *Evangelicalism: The Coming Generation* by James Davison Hunter, *Seattle Pacific University Review* 6 (Autumn 1987): 44–45, 49, and Frank Anthony Spina, "Biblical Scholarship in a Wesleyan Mode: Retrospect and Prospect," photocopy, 1990, 15. Five of the nine colleges Hunter examined in *Evangelicalism* are Wesleyan/Holiness schools. Hunter concluded that the "coming generation" of evangelicals is moving away from fundamentalist beliefs while, in fact, his data from the five Wesleyan/Holiness schools may actually indicate a drifting toward fundamentalism.

9. Hunter, *Evangelicalism*, 7, 47, 62, 140, 141.

10. H. Orton Wiley, *Christian Theology* (Kansas City, Mo.: Nazarene, 1940), 1:141–42, quoted in Paul Merritt Bassett, "The Fundamentalist Leavening of the Holiness Movement, 1914–1940, The Church of the Nazarene: A Case Study," *Wesleyan Theological Journal* 13 (Spring 1978): 66–67. See also 82.

11. Bassett, "Fundamentalist Leavening," 69.

12. Bishop Van Valin, ed., *Free Methodist Book of Discipline* (Indianapolis: Light and Life Press, 1989), 10.

13. John W. V. Smith, "The Bible in the Church of God Reformation Movement: A Historical Perspective," *Centering on Ministry* 6 (Spring 1981): 5.

14. Henry C. Wickersham, *Holiness Bible Subjects* (Anderson, Ind.: Gospel Trumpet, 1894), 18–19, quoted in Smith, "Bible in the Church of God," 4–5.

15. R. R. Byrum, *Christian Theology* (Anderson, Ind.: Gospel Trumpet, 1925), 172–73, quoted in Smith, "Bible in the Church of God," 5.

16. Likewise, evolutionists in the Wesleyan/Holiness movement have referred to themselves as theistic evolutionists, stressing God's role in the evolutionary process. Ronald L. Numbers surveyed attitudes toward evolution in the Wesleyan/Holiness movement and concluded that while many people did not consider themselves evolutionists, they were not as militant about the issue as fundamentalists. See Ronald L. Numbers, "Creation, Evolution, and Holy Ghost Religion: Holiness and Pentecostal Responses to Darwinism," *Religion and American Culture* 2 (Summer 1992): 127–58.

17. Inductive Bible study is "a precursor to some forms of contemporary canonical criticism and some of the newer literary approaches." Spina, "Biblical Scholarship," 23. For instance, see Robert Traina's *Methodical Bible Study* (Grand Rapids, Mich.: Francis Asbury Press of Zondervan, 1980).

18. Donald W. Dayton, "The Holiness and Pentecostal Churches: Emerging from Cultural Isolation," *Christian Century* 96 (Aug. 15–22, 1979): 789.

19. See Bassett, "Fundamentalist Leavening" and Spina, "Biblical Scholarship." Robert Walter Wall noted the addition of fundamentalist concerns to the *Free Methodist Book of Discipline* in "The Embourgoisement of the Free Methodist Ethos," *Wesleyan Theological Journal* 25 (Spring 1990): 122.

20. Bassett, "Fundamentalist Leavening," 79.

21. Ibid., 74. Bassett documents growing sympathy with fundamentalism among Nazarenes during the 1920s but also notes individuals who challenged fundamentalism and offered limited support for modernism.

22. J. Kenneth Grider, "Wesleyanism and the Inerrancy Issue," *Wesleyan Theological Journal* 19 (Fall 1984): 58. Grider also documents accommodation to fundamentalism in the Wesleyan Theological Society, which, from its inception in 1965 through 1969, included the following statement in its doctrinal position: "both the Old and New Testaments constitute the divinely inspired Word of God, inerrant in the originals, and the final authority for life and truth." *Wesleyan Theological Journal* 1 (1966): n.p. Grider attributes the inclusion of *inerrancy* to the fact that the Evangelical Theological Society required its membership to make the same affirmation (52). The Wesleyan Theological Society removed the inerrancy position in 1969 when they adopted a constitution. The revised statement read: "We believe . . . in the plenary-dynamic and unique inspiration of the Bible as the Divine Word of God, the only infallible (i.e., 'absolutely trustworthy and unfailing in effectiveness or operation'—RHD), sufficient and authoritative rule of faith and practice." John G. Merritt, "Fellowship in Ferment: A History of the Wesleyan Theological

Society, 1965–1984," *Wesleyan Theological Journal* 21 (Spring–Fall 1986): 195.
As a result of 1991 by-law changes, members are no longer required to sign a
statement of faith as a requirement for membership.

23. Van Valin, *Free Methodist Book,* 10.

24. Spina, "Biblical Scholarship," 20. Spina reports that inerrancy had been
a "contested point" among Free Methodists prior to 1989 as well, 6.

25. At the general conference the Articles of Religion were amended and
"the canonical books of the two Testaments [were declared] 'to be fully inerrant in their original manuscripts and superior to all human authority.'" Lee
M. Haines and Paul William Thomas, *An Outline History of the Wesleyan
Church* (Marion, Ind.: Wesley Press, 1985), 92.

26. *The Discipline of the Evangelical Church* (n.p., 1982), 3.

27. Steve Wayne Stall, "The Inspiration and Authority of Scripture: The
Views of Eight Historical and Twenty-one Current Doctrinal Teachers in the
Church of God (Anderson, Indiana)" (M.A. thesis, Anderson College School
of Theology, 1980), 27. Brown was a self-proclaimed fundamentalist. See "What
Is Fundamentalism?" *Gospel Trumpet* 59 (Feb. 25, 1939): 2; and "Why I Am
a Fundamentalist," *Gospel Trumpet* 65 (Apr. 7, 1945): 1. He did add the disclaimer that he was not a premillennialist. He admitted to criticism for his
appropriation of the term, which he defined essentially as a modern expression of historic Christianity.

28. Smith, "Bible in the Church of God," 5. F. G. Smith, another early leader, also included inerrancy in his statement on biblical inspiration but he limited inerrancy to matters of faith and practice: "The same promise of the Spirit
which renders the New Testament an unerring and sufficient rule of faith renders it also an unerring and sufficient rule of practice for the church in all
places and times." *The Last Reformation* (Anderson, Ind.: Gospel Trumpet,
1919), 44, quoted in Smith, "Bible in the Church of God," 5.

29. Steve Stall, "Inspiration," 72. The diversity partly reflects the fact that
the Church of God is noncreedal. Stall offered the eighteen participants still
teaching the following four statements and asked them to choose one:

Statement A (the original statement of faith of Fuller Theological Seminary): "The books which form the canon of the Old and New Testaments as
originally given are plenarily inspired and free from all error in the whole and
in the part. These books constitute the written Word of God, the only infallible rule of faith and practice," 4.

Statement B (from the doctrinal position of the Wesleyan Theological Society): "We believe in the plenary-dynamic and unique inspiration of the Bible as the divine Word of God, the only infallible, sufficient, and authoritative
rule of faith and practice," 5.

Statement C (statement of the Fuller Theological Seminary): "Scripture is
an essential and trustworthy record of . . . [the] . . . divine disclosure. All the
books of the Old and New Testaments, given by divine inspiration, are the
written Word of God, the only infallible rule of faith and practice. They are
to be interpreted according to their context and purpose and in reverent obedience to the Lord who speaks through them in living power," 5–6.

Statement D (from the *United Methodist Church Book of Discipline*): "Scripture is the primary source and guideline for doctrine. The Bible is the deposit of a unique testimony to God's self-disclosures. . . . As we open our minds and hearts to the Word of God through the words of persons inspired by the Holy Spirit, faith is born and nourished, our understanding deepens and develops, and both the core of faith and the range of our theological opinions are expanded and enriched. As the constitutive witness to God's self-revelation, Scripture is rightly read and understood within the believing community and its interpretation is informed by the traditions of the community," 6.

30. Information for this paragraph is derived from John E. Stanley, "Unity Amid Diversity: Interpreting the Book of Revelation in the Church of God (Anderson)," *Wesleyan Theological Journal* 25 (Fall 1990): 74–98. I am appreciative to John Stanley for his assistance with this section and his careful reading and advice on this essay as a whole.

31. John W. V. Smith provided this summary in "An Historical Review of Approaches to Church Government in the Church of God," paper prepared for a meeting of the Executive Council and State Representatives, 1961, 1. Smith is quoting from *Gospel Trumpet,* March 1, 1881.

32. Brown, *Apostolic Church,* 118.

33. Most of the other churches in the Wesleyan/Holiness movement adopted an episcopal form of church government. The Church of God (Holiness) shared the understanding of the Church of God (Anderson) about church polity. John Brooks of the Church of God (Holiness) argued that human law in the church was "not only unnecessary, but presumptuous." *The Divine Church* (Columbia, Mo.: Herald, 1891; rpt., New York: Garland, 1984), 27. The flyleaf of Brooks's book describes its contents: "A treatise on the origin, constitution, order, and ordinances of the church; being a vindication of the New Testament Ecclesia, and an exposure of the anti-scriptural character of the modern church of sect." *Church of sect* is Brooks's term for the denominational system.

34. Brown, *Apostolic Church,* 119–21. Brown's view has not gone unchallenged. John W. V. Smith faulted Brown for "spiritualizing the nature of the church and humanizing the work of the church." "Historical Review of Approaches," 4. Merle Strege questioned Brown's concession to organization and called the church to a reconsideration of the shortcomings of organization. "Situation Christianity: Organizing the Church's Work," *Vital Christianity* 110 (Dec. 1990): 10–11.

35. James R. Cook, "Social Consciousness in the Church of God: 1960–1970," *Colloquium* 4 (Mar. 1972): 5.

36. See John W. V. Smith, *The Quest for Holiness and Unity* (Anderson, Ind.: Warner Press, 1980), 326–35, for a summary of the Slacum controversy.

37. L. Earl Slacum to the Directors of the Ministers' and Missionaries' Training School, Inc., Plymouth Ind., and of the World Missionary Society of the Church of God, Inc., Ashland, Kentucky, May 21, 1951, Church of God Archives, Anderson, Ind.

38. Marvin Hartman, "Development of General Ministerial Assembly," in Barry L. Callen, ed., *A Time to Remember—Milestones* (Anderson, Ind.: Warn-

er Press, 1978), 41. See also Marvin Hartman, "The Origin and Development of the General Ministerial Assembly of the Church of God, 1917–1950" (B.D. thesis, Butler University School of Religion, 1958).

39. *1991 Yearbook of the Church of God: United States and Canada* (Anderson, Ind.: Executive Council of the Church of God, Division of Church Service, 1991), 4–33.

40. William R. Hutchison, *The Modernist Impulse in American Protestantism* (Oxford: Oxford University Press, 1976), 183.

41. D. S. Warner, diary, April 2, 1876, quoted in Smith, *Quest*, 51.

42. The Church of God (Holiness) shared the Church of God's anti-sectarianism. See Brooks, *Divine Church*, 266–71. Richard T. Hughes claimed that Brooks was "the architect of the 'come-outer' theory which legitimated separation from the traditional churches." "Christian Primitivism as Perfectionism," 240. The laurels must also be shared with D. S. Warner, who came to his position independently of Brooks.

43. Anderson School of Theology, "We Believe: A Statement of Conviction on the Occasion of the Centennial of the Church of God Reformation Movement" (Anderson, Ind.: Warner Press, 1979), 7.

44. The Church of God initially called itself the church of God to indicate its understanding of unity. To my knowledge, no one has traced the shift from church of God to Church of God.

45. Lawrence, *Defenders of God*, 35. According to Lawrence, the goal of systematizing "is to attempt a holistic reordering of diversity, channeling randomness into a visual, palpable framework that serves the group or groups to which the system applies, and at the same time advances their interest," 31.

46. Anderson School of Theology, "We Believe," n.p.

47. In his social history of the Church of God, Val Clear concluded that it is a denomination. However, he quoted the following description of the Church of God with approval: it is "a self-consciously non-denominational movement with a denominational structure." *Where the Saints*, 122. Clear's quotation is from James R. Cook, "Social Consciousness," 4.

48. See Hughes's preface to this volume.

49. Brown, *Apostolic Church*, 128. Brown further argued: "Any unbiased reader of the New Testament may easily convince himself that for the Christians of the first century the movement of the Spirit of God was the supreme authority in all the work of the church," 165.

50. Ibid., 138. See also 136–37.

51. Ibid., 139.

52. Ibid., 30–31. Brown cited Matt. 23:8, 1 Peter 2:5, 9, and Rev. 1:6 and 20:6 to support his thesis. See 134.

53. Brown, *Apostolic Church*, 134.

54. Ibid., 227.

55. Ibid., 165. See also 166–68.

56. F. G. Smith, an early leader in the Church of God, elaborated on this conviction: "Again, I call your attention to the organization of the church by the Holy Spirit. A man is an evangelist because he has the gift of evangelizing. It is not because he is a man, but because he has that particular gift. The

gift itself is the proof of his calling. If a woman has divine gifts fitting her for a particular work in the church, that is the proof, and the only proof needed, that that is her place. Any other basis of qualification than divine gifts is superficial and arbitrary and ignores the divine plan of organization and government in the church." "Editorial," *Gospel Trumpet* 40 (Oct. 14, 1920): 2.

57. Egalitarian primitivism also serves as the basis of contemporary Christian feminism. The New Testament scholar Elisabeth Schüssler Fiorenza speaks of the first Christians as "a discipleship of equals." See *In Memory of Her: A Feminist Theological Reconstruction of Christian Origins* (New York: Crossroad, 1983), 140–51, 184–88. Modernity is opposed to feminist principles. Enlightenment philosophy advocated inherent human rights but they applied only to males. For example, the Constitution, which was strongly influenced by Enlightenment ideals, guaranteed citizens the right to vote but limited citizenship to white men. Subsequent amendments were necessary to broaden suffrage to include African American men and, later, all women. Efforts to guarantee women's equality of rights under the law by constitutional amendment thus far have been unsuccessful.

58. Susie Stanley, "Church of God Women Pastors: A Look at the Statistics" in Juanita Evans Leonard, ed., *Called to Minister: Empowered to Serve* (Anderson, Ind.: Warner Press, 1989), 175–79. For more information, see also Juanita Evans Leonard, "Women, Change, and the Church," in *Called to Minister,* 149–67. These chapters also consider other reasons for the decline in women clergy.

59. Leon O. Hynson's *To Reform the Nation: Theological Foundations of Wesley's Ethics* (Grand Rapids, Mich.: Francis Asbury Press of Zondervan, 1984) and Mary Alice Tenney's *Blueprint for a Christian World* (Winona Lake, Ind.: Light and Life Press, 1953) outline Wesley's ethic of love.

60. For more information on social holiness, see Timothy L. Smith, *Revivalism and Social Reform: American Protestantism on the Eve of the Civil War* (Baltimore: Johns Hopkins University Press, 1980), and Norris Magnuson, *Salvation in the Slums,* ATLA Series, no. 10 (Metuchen, N.J.: Scarecrow Press, 1977).

61. For an account of ethnic ministries in the Church of God, see David A. Telfer, *Red and Yellow and Black and White and Brown* (Anderson, Ind.: Warner Press, 1981).

62. Susie Cunningham Stanley, *Feminist Pillar of Fire: The Life of Alma White* (Cleveland: Pilgrim Press, 1993), 111–14.

63. Hutchison, *Modernist Impulse,* 79. See also 121.

64. Hunter, *American Evangelicalism,* 15.

65. Fred Burnett has utilized poststructuralism in biblical studies. See Fred W. Burnett, "Postmodern Biblical Exegesis: The Eve of Historical Criticism," *Semeia* 51 (1990): 49–80. In the field of ethics, Merle Strege has employed narrative in the context of community. See Merle Strege, *Tell Me the Tale: Historical Reflections on the Church of God* (Anderson, Ind.: Warner Press, 1991).

66. Poloma, *Assemblies of God,* 239.

8

Searching for Eden with a Satellite Dish: Primitivism, Pragmatism, and the Pentecostal Character

GRANT WACKER

The date was Monday, April 9, 1906. The place, a four-room house on Bonnie Brae Street in the downtown industrial section of Los Angeles. After the supper dishes had been cleared away, a half-dozen black saints gathered to seek the baptism of the Holy Ghost. They assumed that when the power fell they would be enabled to speak an array of unlearned foreign languages, just as the apostles had done in the book of Acts. In the preceding weeks the little band had met many times to no avail. But on that memorable spring evening the Spirit finally moved. First one, then another, and then another began to stammer in unfamiliar tongues. Before the night was over nearly all found themselves singing and shouting in the mysterious cadences of Africa, Asia, and the South Sea Islands. The worshippers concluded, naturally enough, that after a spiritual drought of nearly two thousand years, the wonder-working power of the Holy Ghost once again had fallen upon Christ's humblest followers.

Word raced through the black community. Visitors gathered night after night, spilling out onto the porch and front lawn. Tradition has it that the weight of the enthusiasts soon crushed the porch. Realizing that they needed larger quarters, the band scraped together funds to lease an abandoned meetinghouse several blocks away on a short dirt road called Azusa Street. The following Tuesday evening, eight days after the initial manifestation of tongues, the Lord chose to advertise the mission through a most hapless instrument, a secular newspaper reporter, who may have been just walking home from work at the nearby *Los Angeles Times* building. "The night is made hideous . . . by the howlings of the worshippers," he wrote. "The devotees of the weird doctrine practice the most fanatical rites, preach the wildest theories and work themselves into a state of mad excitement." Not surprisingly, the devotees of the weird doctrine saw things differently. Within a week the San Andreas Fault had shifted, San Francisco lay in shambles, and anyone with a pure heart and an open mind could see that the long-awaited worldwide revival had finally begun.[1]

The tinder that caught fire in that ramshackle mission on Azusa Street is commonly said to have been the beginning of the worldwide pentecostal movement. Whether the revival really started among blacks at Azusa or among whites in faith healing services in Topeka, Kansas, a half-dozen years earlier or even in a series of white-hot meetings among North Carolina hill folk in the 1890s, as various historians have contended, there can be little dispute that the pentecostal insurgence mushroomed into one of the most powerful religious upheavals of the twentieth century. A 1979 Gallup poll revealed that in the United States alone, 19 percent—or 29 million—of adult Americans called themselves "Pentecostal or charismatic Christians."[2] Twelve years later the Assemblies of God, the largest and strongest of the pentecostal denominations, posted 2 million American domestic adherents and another 22 million in affiliated bodies in other parts of the world.[3] In 1993, according to David Barrett, a leading scholar of world Christianity, the movement registered 430 million converts worldwide. Except for Roman Catholicism, it ranked as the largest aggregation of Christians on the planet. Barrett projected that the revival would claim 560 million adherents by the year 2000 and well over a billion by the year 2025.[4] Almost certainly those figures swelled in the telling, perhaps wildly so, yet other studies consistently confirmed that within a century of its beginnings pentecostals had managed to claim a massive slice of the religious pie, both at home and abroad.[5]

Exactly who were the Christians who called themselves pentecostals? In the early 1990s, scores of denominations—or fellowships, as they preferred to be called—claimed the label. The best known was the Assemblies of God, which was national in scope but strongest in the Sunbelt states. Other well-known bodies included the mostly black Church of God in Christ, clustered in the states of the old South; the Church of God, concentrated in the Southern Highlands; the Pentecostal Holiness church, centered in the Southeast; and the International Church of the Foursquare Gospel, most visible on the West Coast. The United Pentecostal church and the largely black Pentecostal Assemblies of the World, commonly known as "Oneness" groups because of their insistence that Jesus alone was God, identified themselves as pentecostal but maintained (or were allowed to maintain) few relations with other pentecostal bodies. Both were concentrated in the urban Midwest. Literally scores of smaller sects, many of which were non-English speaking, dotted the religious landscape.[6]

What did pentecostals believe and practice? In the early days they often dubbed their missions Full Gospel Tabernacles, which meant that they preached the "full" or "foursquare" gospel of salvation through faith in Jesus Christ, baptism of the Holy Spirit with the evidence of speaking in unknown tongues, divine healing, and the promise of the Lord's soon return. Late twentieth-century adherents still shared those notions but in other ways they had grown extremely diverse. Run-down urban missions competed with opulent suburban churches; rough-tongued country preachers vied with unctuous television celebrities. More importantly, after World War II an emphasis upon the supernatural gifts of the Spirit as described in 1 Corinthians 12 and 14—pre-eminently the casting out of demons, divine healing, speaking in tongues, and the interpretation of tongues—penetrated some of the long-established Protestant denominations and the Roman Catholic church. The newer enthusiasts commonly called themselves charismatic Christians, partly to distinguish themselves from their unscrubbed pentecostal cousins.[7] Virtually every week in the 1980s and early 1990s the secular press carried an article about pentecostals or charismatics. Often those items focused upon the avarice of a Jim Bakker, the antics of a Jimmy Swaggart, or the presidential ambitions of a Pat Robertson. Yet behind those very public and often less-than-noble tales lay the private stories of millions of ordinary believers whose commitment to the work of the church typically dwarfed the involvement of non-pentecostal mainline Christians.

Scholars have offered various explanations for pentecostalism's apparent success. Some historians have pointed to the numerous continuities between the Wesleyan Holiness and pentecostal traditions back at the turn of the twentieth century, noting that the latter got a head start, so to speak, by appropriating the vast network of periodicals, churches, camp meetings, Bible schools, and faith homes that Holiness folk had carefully cemented in place decades earlier. Other historians have suggested that pentecostalism provided spiritual compensations for the material good things that believers felt they had been denied this side of heaven's gate. Sociologists in turn have focused upon pentecostals' aptitude for providing a place in the sun for ordinary folk displaced by social disorganization or cast adrift by cultural dislocations. Friendly theologians have pointed to the revival's ability to meet enduring needs of the human spirit, while unfriendly ones have suggested that it exploited the gullibility of the masses, offering bogus cures for incurable diseases.[8]

All of these explanations bear a measure of truth, yet none seems entirely adequate. Either too much data contradicts the theory or, more often, the theory explains too much.[9] In this essay I wish to offer an additional possibility. I do not propose that it supplants any of the others, but I do think that it illumines a neglected dimension of the question.

Simply stated, pentecostalism flourished because two impulses perennially warred for mastery of its soul. I shall call the first the *primitivist* and the second the *pragmatic*. The labels themselves are not crucial, but they seem as useful as any in suggesting a range of meanings that we shall explore more fully in a few moments. Here it suffices to say that the primitivist impulse represented a powerfully destructive urge to smash all humanmade traditions in order to return to a first-century world where the Holy Spirit alone reigned. In that realm supernatural signs and wonders formed the stuff of daily life, dreams and visions exercised normative authority, and the Bible stood free of higher criticism. The pragmatic impulse, in contrast, reflected an eagerness to do whatever was necessary in order to accomplish the movement's purposes. Though pragmatism did not logically require acceptance of the technological achievements and governing social arrangements of the postindustrial West—structural differentiation, procedural rationality, centralized management, and the like—as a practical matter that is the way things usually panned out. Moreover, once pentecostals learned that pragmatic attitudes not only worked but also paid large dividends in subjective well-being, they found themselves drawn inch by inch into the assumptions of the therapeutic society where the quest for personal fulfillment reigned supreme.[10]

There are numerous ways to make this argument. In this essay I shall try to make it by asking a simple question: What kind of persons joined the revival in the first place? The answer—to skip way ahead in the story—is that the pioneer generation evinced, to a striking degree, *both* primitive and pragmatic character traits. More significantly, they displayed those traits at the same time, without compromise, in a knot of behavior patterns so tangled and matted as to be nearly inseparable. Not everyone fit the prototype, of course. As with any large social aggregation—fifty thousand by 1910, maybe twice that number by 1920[11]—a great rainbow of human types joined the revival. Some exhibited consistently primitivist urges, while others found more pragmatic values congenial. Thus the doubleness of the pentecostal character did not necessarily manifest itself with equal force within the same persons all of the time. But among the aggregate it did.

Before turning to those early materials one caveat is needed. Exactly how the founding figures came to acquire these prominent traits generally falls outside the scope of this essay. Some clearly brought them to the movement,[12] while others just as clearly absorbed them after they joined.[13] Probably most fell somewhere in between, discovering something like an elective affinity between long-standing predispositions on the one hand and newly acquired ideals on the other. At this distance it is hard to sort out the exact mix and probably matters little if we could.

The main point is that apparently conflicting impulses energized the initial generation as a whole, and that pattern persisted into the 1990s. The clue lies in the faces of the day laborers and washwomen who crowded the Azusa mission. In their determination to see the lame healed and the dead raised, whatever the cost—and that is the key phrase: *whatever the cost*—they proved themselves as worldly wise as their well-heeled great-grandchildren who frequented the glass-and-steel Christian Life Centers scattered along the interstate bypasses.

The Primitivist Impulse

Since pentecostals themselves acknowledged only the primitivist side of their lives, we shall begin with that part of their story. *Primitivism* has borne a score of meanings in the historical and theoretical literature of religious studies.[14] I shall define it quite simply as a yearning somehow to return to a time before time, to a space outside of space, to a mythical realm that Alexander Campbell memorably called the "ancient order of things." It is important to note that among early pentecostals primitivism was not simply restorationism, or at least what is commonly called restorationism. The latter suggested a rather self-conscious effort to sit down, figure out what the New Testament blueprint called for, then quite rationally reproduce it in the modern world. Campbellites, Mormons, Landmark Baptists, and other so-called restorationist sects of the nineteenth century readily come to mind.[15] Pentecostal primitivism certainly included all of that, but it was more. It was the dark subsoil in which restorationist and, for that matter, millenarian visions germinated. It was the urge to destroy all recently made traditions in order to return to the ancient tradition of the New Testament where the Holy Ghost, and only the Holy Ghost, ruled the hearts and minds of the faithful. That long-lost world was, in a sense, an Edenic realm pulsating with supernatural signs and wonders, yet it was also an apocalyptic realm regimented by the timeless truths and universal values of Scripture. First-generation stalwarts sought to reenter that world as literally as possible by breathing its holy air, smelling its sacred fragrances, and luxuriating in its spiritual delights. In the process, they fashioned their own social networks, cultural symbols, and religious rituals. To a remarkable extent they succeeded in creating a primitive garden in a modern wilderness.

On first reading, early pentecostals' rhetoric suggests that they were, above all, heavenly minded pilgrims pursuing otherworldly satisfactions because they harbored little interest in this-worldly delights. Their storefront missions and backlot tents served as sequestered havens where they found inestimable rewards, at least by any ordinary calculus of things. What emerges from the literature is an image of questers determined to exchange the fleeting pleasures of life in the present world for the enduring fulfillments of life in the world to come. Of course, they never explained themselves exactly that way. Indeed, they rarely explained themselves at all. What they did, rather, was leave a long trail of hints, mostly in letters, diaries, and testimonials, suggesting the kind of satisfactions they sought in the sweat-soaked bedlam of the meetings. Those hints enable us to infer the sort of people they were, the hurts they endured, the aspirations they nurtured.

Examples surface everywhere we look in the primary literature. One Chicago partisan put it as plainly as language permitted: "Those who speak in tongues seem to live in another world."[16] Living in another world took a number of forms, however. For some, it engendered something like a sixth sense, a fundamentally new way of seeing even the natural landscape around them. "It seemed as if human joys vanished," a Florida advocate wrote. "It seemed as if the whole world and the people looked a different color."[17] A Wesleyan Methodist pastor in Toronto spoke of a surge of feelings she had never known: "overwhelming power," "absence of fleshly effort," a sensation of walking "softly with God."[18] Some devotees appear to have entered into a sacred zone where time itself was calibrated according to divine rather than human standards. Looking back to the first blush of the revival from the vantage point of the mid-1920s, the evangelist Frank Bartleman judged that he would *rather live six months at that time than fifty years of ordinary time.*"[19] Members commonly spoke of spending hour after hour, sometimes entire days, in prayer and singing without thought of food[20] or awareness that night had fallen or that daylight had dawned.[21] Converts found themselves in a breathtaking era of history in which the old structures had been swept away and new ones erected. In their nightly prayer meetings, a Webb City, Missouri, devotee wrote, "It seemed impossible to distinguish between the earthly and the heavenly anthems. . . . The celestial glory . . . filled the room with a halo of glory. [Some] could scarcely endure the 'weight of glory' that rested upon them."[22] Another recalled that when he underwent the baptism experience, "the fire fell and burned up all that would burn and what would not burn was caught up into heaven. . . . It [was] a salvation indescribable. . . . My spirit long[ed] to be free from a sin-cursed world and be at home with Jesus."[23] One venerable pentecostal historian may have said more than he intended but surely touched an essential chord when he wrote that many onlookers believed they were "either insane over religion, or drunk on some glorious dream."[24]

If the other world of supernatural delights and timeless truths functioned as the all-consuming locus of interest, it is hardly surprising that pentecostals betrayed little interest in earthly affairs such as presidential elections or local politics. Their response to the war then raging in Europe is instructive. A few forthrightly supported American entry into the conflict and a handful opposed it, but the great majority held no opinion at all. What they worried about in letters to the editors was not bloodshed but the likelihood that the conflict would open up new opportunities for sin. "War is a feeder of hell," stormed the *Church of God Evangel.* "This last awful struggle has been the cause of millions of mothers' boys dropping into the region of the damned where they are entering their eternal tortures."[25] Peace proved no more interesting than war. The November 1918 issue of Aimee Semple McPherson's *Bridal Call* characteristically said nothing about the armistice that had just been signed. Six months elapsed before McPherson finally got around to reminding her readers that there was a Red Cross hospital atop Calvary's hill, too.[26]

Spirit-filled believers lost interest in the kind of day-to-day activities that most evangelical Protestants regarded as simple and legitimate pleasures of life. I am not thinking here of a pipe by the fireplace on a winter's night or a frosty beer out on the front porch on a summer afternoon. Worldly enjoyments of that sort remained inconceivable. The point rather is that even officially sanctioned satisfactions such as family, children, and marital sex often lost all appeal.

Diaries and autobiographies reveal a good deal. Aimee Semple McPherson may not have cared much about the war, but she did care about Holy Ghost revivals. She boasted that she kept on traveling and preaching, month after month, even though her young daughter back at home seemed to be dying of influenza. The reason? Abraham never hesitated to sacrifice Isaac.[27] The journal of pioneer educator D. C. O. Opperman, which carefully chronicled his ceaseless travels back and forth across the South between 1905 and 1912, displayed a man so preoccupied with the work at hand that he gave only perfunctory notice to his marriage and the birth of his first two children. He failed to note the name of his third child.[28] The diary of Pentecostal Holiness church leader George Floyd Taylor revealed a similar pattern: a litany of reports on sermons preached, biblical passages meditated upon, Sunday school classes taught, cronies talked with, prayer meetings attended. The entry for August 27, 1908, taken virtually at random, proclaimed, "My soul is a sea of glass. . . . Glory! Glory! . . . My soul secretly cries out for God to hide me away in His presence."[29] Except for a daily report on the weather, Taylor's journal avoided all hints of mundane detail. One would never suspect that this husband and father had ever suffered a trace of disappointment, a pang of hunger, or a tug of lust. Even in death the pattern persisted. Just before the end Richard G. Spurling Jr., a founder of the Church of God, asked that he not be buried facing east, as the custom was among his people, but buried facing his home place. With that gesture Spurling meant to signal that he had spent too much time caring for his family and not enough time doing the only thing that really mattered, preaching the gospel.[30]

Enthusiasts subordinated romance to a calculus of heavenly rewards. Neither the wedding nor the wedding night could be taken as events memorable or pleasurable in their own right. The notice of an Inglewood, California, ceremony reported that it was preceded by a time of "rejoicing and praise before God." Many were saved.[31] A newspaper published by a pentecostal band in San Francisco happily observed that when two of its members married, the ritual concluded with an impassioned "exhortation for sinners to seek the Lord."[32] Things were no different in Britain. In the Welsh hamlet of Llandilo, one paper reported, celebrants carved up the wedding home into a prayer room and a food room. To everyone's joy one "brother received the baptism of the Holy Ghost" in the prayer room, while the rest presumably attended to their appetites in the food room.[33] Back in Oklahoma, a new husband-wife evangelist team trumpeted that their wedding had been a "glorious occasion" because it reminded all present of "Jesus our Heavenly Bridegroom coming in the air."[34] The evangelist Howard Goss primly recorded that his bride, Ethel, spent their wedding night preaching a fiery sermon at a Eureka Springs, Arkansas, revival, with telling effect upon local sinners.[35] A young brother from Canada begged the readers of the *Christian Evangel* to pray that "God will give me the girl of my choice—a baptized saint—for a wife." Why? For love? For family? Perish the thought. If they married, he solemnly explained, they could start a rest home for missionaries.[36]

If pentecostals discountenanced the routine pleasures of life, they were equally prepared to forgo the bonds that tethered them to earth. This helps explain why believers could dismiss digging a storm cellar, an act that surely seems prudent enough today, as a "habit of the flesh."[37] It also helps explain why a sister who claimed to be heaven bound, yet worried about the eternal fate of her children, could become a target of ridicule. If a mother were *truly* heaven bound, the argument ran, she would not be compromised by any earthly interest, even a concern for the souls of her offspring.[38]

Night after night enthusiasts lustily sang, "Take the world, but give me Jesus." But there really was not much to take. They were already living on that distant shore.

The Pragmatic Impulse

If an initial reading of the letters, diaries, and testimonial columns of early pentecostalism leaves an image of pilgrims singlemindedly trekking toward heaven's gate, a second reading creates a strikingly different image. The latter suggests that first-generation converts are better interpreted as eminently practical-minded folk who used the limited resources at their disposal to gain their purposes, sacred or otherwise. According to this second perspective, when all was said and done, pentecostals proved themselves a persistently ambitious lot, considerably less interested in what was said than in what was done. A scenario of mundane sagacity and this-worldly hardheadedness dominates the picture.

Admittedly, it requires a bit of reading between the lines to see how prevalent the pragmatic character trait really was. Pentecostals almost never described themselves with the repertoire of words we associate with this-worldliness: shrewdness, adroitness, savvy, and the like. Indeed, they typically went to great lengths to suggest the opposite. They wanted to believe and, more importantly, they wanted the world to believe that the Holy Spirit alone governed all aspects of their lives. They also hoped to convince themselves and their neighbors that they never gave a second thought to their own interests. But if we turn the data under the light just a little, it tells a very different story. It was no accident that Aimee Semple McPherson, a pentecostal barnstormer, put up the first religious radio station in the United States or that two generations later Pat Robertson, a pentecostal TV preacher, launched the first privately owned communications satellite in the world. That sure sense of knowing the ropes, knowing how to get things done, knowing how to negotiate with local power brokers existed from the beginning, always poised just beneath the surface.

As a deeply rooted character trait, mundane sagacity manifested itself in countless ways. For brevity I shall discuss only two. The first was a maverick streak so pronounced that it bordered upon outright rebelliousness. The historian Timothy L. Smith once wrote that nineteenth-century Holiness come-outers typically found themselves "unable to accept much real discipline save their own."[39] That characterization fit early pentecostals even better than their Holiness parents. Thumbing through the biographical data, one is struck by pentecostals' self-taught inventiveness, their stubborn unwillingness to be instructed, much less bound, by the conventions of the past. While they were never as theologically unbuttoned as other homegrown sects like Mormons and Jehovah's Witnesses, they routinely winked at or even discarded inherited orthodoxies whenever it suited their purposes. Indeed, the tradition's cardinal doctrinal distinctive—namely, that speaking in tongues invariably accompanied the baptism of the Holy Spirit—stood unprecedented in the entire history of Judaism and Christianity. From time to time individual partisans espoused highly imaginative positions, to put it as charitably as possible, on matters as diverse as the origin of the human species, the destiny of Israel, the gold standard, and much else. Standing alone like that may have taken a toll at some deep psychological level. But on the surface at least pentecostals seem not to have suffered a twinge of self-consciousness or embarrassment as they marched in solitary zeal across the theological landscape.

The point I wish to emphasize here is not so much the singularity of pentecostals' theological ideas, as such, but the frame of mind they brought to the task of formulating those ideas. The fundamental animus can be described as exuberant creativity, a kind of swashbuckling inventiveness that prompted them to draw their own conclusions from their own sources in their own way, the devil and the established churches be damned. To take one of countless examples, probably only a small minority ever shared founder Charles Fox Parham's view that the unregenerate dead suffered annihilation rather than eternal torment. But the way that he came to that conclusion was altogether typical. Parham had been reared and schooled as an orthodox Methodist. Upon marriage, his wife's grandfather, a Quaker with annihilationist leanings, challenged him to read the Bible without commentaries in hand or creeds in mind. Parham did and soon reached an annihilationist position himself, which he stubbornly upheld the rest of his life despite relentless vilification from other evangelicals.[40]

The maverick disposition manifested itself in other ways. A disproportionate number of the early leaders had been voluntary immigrants to the United States to begin with, typically coming from Australia, Britain, or western Europe. Most came over not to escape penury or military service but to do better financially or to find ampler scope for their ministries in the rolling religious spaces of the United States.[41] Many proved inveterate travelers, crisscrossing the United States and frequently the Atlantic and Pacific Oceans year in, year out. Sunderland rector A. A. Boddy, for example, sometimes hailed as the father of British pentecostalism, sailed the ocean at least fourteen times, not counting side trips to Africa, Siberia, and the European continent.[42] Some, of course, were forced to travel constantly, whether they liked it or not, because they were overseers or itinerant preachers by trade.[43] But autobiographies make clear that the opposite dynamic often dominated: many became overseers or itinerants in the first place because they could not abide the confinement of a settled pastorate for more than a few weeks at a stretch.[44] Some clearly became foreign missionaries for pretty much the same reason. China missionaries Alfred Garr and Lillian Garr wrote that they gladly suffered the loss of their "old Holiness friends" in order to be the first to herald the pentecostal message in Asia. One can almost feel their expansionist exuberance: "It was like beginning life over, a new ministry . . . not limited to a small fraction of the Holiness people, nor to one country . . . but the 'World our parish.'"[45] Sometimes globetrotting obviously got out of hand. Complaints about the needlessly peripatetic ways of overseas missionaries regularly spiked the editorial columns of early newspapers.[46]

The maverick demon in the pentecostal soul recoiled at the specter of regularization. For the better part of a decade zealots fought off efforts to standardize the funding of missionaries or to impose even minimal rules of financial accountability upon evangelists or local churches.[47] Until after World War I the majority of periodicals were launched, edited, and run as one-man or, equally often, as one-woman operations.[48] A remarkable number of those editors continued to publish and jealously guard their subscription lists long after joining a pentecostal denomination with its own official publication.[49] Pentecostals were never as prone to put up schools as they were to float periodicals. Yet at least a score of elementary and secondary academies and Bible institutes, originally founded and run as largely one-person operations, persisted long after the founder had joined a body with its own centrally sponsored institutions. These independent schools sorely irked denominational bureaucrats determined to rein in such endeavors.[50] Yet in their heart of hearts they too knew that the movement had been born of a defiant temper. In later years patriarch Howard Goss, a denominational bureaucrat himself, acknowledged that the very "foundation for the vast Pentecostal Movement" had been laid by loners and freelancers, by missionaries without board support and pastors without degrees or salaries or "restful holidays."[51]

Besides a maverick disposition, the evidence discloses another eminently pragmatic character trait. Any number of adjectives will do: intrepid, audacious, assertive, pushy. I shall lump them all under the rubric of willfulness. What these terms all suggest, rightly enough, is a singleminded determination to gain the goal at hand, regardless of the obstacles or even of the human cost. One nameless writer hit the nail squarely on the head when he or she judged that the baptism experience steeled believers with "holy boldness."[52] And they were plenty proud of it too. For Church of God general overseer A. J. Tomlinson, the lassitude that came with "long study and . . . deep tiresome thinking" had grievously undermined established Christianity. In his mind it was high time for Christians to get moving, "fired up with holy zeal and undaunted courage."[53] The fainthearted might lament the rush of technology or the secular world's obsession with progress, but not Tomlinson. Why should we, he demanded, allow others, "by going hungry and arising early, to win the prize for energy, wit, longsuffering, perseverance, grit and determination?"[54]

For most enthusiasts holy boldness was as much a practical as a spiritual mandate. Thus M. L. Ryan, pastor of a flock in Spokane, Washington, and editor of one of the earliest periodicals, *Apostolic Light,* led a band of eighteen missionaries to Japan in the summer of 1907 without the endorsement of any board or denomination and apparently without any certain destination in mind or clear notion of how they would support themselves when they got there. No matter. When the band reached Tokyo, Ryan discovered that he would have to pay high customs fees. Undeterred, he offered his typewriter and tent as collateral, somehow secured a two-masted lifeboat, and immediately proceeded to sail around Tokyo harbor preaching the pentecostal message (presumably with an interpreter in tow). Within days Ryan had managed to turn out two issues of an English-and-Japanese edition of *Apostolic Light.*[55]

Pentecostals' notorious anti-intellectualism was more stereotypical than typical. Yet insofar as they were anti-intellectual, much of that trait can be attributed to impatience, to a brash determination to get on with the job at hand rather than waste time on pointless theorizing. One leader probably revealed more than he intended when he declared that "God made grappling hooks of His Pentecostal preachers rather than bookworms."[56] Not all preachers and certainly not all laypersons were grappling hooks. As in any large social movement, pentecostalism also attracted the timid and the bookish.[57] But no one thought to preserve their memory in the evidence because it did not fit the ideal. What we read about, rather, are leaders variously described as "vivid, magnetic . . . incisive,"[58] "erect, clear-eyed, tense and enthusiastic,"[59] filled with "intense dogmatic zeal [and] a firm determination to rule or ruin."[60]

Willfulness fired stamina. Though the evidence is too spotty to warrant confident generalizations about the rank and file, pentecostal leaders appear remarkably vigorous. To be sure, most had experienced serious illness before converting to the movement and many suffered recurring bouts afterward. Yet there is good reason to believe that significantly fewer of them endured debilitating illness than the national norm. Moreover, virtually all enjoyed stunning divine healings in their own bodies.[61] Those landmark events not only brought physical restoration but also stirred converts to proclaim the pentecostal message with renewed vigor. Thus willfulness—defined in this case as a determination to believe that one had been healed, regardless of symptoms, or the certainty that one had been divinely commissioned to do the Lord's work, come what may—ignited and sustained extraordinary levels of physical exertion.

Again, examples readily come to hand. One thinks of missionary heroes like Victor Plymire, who toiled forty-one years on the Tibetan-Chinese border, despite hardship, disease, and persecution from local magistrates, with only a handful of converts to show for his life's work.[62] Yet the exertions of less-heralded leaders illustrate the point better, precisely because they were less heralded. One evangelist remembered that if workers could not afford trains or carriages, "they rode bicycles, or in lumber wagons; some went horseback, some walked. Often they waded creeks. Often men removed their clothes, tied their bundles above their heads and swam rivers" to get to the next night's meeting.[63] In 1908 Winnipeg pastor and businessman A. H. Argue casually remarked that he had led nine services per week every week for the past nine months.[64] Mary "Mother" Barnes achieved local notoriety for shepherding a revival in Thayer, Missouri, from 9 A.M. until midnight, seven days a week, for eight months straight.[65] In 1912, E. N. Bell proudly grumbled that as sole editor of *Word and Witness,* he had mailed out nineteen thousand copies of the paper each month, personally answered six to seven hundred letters each month, and held down a full time pastorate in Malvern, Arkansas, where he preached five times per week and maintained a regular hospital visitation ministry.[66] The diary of A. J. Tomlinson stands as a chronicle of tireless travel on foot, mule, train, auto, ship—whatever was available—and the preaching of, on the average, one sermon a day for nearly forty years. The entries for a July

1925 weekend were typical. At age sixty-five, between Thursday and Sunday, he delivered ten sermons amidst swarming mosquitoes and drenching humidity. "The only rest I got," he added in a telling post-script, "was while the saints were shouting, dancing and talking in tongues."[67]

Allowing for some forgivable exaggeration in such accounts, it is clear that extraordinary faith—read willfulness—prompted extraordinary activity. To be sure, common sense tells us that men and women who could ford rivers and shout the devil into submission were blessed with a tough constitution to begin with. But it was an iron-willed frame of mind that put that constitution rightly to work. One author allowed that feeling blue from time to time was to be expected, yet immediately added that melancholy was a sin to be borne and fought off like any other temptation. The Christian "is never to be sorrowful for a moment, but to be ALWAYS REJOICING."[68] The steel rod that stiffened the pentecostal spinal column revealed itself in the India missionary Elizabeth Sisson. In the dentist's chair, Sisson boasted, she had never used Novocaine because she was determined to retain complete control of her mind and body at all times.[69] That last statement is particularly significant given that Sisson also wrote with luxuriant detail about the frequency and intensity of her ecstatic experiences, events that outsiders would readily categorize as disassociative if not pathological.[70]

Willfulness manifested itself in other ways. Sometimes pentecostal writers sounded like hawkers for a Dale Carnegie course. "It is always better to encourage people to do what they can for themselves," one averred. "People are pauperized by teaching them . . . to ask the Lord to do for us many things which we ought to do for ourselves."[71] Often willfulness expressed itself in a simple premise that outsiders found scandalous if not blasphemous. God has uttered certain promises in Scripture. Therefore, if believers act in the prescribed manner set forth in Scripture, then God will respond in the prescribed manner. "Getting things from God is like playing checkers," wrote F. F. Bosworth, the most respected healing evangelist of the 1920s. "He always moves when it is His turn. . . . Our move is to expect what he promises."[72]

Pentecostals applied that reasoning most frequently to the matter of physical health. Since God had promised to heal the body if one prayed with genuine faith, the only possible result was immediate and complete restoration of the body. Carrie Judd Montgomery, one of the most prolific and articulate figures in the early history of the movement, made the case with memorable clarity: "If, after prayer for physical healing, we reckon the work as already accomplished in our bodies, we shall not fear to act out that faith, and to make physical exertions which will justify our professed belief in the healing." Then came the knock-out punch: "I have never failed to receive according to my faith."[73] The import was as clear and hard as glass: the genuineness of one's faith was directly and exactly commensurate with one's ability to get up and subdue the afflicting disease. If the symptoms persisted that meant either that one's faith was weak or that they were nothing but "counterfeit symptoms" to begin with. As one physician convert put it, you must not "wait to see the evidence of your healing. There will be no evidence until it is done, and it will not be done until you believe without visible or tangible evidence of any sort."[74] One nameless grandmother, who had worn eyeglasses for twenty years, tossed them out when she decided to pray for restoration of her eyesight. From that point on, she forced herself to read ten chapters of her Bible each day without glasses because God had promised that he would answer the prayer of faith. Therefore he *did*. "Why, salt water is good for the eyes," she wrote, tears tumbling onto the page.[75]

Express your needs in prayer. Assume that you possess your healing the instant you pray for it. Get up and act on that assumption. If counterfeit symptoms persist, disregard them. After all, the Lord promised: "'I'll do anything you want *me* to do.'"[76]

The formula worked every time. All it took was the grit and the moxie to make it work.

Primitive and Pragmatic: Assessing the Fit

The world has changed dramatically since that nameless grandmother flung her glasses aside, and in many ways pentecostals have changed with it. But only superficially.

In 1990, the essential structural tension between the primitive and the pragmatic persisted as acutely as ever. On one hand, the theology and worship patterns, or what religion scholars might call the myths and rituals, that energized the movement's inner life survived largely untouched by the assumptions of the secular culture. Biblical inerrancy and literalism hovered as close to the ground as they did at the turn of the twentieth century. Darwin, Marx, and Freud, not to mention more recent icons of the secular academy such as Mary Daly, Richard Rorty, and Stephen Jay Gould, remained wholly outside the horizon of pentecostal consciousness. More significantly, the longing for vital manifestations of the supernatural gifts of the Holy Spirit thrived with unabated fervor. Pentecostal periodicals brimmed with stories of stunning healings and divine interventions in daily life. Miracles may not have danced before believers' eyes quite as often as they once did, but one thing was sure: no child of the revival would have counted it a good thing if it were true.[77]

At the same time, however, latter-day enthusiasts rushed to embrace the therapeutic rewards and technological amenities of modernity with scarcely a second thought. Although a few still gathered in storefront missions and avoided the trappings of the good life, the majority worshipped in carpeted, air-conditioned buildings indistinguishable from the local United Methodist church. Adherents propagated their message with state-of-the-art publishing and communications technology. They hobnobbed with the rich and the powerful. Indeed, many of them *were* the rich and the powerful. On the whole, then, they dressed, worked, and played like anyone else who hailed from the same region and occupied the same position in the social system. Sometimes it appeared that the only difference between pentecostal Christians and mainline Christians was that the former got there first and did it bigger, better, and less tastefully.[78]

Taken together, then, pentecostals of 1990 presented an arresting spectacle. They appeared to believe and worship by one set of rules but to work and play by quite another. Stalwarts spent their evenings at full gospel rallies, rapturously speaking in tongues, and their days in university computer labs unraveling mysteries of another sort. Spirit-filled medical missionaries cast out demons in the morning and adjusted CT scanners in the afternoon. Partisans asked the Holy Spirit to help them find their car keys as nonchalantly as they invited a neighbor to drop by for coffee. Though scenarios of this sort could have been witnessed in virtually any large urban pentecostal church—and for that matter a great many small rural ones, too—we are not limited to impressions. The hard data sniffed out by social scientists told very much the same story. Case studies of pentecostal converts strongly suggested that the primitive and the pragmatic actually co-varied: the more fervent the former, the more determined the latter.[79]

Any number of outsiders looked at this spectacle and came away scratching their heads, wondering how it all fit together. In their minds it was nothing short of remarkable that pentecostals' taste for other-worldly ecstasies and for ahistorical dogmatisms had survived as long as it had. Surely it could not last indefinitely, they supposed. Surely pentecostals were destined either to go the way of the United Methodists—that is, move uptown culturally as well as socially—or, like Old Order Mennonites, to recede to a picturesque but obscure corner of contemporary life.[80] What most of those observers presupposed, of course, was that cultural modernism and social modernization came together as a package deal, something like a solid-state appliance with no customer-removable parts.

But that is precisely where the problem arises. Recent history proves that no one owns the franchise on modernity. Everywhere we look we see ardent Christians selectively shopping in the warehouse of the times, choosing what they like, ignoring what they do not like, and rarely giving the matter a second thought. The plain fact is that religious folk put their lives together in a dizzying variety of ways.

Examples abound. In the midnineteenth century Oneida Perfectionists, fired by a potent mix of apocalyptic Scripture and ecstatic religious experience, implemented systematic work habits and careful accounting procedures that led to the redoubtable Oneida Silverware Company. In the late nineteenth century evangelical missionaries fanned out around the world heralding a darkly primitivist vision of the imminent fiery climax of history. Yet the very urgency of their message also impelled them to adopt the most efficient means of transportation and publication known, along with a streamlining of mission boards at home that should have made Wall Street envious. Anyone familiar with the corpus of missionary biographies and autobiographies of the eighteenth and nineteenth centuries knows how often the primitive and the pragmatic, or at least facsimiles thereof, presented themselves in the same souls. "A strange compound of fiercely practical common sense and profound mysticism" was the way that Pearl Buck described her China missionary mother.[81] After World War II ultra-traditionalist insurrectionaries around the world distinguished themselves by their deployment of the best and latest in mass communications technology—not to mention weaponry. And lest anyone doubt that all sorts of primitivisms could promenade arm-in-arm with the most advanced forms of social modernization, we need only observe the daily lives of millions of mainline Christians in the 1990s. Episcopalians confronted the mystery of the Eucharist on Sunday mornings and ran corporate board meetings on Monday afternoons. Roman Catholics earnestly confessed the Apostles' Creed one day and negotiated high-priced real estate deals the next.

All of this is to say that at one time or another, virtually every tradition within the Christian family (and for that matter a good many outside the Christian family) confronted a roughly similar set of polarities: piety versus intellect, supernature versus nature, prophetic critique versus priestly legitimation, ancient wisdom versus modern insight, right belief versus right result. In this respect, Spirit-filled believers proved themselves no different from countless faithful before them.

But the story does not end there. In other ways, first-, second-, and third-generation pentecostals consistently showed themselves very different indeed. If they drew threads of inspiration from the heritage of

Christian belief and behavior, they also wove those threads into a distinctive tapestry that was very much of their own making. And one feature of that distinctiveness was the sheer bravura with which they maintained *both* the primitive and the pragmatic sides of their identity at once. Though it would be difficult to prove, looking back over the twentieth century, it is at least arguable that the contrast between transcendent visions and mundane sagacity manifested itself more dramatically among pentecostals than among any other large group of Christians of modern times (except perhaps the Mormons). That was particularly true in developing countries where, especially after World War II, the transcendent and the mundane flourished side by side with riotous abandon.[82]

To be sure, the exact nature of the interaction between the primitive and the pragmatic in the pentecostal subculture is not entirely clear. We grope for metaphors. Is that relationship best construed as a struggle between antagonists? Or as an alliance between partners? Or is it more accurate to picture it as both at once—something like the inexplicable chemistry of a combative but invigorating marriage?

Subtler images that intimate more complex modes of interaction also come to mind. The trickster figure of American folklore offers one possibility. In those stories a mythic character such as Brer Rabbit presents itself in one form in one context, but in a dramatically different form in another context. This analogy suggests that perhaps we should think of the primitive and the pragmatic not as two distinct impulses at all, but rather as a single reflex that changes faces according to situation. The signal benefit of the trickster construct is that it reminds us that a given act, such as obliviousness to conventional family ties, may have served fiercely primitive ends in one setting and crassly pragmatic ones in another.[83]

Another possibility presents itself. Literary critics have taught us that all texts can be read at two levels (or at least at two levels). Wherever there is a surface text there is also always a submerged text; what is said gains force and meaning when we peel back the explicit words, so to speak, and expose the implicit ones beneath. Arguably religious cultures too can be read as "texts." In that case, pentecostals' primitivist behavior can be construed as the surface text, while their pragmatic inclinations can be construed as the submerged text. The task then is not to prove that one was more real or even more important than the other, but to recognize that the revivals' spiritual power and cultural meaning emerged from the perennial interplay of the two.[84]

A metaphor drawn from the realm of the theater offers one more option and, given the intractable doubleness of the evidence, a particularly compelling one at that. By this reckoning the primitive invariably stood front and center stage, carrying the burden of the plot, reveling in the applause of the faithful, and, of course, bravely bearing the jeers of the faithless. The pragmatic, on the other hand, normally served as the stage manager, standing behind the curtains, orchestrating all of the moves—with the cash till never far from mind. This scenario suggests that when pentecostals were wearing their primitivist garb, they may have been, first and foremost, following a script: a preapproved story carefully designed to edify the committed and win the uncommitted. It also suggests that if believers played to the galleries more often than they admitted, journalists and historians bought the ruse more often than they knew.[85]

All of these metaphors may well help us conceptualize the inner workings of pentecostal culture, but they also pose risks, for they may beguile us into thinking that the primitive and the pragmatic were somehow substantive things in themselves. Obviously they were not; they are only labels that we apply to conspicuous and persistent patterns of behavior. Thus pinning down the exact configuration of the interaction—be it antagonistic, complementary, competitive, invertible, dialectical, theatrical, or whatever—seems less important than recognizing its pervasive and vital presence in the movement's life. The real task before us, then, is to divine the functions that the interaction performed in the lives of ordinary believers.

At least two functions come to mind. The first might be called institutional success, the second ethical immaturity.

Institutional success arose from a delicate balancing of primitive and pragmatic energies. On one side, the primitive fueled the revival by offering certitude about the truthfulness of inherited theological claims and the reality of the supernatural. It gave ordinary Christians life-giving energies. It guaranteed that the pentecostal message would not fall into the deadening routines of pragmatic implementation or, worse, of self-serving manipulation. Moreover, otherworldly yearnings distanced the tradition from the conventions of the surrounding culture, making it possible for believers to chart their own spiritual course in a world that was not so much hostile as simply uncomprehending. The pragmatic, in contrast, stabilized the movement by keeping adherents from squandering their energies in ecstatic excesses. It imposed standards of efficiency, economy, and institutional order. It kept the revival from rendering itself, in Emerson's memorable words, "frivolous and ungirt." Most importantly, perhaps, the pragmatic enabled believers to reproduce their culture among succeeding generations by fostering stable educational structures. If primitivist aspirations inspired a vision of life as it might be, pragmatic values afforded the means for preserving it.

Less happily, the interplay of impulses also engendered ethical immaturity. The primitive freed enthusiasts from worrying very much about the propriety of their social attitudes. To be sure, they avoided personal vices such as drinking and smoking and, except for the question of conscription during World War I, they took pride in their obedience to the laws of the land. But until very recently at least, pentecostals displayed little or no concern with larger questions of responsible social and political behavior. It almost never occurred to them that a Christian ought to take a thoughtful stand, any stand, regarding suffrage, prohibition, civil rights, environmental pollution, or famine in other countries. Only the Holy Spirit reigned in their lives, they wanted to believe, and since the Holy Spirit had nothing to say about those pesky questions, there was no reason to trouble themselves with them either. In the meantime, the pragmatic impulse spurred pentecostals to build the biggest and buy the best of everything, mainly for the Lord of course, but sometimes a little for themselves too. Where other more historically seasoned Christians had learned that it was not so easy to live godly lives in a godless world, pentecostals experienced few qualms about their ability to shuttle from celestial heights to terrestrial plains and back again. The impregnable conviction that they— and often enough, that they alone—had seen the Promised Land enabled them to relish the satisfactions of spiritual separation from modern life and, at the same time, to savor most of its benefits without a trace of guilt. The formula proved golden, in more ways than one.[86]

Conclusions

As the movement matures, of course, some of this may change. We need not accept the conclusions of extreme cultural evolutionists who expect the primitive side of the pentecostal character to wither up and die in the bright sun of modern civilization in order to suppose that time and experience will temper the wildest of visionaries. And in the process, pentecostals are sure to tumble into the dark turbulences of history, where life is neither simple nor solutions clear-cut. Awareness that the movement did not fall from the skies like a sacred meteorite but emerged at a particular time and place, and thus bore the earmarks of its time and place, may make it more difficult to sustain the power of first-century signs and wonders. But if immersion in the messy details of history threatens a slowdown of institutional growth, it also promises a deepening of ethical self-awareness.[87]

At the same time, modern secular culture, smugly secure in its relativist premises and its quest for personal gratification, may find that unruly movements like pentecostalism really do have something to say that is worth hearing. "The Lord hath more light yet to break forth out of his Holy Word," Pilgrim John Robinson observed some four centuries ago.[88] Pentecostals were not the first and almost certainly will not be the last of American-born sectarians to capture the religious world's attention. And they may demonstrate, in ways that other Christians have not often matched, that the ancient book and the ecstatic visions it harbors still bears the power to change lives and to transform cultures.

Notes

1. "Weird Babel of Tongues," *Los Angeles Times*, April 18, 1906, 1.

2. The Gallup poll is described in Kenneth S. Kantzer's "The Charismatics among Us," *Christianity Today* 24 (Feb. 22, 1980): 24–29.

3. *The Assemblies of God: Current Facts 1991*, a pamphlet published by that body's Office of Information in Springfield, Missouri, in 1992, claims a U.S. constituency of 2,234,708, a U.S. membership of 1,324,800, and a world constituency of 22,723,215.

4. David B. Barrett, "Annual Statistical Table on Global Mission: 1993," *International Bulletin of Missionary Research* 17 (Jan. 1993): 23. It should be remembered that many charismatics are Roman Catholics.

5. In 1991 membership for the major pentecostal bodies in the United States totaled 7,698,547. *Yearbook of American and Canadian Churches, 1991* (Nashville: Abingdon, 1991), 258–64. A research assistant and I compiled these figures by adding up the totals for all of the groups that are traditionally categorized as pentecostal. Random telephone sampling of the adult U.S. population in 1990 yielded adherence figures of 4,032,000. Graduate School and University Center of the City University of New York, "Research Report, the National Survey of Religious Identification, 1989–90." (I have not included 442,000 self-professed adherents of the "Church of God," since there are several decidedly nonpentecostal Wesleyan Holiness bodies that go by the same name.)

6. For a concise, perceptive overview of the history of American pentecostalism, see R. G. Robins, "Pentecostal Movement," in Daniel G. Reid, Robert P. Linden, Bruce L. Shelley, and Harry S. Stout, eds. *Dictionary of Christianity in America* (Downers Grove, Ill.: Inter Varsity Press, 1990).

7. The insurgence of the world charismatic movement is ably described in Vinson Synan's *The Twentieth-Century Pentecostal Explosion* (Altamonte Springs, Fla.: Creation House, 1987).

8. I have elaborated the range of explanations that have been offered by scholars in "Bibliography and Historiography of Pentecostalism (U.S.)" in Stanley M. Burgess and Gary B. McGee, eds., *Dictionary of Pentecostal and Charismatic Movements* (Grand Rapids, Mich.: Zondervan, 1988), 65–76.

9. Reductionist approaches predominate, at least in the nontheological scholarly literature. For critiques of such, see Virginia H. Hine, "The Deprivation and Disorganization Theories of Religious Movements," in Irving I. Zaretsky and Mark P. Leone, eds., *Religious Movements in Contemporary America* (Princeton: Princeton University Press, 1974), 646–64; Margaret M. Poloma, "An Empirical Study of Perceptions of Healing among Assemblies of God Members," *Pneuma: The Journal of the Society for Pentecostal Studies* 7 (Spring 1985): 61–77; and Grant Wacker, "Taking Another Look at the Vision of the Disinherited," *Religious Studies Review* 8 (1982): 15–22. See also the fine survey of the assumptions and conclusions of the dominant social scientific literature in H. Newton Malony and A. Adams Lovekin's *Glossolalia: Behavioral Science Perspectives on Speaking in Tongues* (New York: Oxford University Press, 1985), chap. 7. More generally, see R. Stephen Warner, "Theoretical Barriers to the Understanding of Evangelical Christianity," *Sociological Analysis* 15 (Spring 1979): 1–9.

10. My understanding of the differences between cultural modernism on one hand and technological and social modernization on the other has been informed by Mary Douglas's "The Effects of Modernization on Religious Change," *Daedalus* 3 (Winter 1982): 1–19; Bruce B. Lawrence's *Defenders of God: The Fundamentalist Revolt against the Modern Age* (San Francisco: Harper and Row, 1989), especially chap. 1; and John F. Wilson's "Modernity and Religion: A Problem of Perspective," in William Nicholls, ed., *Modernity and Religion* (Waterloo, Ontario: Wilfrid Laurier University Press, 1987), 9–18. Obviously there is no necessary link between pragmatism and modernity. Many ancients displayed highly pragmatic behavior and many moderns do not. But the present point is that pentecostals' pragmatic behavior normally led to an appropriation of the technological achievements and social arrangements of the post-industrial West.

11. Reliable figures on the size of the movement in the early years of the twentieth century are hard to come by, to say the least. In 1908, in the first attempt to construct a historical overview, India missionary Max Wood Moorhead estimated 50,000 adherents in the United States alone. Two years later Arthur S. Booth-Clibborn, a thoughtful and widely traveled early leader, put the figure at 60,000 to 80,000 fully committed members, plus another 20,000 to 40,000 active supporters worldwide. See Moorhead, "A Short History of the Pentecostal Movement," *Cloud of Witnesses,* 1908, 16; Booth-Clibborn, *Confidence,* Aug. 1910, 182. In 1936, the United States Bureau of the Census listed 356,329 members for twenty-six known pentecostal sects. Given pentecostals' propensity to worship in homes, skid-row missions, and rural meeting houses, many of which surely escaped the eye of the enumerators, it is safe to assume that the actual number was greater. I have taken these census figures from Robert Mapes Anderson's *Vision of the Disinherited: The Making of American Pentecostalism* (New York: Oxford University Press, 1979), 117.

12. The entwining of primitivist and pragmatic strains revealed itself in the behavior of the Holiness pastor A. G. Garr years before his conversion to pentecostalism. See, for example, the wide-eyed supernaturalism and the street-

wise bravura of Garr's actions at a 1903 street meeting in Dillon, Montana, in *Burning Bush,* Sept. 10, 1903, 7.

13. Some of the faithful acquired the signature blending of primitive and pragmatic traits only after they converted. Consider, for example, one missionary correspondent in China who wrote to the Nazarene leader A. M. Hills about the personality transformation that overtook Holiness defectors to pentecostalism: "Quiet, retiring, teachable natures, who were charitable to a fault, were transformed into dogmatic, unteachable, schismatic and anathema-breathing souls." A. M. Hills, *The Tongues Movement* (Manchester, England: Star Hall, ca. 1914), 26.

14. George Boas, s.v. "Primitivism," in Philip Wiener, ed., *Dictionary of the History of Ideas* (New York: Scribner's, 1973).

15. The story of these and other explicitly restorationist bodies is ably told by Richard T. Hughes and C. Leonard Allen in *Illusions of Innocence: Protestant Primitivism in America, 1630–1875* (Chicago: University of Chicago Press, 1988).

16. *Apostolic Faith* (Los Angeles), June–Sept. 1907, 3.

17. *Apostolic Faith* (Los Angeles), Jan. 1907, 1, quoted in Edith L. Blumhofer, *The Assemblies of God: A Chapter in the Story of American Pentecostalism* (Springfield, Mo.: Gospel, 1989), 1:143.

18. Addie A. Knowlton, *New Acts,* June 1907, 8.

19. Frank Bartleman, *Azusa Street* (Plainfield, N.J.: Logos International, 1980), 21. Except for the title, this work is an unaltered reprint of Bartleman's 1925 classic, *How "Pentecost" Came to Los Angeles—How It Was in the Beginning.*

20. Ardell K. Mead, *Apostolic Faith* (Los Angeles), Nov. 1906, 3; A. A. Boddy, quoting the letter of "a working-man," *Christian* (England), Aug. 1, 1907, n.p.; Mrs. Hebden, *Promise* (Toronto), May 1907, 2.

21. *Word and Work,* May 1910, 14; *Apostolic Faith* (Los Angeles), Dec. 1906, 3; typescript of interview with Azusa pioneer A. G. Osterberg, "Second Tape," Assemblies of God Archives, Springfield, Mo.

22. A. R. Haughawout, *Apostolic Faith* (Baxter Springs, Kans.), June 1914, 3.

23. J. M. Vawter, *New Acts,* Aug. 16, 1906, 6.

24. Howard A. Goss, *The Winds of God: The Story of the Early Pentecostal Days (1901–1914) in the Life of Howard A. Goss, As Told by Ethel E. Goss* (New York: Comet Press Books, 1958), 78.

25. *The Church of God Evangel,* Feb. 24, 1917, 1.

26. Aimee Semple McPherson, *Bridal Call,* May 1919, 2.

27. Aimee Semple McPherson, *This Is That: Personal Experiences, Sermons, and Writings* (New York: Garland, 1985), 205–7.

28. Daniel C. O. Opperman, diary, 1905–12, Assemblies of God Archives, Springfield, Mo..

29. George Floyd Taylor, diary, North Carolina State History Archives, Raleigh, N.C. This diary was kept for the years 1896, 1901, and 1908. Of course, pentecostals' autobiographies and diaries, like all such texts, may have been penned more for the edification of potential readers than as a record of actual experiences. If so, that would make my argument stronger, for it shows that they regarded singleminded otherworldliness as the ideal.

30. James Glover Marshall and June Glover Marshall, "R. G. Spurling Jr.: The Origins of the Church of God," *Reflections . . . Church of God Heritage,* Winter 1990, 3.

31. *Glad Tidings* (San Francisco), July 1928, 10.

32. *Glad Tidings* (San Francisco), May 1926, 8.

33. *Showers of Blessings* 8 (ca. 1910): 9.

34. Agnes N. O. LaBerge, *What God Hath Wrought: Life and Work of Mrs. Agnes N. O. LaBerge* (New York: Garland, 1985), 54.

35. Goss, *Winds,* 136.

36. *Christian Evangel,* Oct. 17, 1914, 2.

37. *Pentecostal Evangel,* Apr. 4, 1914, 6.

38. *Pentecostal Evangel,* Nov. 1, 1919, 5.

39. Timothy L. Smith, *Called unto Holiness: The Story of the Nazarenes: The Formative Years* (Kansas City, Mo.: Nazarene, 1962), 37.

40. Charles Fox Parham, *The Life of Charles F. Parham: Founder of the Apostolic Faith Movement,* comp. Mrs. Charles Fox Parham (Baxter Springs, Kans.: Apostolic Faith, 1930), 14.

41. For example, John Alexander Dowie, Fred Vogler, and Frank Ewart emigrated from Australia; Stanley Frodsham, A. W. Frodsham, Noel Perkin, and George T. Studd from Britain; and Andrew Urshan from Persia.

42. A. A. Boddy, *Confidence,* Sept. 1914, 176. For Boddy's incessant globe-trotting, which was, if not typical, at least not rare among early leaders, see the typescript biography by his daughter, Mother Joanna Mary Boddy, "Alexander Alfred Boddy, 1854–1930," Assemblies of God Archives, Springfield, Mo.

43. See, for example, the fat file of newspaper clippings tracking the continental crisscrossings of evangelists John S. and Hattie McConnell, Assemblies of God Archives, Springfield, Mo.

44. Bartleman, *Azusa,* 146–47.

45. Alfred Garr and Lillian Garr, quoted in B. F. Lawrence, *The Apostolic Faith Restored* (St. Louis: Gospel, 1916), 98.

46. Gary B. McGee, *"This Gospel . . . Shall Be Preached": A History and Theology of Assemblies of God Foreign Missions to 1959* (Springfield, Mo.: Gospel, 1986), 77.

47. For missionaries, see Joseph H. King and Blanch L. King, *Yet Speaketh: Memoirs of the Late Bishop Joseph H. King* (Franklin Springs, Ga.: Pentecostal, 1949), 191. For local churches see *Glad Tidings* (Kenedy, Tex.), Sept. 1924, 1–2. See also the verbal altercation between patriarchs J. R. Flower and George Brinkman over financial accountability, recounted from one perspective in *Pentecostal Evangel,* Nov. 15, 1918, 7, and from the opposite in *Pentecostal Herald,* Oct. 1919, 3.

48. See Wayne E. Warner, "Publications," in *Dictionary of Pentecostal and Charismatic Movements.* Examples of publications launched by women include *Apostolic Faith* (Portland), edited by Florence Crawford and Clara Lum; *Bridal Call,* edited by Aimee Semple McPherson with assistance from her mother, Minnie Kennedy; *Bridegroom's Messenger,* edited by Elizabeth A. Sexton; *Elbethel,* edited by Cora McIlray; *Latter Rain Evangel,* edited by Lydia Piper

and Anna C. Reiff; *Triumphs of Faith,* edited by Carrie Judd Montgomery; and *Trust,* edited by Elizabeth V. Baker and Susan Duncan.

49. For example, D. W. Kerr edited and published the *Pentecostal Missionary Report* out of his church in Cleveland; Robert Craig edited and published *Glad Tidings* out of his church in San Francisco; Samuel G. Otis edited and published *Word and Work* at the camp meeting grounds in Framingham, Massachusetts.

50. Michael G. Owen, "Preparing Students for the First Harvest," *Assemblies of God Heritage* (Winter 1989–90): 3–5, 16–18; Lewis Wilson, "Bible Institutes, Colleges, Universities," in *Dictionary of Pentecostal and Charismatic Movements*.

51. Goss, *Winds,* 154.

52. *Apostolic Faith* (Los Angeles), Oct. 1906, 2.

53. A. J. Tomlinson, *The Last Great Conflict* (New York: Garland, 1985), 68–69.

54. Ibid., 38.

55. *Apostolic Faith* (Houston), Oct. 1908, 2; *Midnight Cry,* Nov. 1907, 2; *Pentecost,* Apr.–May 1909, 4; *Seattle Post Intelligencer,* Aug. 29, 1907, 6, and Sept. 3, 1907, 4. There is no reason to believe that Ryan knew a word of Japanese, which makes his venture to Japan all the more audacious. I owe the *Pentecost* reference to Wayne Warner, and the *Post Intelligencer* references to Professor Cecil M. Robeck of Fuller Seminary.

56. Goss, *Winds,* 65.

57. Stanley F. Frodsham, longtime editor of the Assemblies of God's *Pentecostal Evangel,* won lasting notoriety for remaining lost in the heavenlies. "Brother Frodsham had many gifts," a colleague recalled years later, "but discernment was never one of them." Interview with Wayne Warner, August 29, 1992.

58. Goss, *Winds,* 17.

59. Lewiston, Maine, newspaper reporter describing Frank S. Sandford, quoted in Shirley Nelson, *Fair, Clear, and Terrible: The Story of Shiloh, Maine* (Lathan, N.Y.: British American, 1989), 78.

60. Charles William Shumway, "A Study of 'The Gift of Tongues'" (A.B. thesis, University of Southern California, 1914), 179.

61. Anderson, *Vision,* 103–4. It is difficult to determine the life expectancy of first-generation leaders, partly because the records are spotty and partly because there is no consensus as to who should be included. With those qualifications in mind, I selected one hundred persons from the *Dictionary of Pentecostal and Charismatic Movements* whose birth and death dates are known and who, in my judgment, served as pathfinders during the formative years from 1905 to 1920. The median birth and death dates for those leaders was 1869 and 1943, yielding a life span of seventy-four years. In contrast, the typical American born in 1866 (the year closest to 1869 for which census figures are available) lived only fifty-four years. Though this is hardly a scientific sampling, these figures do suggest that far from being sickly, as charged, pentecostal trailblazers exhibited unusual vitality. See National Center for Health

Statistics, "Years of Life Expected at Birth," in *The World Almanac and Book of Facts 1992* (New York: World Almanac, 1992), 956.

62. Victor G. Plymire, typed autobiography, no title, Assemblies of God Archives, Springfield, Mo.

63. Goss, *Winds,* 73.

64. A. H. Argue, *Apostolic Messenger,* Feb.-Mar. 1908, n.p.

65. *Pentecost,* Aug. 1909, n.p.

66. A. N. Bell, *Word and Witness,* Dec. 20, 1912, 2. Bell did not acknowledge that volunteers helped him mail out the periodical, which may say something about the image he desired to project. Interview with Wayne Warner, August 31, 1992.

67. *Diary of A. J. Tomlinson,* ed. Homer A. Tomlinson (Jamaica, N.Y.: Erhardt Press, 1955), 3:104–5. See also 140.

68. Henry Proctor, *Trust,* May–June 1930, 14.

69. Elizabeth Sisson, *Latter Rain Evangel,* May 1909, 6–10. Members of the quasi-pentecostal Shiloh community near Durham, Maine, routinely refused Novocaine for the same reason. Nelson, *Fair,* 332 of galleys, omitted from published edition.

70. See, for example, Elizabeth Sisson, *Latter Rain Evangel,* May 1909, 10. A graduate student who read this paper responded that Sisson's willfulness in the dentist's chair seemed more a reflection of primitivist otherworldliness than of pragmatic this-worldliness. Perhaps so. At the margins the two traits blended and often it is hard to know where to draw the line.

71. *Living Water,* reprinted in *Triumphs of Faith,* June 1908, 123.

72. F. F. Bosworth, *Christ the Healer: Sermons on Divine Healing* (privately printed, 1924), 98–99.

73. Carrie Judd Montgomery, *Faith's Reckonings,* ca. 1920, 9.

74. Dr. J. A. Krumrine, *Trust,* Sept. 1915, 12–13.

75. Anecdote related by the daughter, Mildred Edwards, *Trust,* Feb. 1915, 13.

76. Maude Craig, *Tongues of Fire,* Aug. 15, 1900, 146. This periodical, which bore the subtitle *From the Church of the Living God the Pillar and Ground of the Truth,* was published by the quasi-pentecostal Shiloh community.

77. Margaret Poloma, *The Assemblies of God at the Crossroads: Charisma and Institutional Dilemmas* (Knoxville: University of Tennessee Press, 1989), chap. 9, especially 161; Arthur E. Paris, *Black Pentecostalism: Southern Religion in an Urban World* (Amherst: University of Massachusetts Press, 1982).

78. Edith L. Blumhofer, *Restoring the Faith: The Assemblies of God, Pentecostalism, and American Culture* (Urbana: University of Illinois Press, 1993), 254–60; Mickey Crews, *The Church of God: A Social History* (Knoxville: University of Tennessee Press, 1990), esp. chap. 7. For a one-sided though partly defensible exposé of pentecostals' relentless pursuit of the good life, see Robert Johnson, "Heavenly Gifts," *Wall Street Journal,* Dec. 11, 1990, 1. See also Poloma, *Assemblies of God,* 153.

79. See, for example, Poloma, *Assemblies of God,* 48–49; William J. Samarin, *Tongues of Men and Angels: The Religious Language of Pentecostalism* (New York: Macmillan, 1972), 213; Luther P. Gerlach and Virginia H. Hine,

People, Power, Change: Movements of Social Transformation (Indianapolis: Bobbs-Merrill, 1970), 4–5; H. Newton Malony, "Debunking Some of the Myths about Glossolalia," in Cecil M. Robeck Jr., ed., *Charismatic Experiences in History* (Peabody, Mass.: Hendrickson, 1985), 105–6. This article was originally published in the *Journal for the Scientific Study of Religion* 34 (1982): 144–48. According to this data, better-educated and more-prosperous adherents are more, not less, likely to speak in tongues and to espouse first-century (or at least what outside journalists and academics like to think are first-century) assumptions in religious matters than their less-accomplished counterparts. Admittedly, these studies tested for the correlation between speaking in tongues and position in the social system, which is not exactly the same as pragmatism as I have defined it (that is, a willingness to appropriate the technological achievements and social arrangements of the modern West whenever it suits their purposes). But it is plausible to assume that above-average education and wealth normally betoken a measure of pragmatic aptitude for getting along in the modern social system.

80. See, for example, Vance Packard, "The Long Road from Pentecostal to Episcopal," *The Status Seekers* (New York: David McKay, 1959), 200–201, described in Martin E. Marty, *A Nation of Behavers* (Chicago: University of Chicago Press, 1976), 106. The same outlook undergirds Robert Mapes Anderson's otherwise superior study of pentecostal origins, *Vision of the Disinherited.* Anderson claims that pentecostals sought redress for the various deprivations they suffered in "other-worldly, symbolic, and psychotherapeutic" measures. By implication, once those deprivations disappear, the otherworldly measures will disappear too. See especially 229. See also James Davison Hunter, *American Evangelicalism: Conservative Religion and the Quandary of Modernity* (New Brunswick, N.J.: Rutgers University Press, 1983), especially 5–6, 131; for a sophisticated reworking of the argument, see Hunter's *Evangelicalism: The Coming Generation* (Chicago: University of Chicago Press, 1987), especially 238–41. William G. McLoughlin used a different path to arrive at the same destination. He claimed that pentecostals, however numerically impressive, will remain mere "effluvia," incapable of "seriously threatening the old order," as long as they distance themselves from modern mainstream culture. See "Is There a Third Force in Christendom?" in William G. McLoughlin and Robert N. Bellah, eds., *Religion in America* (Boston: Beacon Press, 1968), 45–72, especially 47, and McLoughlin, *Revivals, Awakenings, and Reform: An Essay on Religion and Social Change in America, 1607–1977* (Chicago: University of Chicago Press, 1978), chap. 6, esp. 212–16.

81. Pearl S. Buck, *The Exile* (New York: John Day, 1936), 58.

82. David Martin, *Tongues of Fire: The Explosion of Protestantism in Latin America* (Cambridge, Mass.: Basil Blackwell, 1990), 122, 140, 164; David Stoll, *Is Latin America Turning Protestant?: The Politics of Evangelical Growth* (Berkeley: University of California Press, 1990), 13, 36, 94; Everett A. Wilson, "Sanguine Saints: Pentecostalism in El Salvador," *Church History* 52 (1983): 186–98; Everett A. Wilson, "The Central American Evangelicals: From Protest to Pragmatism," *International Review of Mission* (Jan. 1988): 93–106. More generally, see Martin E. Marty's astute assessment of the functions of the interac-

tion of primitivism and pragmatism in "Sophisticated Primitives Then, Primitive Sophisticates Now," *Christian Century,* June 7–14, 1989, 586–91.

83. See, for example, Catherine Albanese, *America: Religions and Religion,* 2d ed. (Belmont, Calif.: Wadsworth, 1992), 28–32.

84. See, for example, Virginia Lieson Brereton, *From Sin to Salvation: American Women's Conversion Narratives, 1800–1980* (Bloomington: Indiana University Press, 1991), chaps. 3, 7.

85. I owe this insight to David D. Hall's *Worlds of Wonder, Days of Judgment: Popular Religious Belief in Early New England* (New York: Alfred A. Knopf, 1989), 239–45. The signal exception to my generalization about historians of pentecostalism is Robert Mapes Anderson, who, in *Vision of the Disinherited,* moved to the other extreme, discountenancing the approved script almost entirely.

86. Dan Morgan's *Rising in the West* (New York: Alfred K. Knopf, 1992) offers an intriguing case study of an extended family of sharecroppers who migrated from Oklahoma to California in the 1930s and quite literally made a fortune in construction, junk dealing, real estate, sports franchises, and retirement homes in the burgeoning economy of the Southwest. Morgan shows that the family's fervent pentecostal faith provided spiritual and communal legitimation for their perfectly legal yet financially aggressive (if not avaricious) behavior every step of the way.

To be fair, pentecostals often responded to the material needs of their own members at least by providing food, clothing, rent money, and the like when those privations arose. But typically they acted on a purely case-by-case basis, uninformed by any systematic social ethic or recognition of the structural dislocations that might have caused such problems in the first place. More significantly, their leaders consistently refused to permit self-criticism of ease of lifestyle or of the use of money by themselves or by the rank and file. In the 1970s and 1980s a few "mainline" pentecostal writers critiqued the "Faith Confession" movement, a subtradition that explicitly sanctified the pursuit of boundless personal wealth. But that critique proves my larger point precisely because it focused upon—and only upon—egregious and flaunted excess, not routine preoccupation with the good life. A signal exception to all of this is the work of the pentecostal ethicist Murray Dempster of Southern California College. See, for example, his "Pentecostal Social Concern and the Biblical Mandate of Social Justice," *Pneuma: The Journal of the Society for Pentecostal Studies* 9 (Fall 1987): 129–54, and "Christian Social Concern in Pentecostal Perspective: Reformulating Pentecostal Eschatology," *Journal of Pentecostal Theology* 2 (1993): 51–64.

87. A profounder ethical sense may be coming into being. Pentecostals' preoccupation with laws pertaining to abortion and homosexuality in the 1980s and 1990s betokened a narrow yet very important entry into the broader sphere of public policy.

88. Robinson is quoted in Winthrop S. Hudson and John Corrigan, *Religion in America,* 5th ed. (New York: Macmillan, 1992), 32–33.

9

Mormon Primitivism and Modernization

THOMAS G. ALEXANDER

Scholars have written a great deal on the relationship between religion and modernization in society.[1] A number of older studies, following the lead of Max Weber, have seen secularization as a consequence of modernization. In 1904, Weber wrote, "Closer scrutiny revealed the steady progress of the characteristic process of 'secularization,' to which in modern times all phenomena that originated in religious conceptions succumb."[2]

In recent years, however, sociologists and historians have come to recognize what Peter Berger seems to have anticipated but tried to explain away, that in the United States the positive correlation between secularization and modernization does not exist. At least since Andrew Greeley's work in 1972, some scholars have understood that while American culture has become thoroughly modern, our citizens have remained unabashedly religious.[3] More recently, historians such as Peter Williams and sociologists such as Robert Bellah have recognized the vitality of religion in its various forms in modern American society.[4] Moreover, Stan Albrecht and Tim Heaton have shown among Mormons a positive correlation between religiosity and level of education, suggesting that the most modernized sector of Latter-day Saint society is, in fact, its most religious.[5]

In this essay I will investigate the relationship between the historical process through which Mormonism, as a Christian primitivist and restorationist religion, adapted to modernization.[6] I will address such questions as What forces drove the process of modernization within the Latter-day Saint Church and community? How did the Mormons respond to the forces impelling modernization? What was the relationship between modernization and Mormon Christian primitivism?

At the outset we should understand, as Grant Underwood has observed, that it helps little in our analysis simply to say that Mormons were primitivists. Virtually every Christian group has tried to pattern its practices and teachings on the biblical model.[7] The Mormons were no exception. Unlike most other Christian primitivists, however, Mormons, as radical restorationists, did not content themselves with sole reliance on the authority of the Bible.[8] Some other primitivist groups, such as the Shakers, accepted modern revelation as well, but none seems to have applied the practice as extensively as did the Mormons.[9] Since God's revelations through prophets had guided the Israelites and primitive Christians and had given Christianity the Bible, Latter-day Saints concluded that revelation and its corollary, additional canonical Scripture, should continue to guide the church in modern as well as ancient times.[10]

In order to understand the response of Mormonism to modernization, it has been necessary to reconceptualize a series of events in Latter-day Saint history and its relationship to American society during the nineteenth century and the early twentieth. I found the most useful model for such reconceptualization in Stephen Toulmin's book *Cosmopolis: The Hidden Agenda of Modernity.*[11] Toulmin argues that we can best understand the process of modernization by "recontextualizing" the work of a number of seventeenth-century philosophers and scientists, most particularly René Descartes, Isaac Newton, and Gottfried Wilhelm Leibniz. Traumatized by the bloody religious conflict of the Thirty Years' War (ca. 1615–48), these men created modern physics in part to reorder what they and others perceived to be a disorderly universe. At the same time, unlike Baron d'Holbach and others of the eighteenth-century French Enlightenment who made of Newton's theistic universe a vehicle driven by atheism, the seventeenth-century thinkers conceptualized an orderly world in which God played a central role.

In the most profound sense, the modernization of Mormonism grew out of a similar conflict. In a pattern not unlike the nations and principalities of seventeenth-century Europe, Evangelical Protestantism and the federal government battled the Latter-day Saints over religion. Begun in the horrors of the civil war in Missouri during the 1830s; nurtured by the assassinations of Joseph Smith and Hyrum Smith and the Hancock County war in Illinois in the 1840s; fed by the Mormon war of the late 1850s and the tragic Mountain Meadows Massacre; and consummated in the judicial crusade of the 1880s, this conflict lasted more than sixty years. From 1833 until 1894 when Congress passed an enabling act authorizing the admission of the state of Utah, Mormons remained in perpetual conflict with the dominant Protestant society of the United States.

Like the group of scientist-philosophers who envisioned theistic physics as a way out of the chaos of the Thirty Years' War, a group of Mormon General Authorities, theologians, and scientists fashioned Mormonism's accommodation with modernity. Most important in this regard were President Wilford Woodruff, First Counselor George Q. Cannon, journalist and publicist Charles W. Penrose, legal counsel Franklin S. Richards, academics James E. Talmage and John A. Widtsoe, and self-taught theologian Brigham H. Roberts. Thoroughly bloodied by sixty years of conflict, these men shepherded Mormonism into accommodation with the United States, enthroning modernization, revisioning the apocalypse as an event in the distant future, and at the same time leaving the church's primitivist doctrines substantially intact. The church leadership accomplished this process by separating two previously inseparable spheres—the temporal and the spiritual—into reasonably distinct fields and by defining the content of each arena in ways generally acceptable to a hostile American society.

Before we investigate the historical aspects of this process—to "recontextualize" the process, in Toulmin's phraseology—we need to understand just what Mormons mean by the terms *temporal* and *spiritual*. In Mormon terminology, *temporal* refers to the arena or sphere encompassing those activities taking place on this earth and in time. Most emphatically, *temporal* is not a synonym for *secular*, since the latter word implies desacralization and the rejection of religion. For the Mormons, as for the seventeenth-century scientist-philosophers, temporal activities might take place in the physical universe, but they possess religious significance as well.

As used in Mormonism, then, the term *temporal* came to connote those activities and symbols associated with life on the earth and in the physical world. The church as an organization often took an interest in temporal matters and church leaders expressed opinions on them that they often urged members to heed. Before the division of the temporal and spiritual, leaders subjected church members to ecclesiastical discipline for offenses in the temporal as well as the spiritual arena. After the division, however, in matters perceived as purely temporal, church leaders generally left lay members free to follow their own consciences and cooperate with people outside the church—generally called Gentiles in the nineteenth century—should they choose to do so. Leaders continued to provide counsel in the temporal sphere but generally did not subject members to church discipline for failure to heed that counsel.

The term *spiritual,* on the other hand, designates the sphere of the
sacred and eternal. The spiritual arena encompasses those matters of
ultimate concern, particularly in the relationship between the Saints and
their God. It includes aspects of such matters as worship, rituals, revelation, religious experiences, worldview, and doctrine. In this sphere, the
church leadership has frequently punished deviance by disfellowship-
ment or excommunication both before and after the division of temporal and spiritual.

As the church leaders promoted modernization and worked their way
out of the conflict with the United States government and Evangelical
Protestantism, they assigned certain categories to the temporal arena
and certain to the spiritual. As the leaders more carefully defined the
separation between the temporal and spiritual arenas, they found it
necessary to more carefully define doctrine and practice within the
spiritual arena, in part because church leaders could subject members
to discipline for offenses within that arena whereas within the temporal arena pluralism generally prevailed.

The Temporal and Spiritual Fused

Perhaps we can best see the early relationship between the temporal
and spiritual spheres during Joseph Smith's time. In a number of revelations, Joseph Smith made clear the congruence of the temporal and
the spiritual. Speaking for the Lord, he said in September 1830, "Ver-
ily I say unto you that all things unto me are spiritual, and not at any
time have I given unto you a law which was temporal." Speaking of
Adam, he said, "No temporal commandment gave I unto him, for my
commandments are spiritual; they are not natural nor temporal."[12]

Mormons saw no incongruity in occupying the Kirtland Temple
both for temporal education in everyday subjects and for deeply spiritual rituals and charismatic experiences. This dual use underscored
the undifferentiated temporal and spiritual life devout Mormons
lived.[13]

Under these circumstances, devoted members lived in a psychically
undifferentiated secular and religious world, a world we might call for
want of a better word a holistic temporal and spiritual world. No effective separation existed between the temporal and spiritual spheres.
Nearly 80 percent of the revelations on spiritual subjects given by Joseph Smith contained what we would perceive today as some temporal—generally economic—instructions.[14] This failure to differentiate
between the temporal and spiritual arenas contributed to the conflicts
the Saints experienced in the Midwest.

After the Saints arrived in Utah, as in Missouri and Illinois, they continued to live in a holistic temporal and spiritual world. Building communities, starting businesses, administering God's kingdom, which they called Zion, worshipping, praying, and performing rituals were all of a piece for the Mormons.[15] Sermons by Brigham Young and others emphasized that the temporal and spiritual were "one."[16]

Living in a holistic world facilitated rather than retarded scientific and technological modernization. In the Mormon community such modernization enjoyed the force of official church sponsorship. In Utah, voluntary organizations promoted by church leaders, like those that Tocqueville had seen as the life blood of early nineteenth-century America, facilitated scientific, technological, and educational improvement of the community.[17]

For example, in December 1854, eighty men and one woman led by Wilford Woodruff organized the Universal Scientific Society as an association for "the universal diffusion of knowledge and science."[18] In his presidential address inaugurating the society's activities on February 17, 1855, Woodruff drew on his own temporal and spiritual background to emphasize that he and his associates had established the USS to acquaint the members, as far as possible, with every law, truth, and principle belonging to art, science, or any subject that might benefit God, angels, or people. Such lectures and discussions, he said, could provide an exchange of information among interested parties. In addressing the members, he outlined several possible areas of study ranging from the earth to the heavens, and as one illustration he described the mathematical formula used to calculate the orbit of planets. He expected, he said, by learning the laws of nature, human beings could banish the mysteries and wonders of the universe.[19]

In spite of these high hopes, the society appears to have functioned less than a year—until November 10, 1855. Until its demise, the members held regular Saturday evening meetings consisting of lectures by the members on subjects of common interest drawn from inside and outside Utah. Lecturers included George D. Watt and Wilford Woodruff on orthographic reform, John Hyde on natural philosophy, George A. Smith on chopping wood and Saracen history, William W. Phelps on the Ten Tribes of Israel, John Lyon on poetry, Thomas Hawkins on conservation of natural resources, David Candland on subjects ranging from public opinion to phrenology and the Crimean War, Jonathan Grimshaw on music, Dr. Darwin Richardson and Dr. William France on the principles of genetics, Gilbert Clements on the discipline of the mind, Orson Pratt on the operation of the planetary system, Almon W. Babbitt on the organization of the American government, Wilford

Woodruff on home manufacture and horticulture, and William Paul and Brigham Young on the principles of architecture.[20]

They drew on both temporal and religious sources and from reading and experience both in and outside Utah to enlighten one another. Given the limited size of the intellectual community and the narrow range of experience upon which they had to draw, it is not surprising that they soon exhausted the expertise and interests of members and associates. Attendance then lagged and the society died.[21]

The failure of the USS did not discourage the Latter-day Saints from seeking other means to promote the technological and scientific aspects of the modern world. During the 1850s, they established horticultural and pomological societies to introduce improved varieties of trees and plants. They set up the Deseret Agricultural and Manufacturing Society to import the latest plants, animals, and technology and to carry on experiments. In May 1856, for instance, Wilford Woodruff began corresponding with Sir William J. Hooker of London, Chief Director of Her Majesty's Royal Gardens (Kew Gardens). Writing to Woodruff, Hooker proposed to obtain any "specimens, seeds, or plants of any trees, shrubs, flowers, or vegetable." In return, he said he would forward to Utah any similar plants Woodruff wanted to order from Kew Gardens. With Brigham Young's support, Woodruff continued the correspondence. Later taking advantage of Hooker's offer, Woodruff secured some strawberry plants.[22] Woodruff also corresponded with Dr. Asa Fitch of New York, exchanging information and examples of insects and vermin.[23] He also imported fruit trees and other plants from California and the eastern states, which he planted in a garden plot on temple block.[24]

As early as the 1850s, the church leadership continued to expand contacts with the outside world, developing the industrial base of the kingdom. Utilizing the water courses for power to establish grist mills and sawmills, the church leadership also sent out specialized missions to establish iron works at Cedar City, lead mines in Las Vegas, and gold mines in California. They introduced improved turbines for water power, McCormick reapers, and numerous other technological improvements. During the 1850s, physicians in Salt Lake City began performing operations under anesthesia. In addition, the Mormons formed an express and carrying company in 1857 to facilitate useful commerce with the outside world.[25]

In the 1850s, however, the Latter-day Saints' holistic temporal and spiritual ideology did not allow the creation of anything like a democratic or pluralistic political or economic system. Those aspects of modernization lagged until the late 1880s and early 1890s.

To nineteenth-century Americans inured to the rough and tumble of politics, the Mormons' temporal and spiritual universe seemed positively un-American. Within the holistic unity, the Mormons intended neither to set up a two-party system nor to relinquish political control to outsiders. On several occasions, Brigham Young emphasized that instead of offering two candidates for election, the Saints should meet together and agree on a single nominee for each political office. The two-party system, he said, was Satan's plan, inaugurated in the preexistence when Lucifer rebelled against the authority of God and Christ.[26] Parley P. Pratt agreed in a conference of the Quorum of the Twelve in December 1852, when he argued that priesthood authority constituted the only true basis for government.[27] As a result, the church leadership made important political decisions either through the First Presidency and the Quorum of the Twelve or the Council of Fifty, which they created either for empire or refuge, depending on which interpretation you accept.[28]

Such an intermingling of church and state would probably have generated little opposition in early nineteenth-century Protestant-dominated communities. Mormon domination was another matter. The practice of plural marriage, the preaching of other unorthodox doctrines, the political exclusion of non-Mormons in Utah, and the long-standing alienation of Mormons from other Americans fueled antagonism between the two communities.

In the belief that members had become lax in their observance of things spiritual, the Mormon leadership attempted to revitalize the temporal and spiritual community in a reformation during 1856 and 1857.[29] Summing up the feelings of a number of the First Presidency and the Twelve, Brigham Young said that Mormons only wanted "to know how they can get this House built or a farm, Horses cattle &c. Their whole soul," Young opined, "is in the work of the world not the building of the kingdom of God." In commenting on this tendency, Young said that "any man that gets property upon this principle it will Carode him."[30]

In various sermons aimed at reinforcing the spiritual and maintaining the temporospiritual union, Brigham Young, Heber C. Kimball, and Jedediah M. Grant "sent arrows into the harts of men." In one sermon, Young preached the doctrine of blood atonement, saying that "for some sins no blood would be acceptable except the life & blood of the individual." Thereafter at various times during the reformation, authorities preached similar doctrines.[31] Subsequent events in the reformation, however, indicate that Young had engaged in hyperbole and that he and the other church leaders really wanted internal revitalization not ritual murder. Some members, however, may have taken him seriously.[32]

Modernization: The Temporal Sphere

During the 1850s, the federal government had received numerous complaints about the Mormon kingdom. Responding to these charges in 1857, President James Buchanan removed Brigham Young as territorial governor and sent Alfred Cumming of Georgia as his replacement. To escort the new governor, Buchanan sent an army of 3,500 under Colonel Albert Sidney Johnston. Learning of the expedition, the Mormons declared martial law and conducted a guerrilla campaign of harassment that forced the army into winter quarters at Fort Bridger. The Mountain Meadows Massacre occurred during this war as well. Mediation by Thomas L. Kane, a Pennsylvania aristocrat and friend of both Buchanan and the Mormons, and negotiations with Lazarus W. Powell, former governor and senator-elect from Kentucky, and Major Ben McCullough of Texas led to a presidential pardon and amnesty for the Mormons.[33]

Nevertheless, in the aftermath of the Utah war, federal troops and officials cracked and weakened the cement that had held the temporal and spiritual spheres together. Confrontation and violence in the streets of Salt Lake City became commonplace as saloons, houses of prostitution, and other resorts of footloose and free-spending soldiers opened in the city of the Saints.[34] A Missouri reporter named Kirk Anderson began the publication of a Gentile tabloid—the *Valley Tan*—a title adopted from the nickname for local home-brewed liquor.[35]

As events progressed, the Gentiles entered Utah political life, splitting the temporal and spiritual spheres even further. Cumming and District Attorney Alexander Wilson sided with the Mormons. Federal judges Charles Sinclair and John Cradlebaugh secured soldiers from Colonel Johnston to oppose them. Cumming and Wilson eventually stopped the judges' marshaling of federal troops to harass the Mormons by appealing to the Buchanan administration and securing orders from Attorney General Jeremiah S. Black telling them to obey the civil authority rather than to rely on martial law.[36]

Fallout from the Utah war affected the Latter-day Saints even more profoundly than indicated by the surface manifestations of political conflicts over civil jurisdiction or the social impact of violence, prostitution, and drunkenness. Although the number of troops in Utah declined rapidly during 1860 and 1861 as Buchanan and Lincoln relocated the soldiers to other posts on the West Coast and in the Midwest, many of the Gentiles remained. Moreover, the outbreak of the Civil War led, in 1862, to the reestablishment of a federal military presence in Zion—this time at Fort Douglas in Salt Lake City.[37]

In the minds of the Mormons, the flood of Gentiles had desecrated the land of Zion—God's kingdom on earth prepared for Christ's Second Coming. Shamed by their inability to protect their kingdom from outside intrusion, the Latter-day Saints began to rethink their relationship with God and the nation and, most importantly, they began to differentiate the temporal from the spiritual. In the summer of 1858, the Latter-day Saints responded to the disruption of their community by moving their worship out of the public eye. Disheartened by the desecration of their land, Brigham Young and the church leadership suppressed public expressions of piety for a time. As a result, the Mormons held no public worship—at least in Salt Lake City—from May 30, 1858, to January 2, 1859. Instead, the First Presidency had each of the Twelve organize a prayer circle consisting of a group of priesthood holders who met regularly in private to discuss the gospel and current affairs and to conduct formal prayers.[38]

The church leadership reestablished public worship early in 1859, but in the wake of the invasion they began to place more emphasis on the private side of spiritual life, and the breach in the temporal and spiritual spheres widened even more. Wilford Woodruff, for instance, began to spend more time officiating in exclusive and sacred services of the Endowment House. In 1866, the leadership began to expand the performance of Second Anointings, the most sacred of the temple rituals.[39] They also promoted the increase in the number of temple rituals for the dead in 1869.[40]

Although the temporal and spiritual spheres began to divide, the church leaders continued to maintain their authority over the temporal sphere. Though they sought Utah's admission as a state in 1862, a locally popular but essentially futile tactic followed at a number of critical junctures during the latter half of the nineteenth century. Considering the growth of military power associated with the Civil War, Brigham Young argued that the "whole country will soon be a military despotism" and that the Saints "must soon take care of" themselves.[41] In view of the nascent separation of temporal and spiritual, the Saints sought and secured the support of a number of Gentiles, including former governor James Duane Doty and federal judge John F. Kinney in their efforts for statehood. They also elected Kinney as territorial delegate to Congress.[42]

After Congress refused to admit Utah into the Union, the residents operated a provisional government of their own with an apocalyptic agenda. During the early 1860s, after the legislature of the territory of Utah adjourned, its members reconvened as the State of Deseret. After hearing a message from Provisional Governor Brigham Young, they conducted such business as seemed appropriate. In his January 1863 message Young said that "we are Called the State Legislature but when the time Comes [at Christ's reappearance] we shall be Called the kingdom of God."[43]

During the 1860s, the church leadership promoted a series of other measures containing both temporal and spiritual elements. These included the establishment of the School of the Prophets, women's relief societies, retrenchment organizations for young women, cooperative marketing ventures, and Zion's Cooperative Mercantile Institution (ZCMI). During the 1870s, they promoted short-lived united orders—communitarian organizations—in various communities.[44]

Congruent with their general support of technological improvement, the Mormons facilitated the construction of the transcontinental railroad to Utah and the extension of branch lines throughout the territory. Transportational change transformed relations of space and time and altered both the physical and psychic landscape. In practice, however, it facilitated continued temporal control and retarded the rate of separation of the temporal and spiritual into two spheres.[45] In effect, the east-west entry of the railroad into Utah in 1869 and its north-south expansion along the Wasatch Front in succeeding years integrated the agricultural towns and commercial and industrial cities into a suburban-urban oasis. The entry of rapid transportation facilitated easy access so the bulk of the Mormon population could market farm and manufactured goods, conduct business transactions, and promote intercommunity association. At the same time, the access provided by the railroad allowed General Authorities to work more closely with local religious leaders in such matters as holding stake conferences and settling disputes. The railroad also facilitated a reciprocal interaction by providing members with easier access to the General Authorities and to the semiannual general conferences and by providing cheaper fares for Mormon immigrants traveling to Zion. Technological modernization proved a boon rather than a disadvantage to the Mormons.

At the same time, the enticements that led the railroad companies to build to Utah—especially the potentially rich store of minerals—led to divisions in the Mormon community. In the late 1860s, a group of solidly upper middle-class businessmen and literati in Salt Lake City who served in the local church leadership and counted friendships among the General Authorities and other LDS leaders favored the severing of the temporal and spiritual spheres in the economic sector.[46]

Most of the group had converted to Mormonism in the British Isles, and they knew intimately returned missionaries such as Wilford Woodruff, Orson Pratt, Brigham Young, George A. Smith, George Q. Cannon, and the late Heber C. Kimball. William S. Godbe, a prominent businessman, counselor in the bishopric of the Salt Lake Thirteenth Ward, member of the School of the Prophets, city councilman, and polygamist, led the group. Others included such businessmen as Eli B. Kelsey, William H. Shearman, Thomas B. H. Stenhouse, and Henry W. Lawrence; literary figures such as Elias L. T. Harrison, George D. Watt, and Edward W. Tullidge; and John Tullidge, a noted artist and musician. Articulate and persuasive, they had established the *Utah Magazine* to publish their views.

Like other Mormons, and a number of late nineteenth-century reformers, these men approached their problems from both religious and temporal perspectives.[47] Convinced of the efficacy of messages from beyond the grave, Godbe and Harrison began holding spiritualistic seances. They used both the nationally prominent New Yorker Charles Foster and Godbe's wife, Charlotte, a stepdaughter of Brigham Young, as mediums. Eventually, the group included in their circle the excommunicated LDS apostle Amasa Lyman, who had been influenced by such spiritualists as Andrew Jackson Davis and Henry J. Horn. They came to perceive their spiritualistic revelations as effective cures for the problems of Mormonism.

Beyond their search for enlightenment through spiritualism, the Godbeites came to believe the General Authorities' efforts to control the temporal sphere had shortsightedly closed the obvious avenues to community prosperity. Like many late nineteenth-century reformers, the Godbeites held essentially laissez-faire attitudes. As such, they expressed disdain at the pressure for business conformity through the cooperative movement and the promotion of ZCMI and wage reductions designed by church leaders to meet national competition. Most important, they feared the loss of business initiatives caused by the effort to discourage Mormons from engaging in mining.

Although the Mormon leadership never capitulated to the siren call of spiritualism, they eventually modernized their economic policies, creating a pluralistic economic system. Thus, in the economic realm, these businessmen had simply raced ahead of their time. Within four years, the initial impact of the railroad had passed and Brigham Young began to encourage enterprising Mormons to help develop the territory's mining resources. William Jennings rode that wave to become the territory's first millionaire; and as early as 1871, Daniel H. Wells, John Taylor, George Q. Cannon, and other church leaders themselves owned mining property.[48] Moreover, after an initial effort to use cooperative ventures to promote equality, prominent Mormon capitalists began to accumulate stock in these enterprises, effectively changing community undertakings such as ZCMI into business corporations. After Young's death in 1877, John Taylor widened business opportunities by lifting the boycott against non-Mormon companies and Mormons and Gentiles inaugurated joint business ventures, especially during Woodruff's administration.

In the meantime, church leaders excommunicated the Godbeites for breaches of temporal decorum.[49] Godbe and Elias L. T. Harrison challenged the hierarchy's right to dictate in all matters temporal or spiritual. Arguing that he had not apostasized, Godbe testified that he loved the church and its doctrines and said that he had not opposed the church's economic policy in a disrespectful spirit. Harrison believed in priesthood authority but denied priesthood infallibility. He thought members should not attack or ridicule the church leadership, but insisted on the right to an honest difference of opinion provided he expressed that difference "respectfully and moderately."[50]

Although the church leaders no longer promoted a completely holistic temporal and spiritual world, they continued to demand control within the temporal arena in the interest of building the kingdom. Under the circumstances, the Godbeites' insistence upon respectful independence moved the trial toward a predictable conclusion. Speakers against the accused included Young, George A. Smith, Woodruff, and Cannon. The High Council of the Salt Lake Stake excommunicated Harrison and Godbe, and Young asked the assembled congregation for a sustaining vote. All present except Eli Kelsey, the Tullidge brothers, and two others voted with the church leadership. Because of his vigorous opposition, the congregation voted to cut off Kelsey immediately as well.[51]

During the early 1870s, Mormons faced a new challenge to their dominance of the temporal sphere in a battle with federal officers appointed by President Ulysses S. Grant—particularly Utah chief justice James B. McKean, a devoted Methodist and fervent anti-Mormon. Bringing Young before his court, McKean said that the case should be titled "Federal Authority versus Polygamic Theocracy."[52] The Mormons weathered this conflict, however, and Grant sacked McKean.

Modernization: The Spiritual Sphere

More ominously, the federal government invaded what the Latter-day Saints perceived as the spiritual arena by beginning the prosecution of polygamists. As an aspect of Christian primitivist restorationism, Mormons had instituted plural marriage, or polygyny—generally called polygamy—on the biblical model and on the basis of new revelations to Joseph Smith during the 1840s.[53] Prosecution could not begin immediately after Congress's passage of the anti-Mormon Morrill Anti-bigamy Act in 1862 since Mormon-dominated grand juries would not return indictments. After the 1874 passage of the Poland Act changed the method of empaneling juries, a federal court convicted George Reynolds on the testimony of his second wife. On appeal, the United States Supreme Court ruled against Reynolds, arguing that the free exercise clause of the First Amendment protected beliefs but not action injurious to good public order.[54]

In 1872, during the height of the controversy with Judge McKean, the Mormons embarked on yet another attempt to achieve statehood. On this occasion, instead of simply securing Gentile support, the gradual separation of temporal and spiritual spheres allowed the church leaders to include non-Mormons as convention delegates. Thus, Gentiles like former territorial secretaries S. A. Mann and Frank Fuller appeared in both the constitutional convention and the slate of state officers offered to the electorate.[55]

In spite of such gestures toward friendly non-Mormons, the church leadership still maintained a tight control on local politics and encouraged members not to open political participation to Gentiles generally. In July 1877, Brigham Young sent Wilford Woodruff and Erastus Snow to Beaver, a predominantly Mormon town with a sizeable Gentile population swollen by nearby mining operations, to look into allegations of political and social cooperation between the Mormons and local apostates and Gentiles. "It will not do," he wrote, "for LDS to mix with the world." If the leaders did not correct conditions in that southern Utah community, Young thought the people there might possibly get "into the same condition as Tooele," where the Gentiles had captured control of the government.[56]

Apparently in response to Young's concerns, Woodruff and Snow met with the priesthood in Beaver. In the meeting, Woodruff "reproved them sharply for mingling with the Gentiles as they were doing and for their folly in dividing on their Election."[57]

At the same time, while church leaders continued to urge temporal unity, they seem to have recognized that future success for the Mormon community lay in the spiritual sphere, particularly in personal piety rather than in conflict with the larger American society. In inaugurating rituals for the dead at the St. George Temple in 1877 and particularly in expanding that work by offering vicarious redemption to prominent men and women of the past, Wilford Woodruff led the movement in refocusing the religious energies of the Mormon people on personal piety rather than on conflict with outside political, religious, and economic interests.

In common with many of the Evangelical Protestants who opposed
them so vigorously, Latter-day Saints believed strongly in dispensational
premillennialism.[58] Central to their belief was the proposition that
Christ would return soon to save them from their persecutors, protect
plural marriage, assume the leadership of the kingdom they had established, and punish their enemies. A revelation—generally called the
Wilderness Revelation—Woodruff received in 1880, which the other
apostles accepted and supported strongly, reaffirmed that proposition.[59]

As the 1880s progressed, however, political and social pressures
forced the Latter-day Saints to temporize. These same Protestants who
shared the Mormon beliefs in millennialism, working with many others less sure about the imminence of Christ's Second Coming, had become outraged by Mormon practices—especially polygamy and political control. Under the circumstances, they pressed a compliant
Congress to enact legislation to suppress both plural marriage and the
temporal power of the church.[60] Embodied in the Edmunds Act of 1882
and the Edmunds-Tucker Act of 1887, attacks on Mormon practices
were carried out by the federal government by putting polygamists in
jail and by undercutting the financing for the gathering of the Saints
through immigration. In addition, they undermined the political, social, and economic power of the church itself by disfranchising practicing polygamists and all women, turning control of Utah's election
machinery and a number of other local institutions to federal appoin-
tees, and confiscating church property.

Moreover, and perhaps most important, the vigor and success of the
enforcement of these laws began to undermine the basic premise of
Mormon premillennialism since the success of the anti-Mormon campaign led Latter-day Saints to doubt the proximity of Christ's Second
Coming and the imminent salvation from their enemies. Increasingly,
talk of the signs of the times replaced expectations that Christ might
return soon. These changing perceptions forced the LDS community
in general and Wilford Woodruff in particular, who assumed the leadership of that community in 1887, to undertake a series of initiatives
essentially at odds with the previous millennialist ideology, with the
emphasis on the necessity of plural marriage for salvation, and with the
strident antipluralism that had characterized the LDS community since
Joseph Smith's time. Increasingly, the force of circumstance caused by
the conflict with the larger American society pressed the Latter-day
Saints to rethink the proposition that their community could remain
politically and socially separated and to take actions that made them
increasingly interdependent, both politically and socially, with others
in the United States.

During the period from 1887 to about 1894, the Latter-day Saints drafted the intellectual rationale for the separation of the temporal and spiritual spheres, began some of the separation, and started to define more carefully the scope of each. In the process, they accepted the corollaries of modernization and pluralism in the political and economic arenas.

In yet another attempt to secure statehood, the Utahns drafted a new constitution in 1887. In this case, they hired some rather formidable legal talent, including Senator Joseph E. McDonald of Indiana and Judge Jeremiah Wilson. With the approval of the First Presidency, Charles W. Penrose formulated a number of temporizing arguments focusing on church doctrine and practice, McDonald and Wilson argued the constitutional case for admission, and Franklin S. Richards addressed the two main objections—polygamy and the domination of politics by the Mormon hierarchy.

Using a textual argument, Richards interpreted the words of Joseph Smith's revelation on plural marriage to mean that the church considered the practice permissive rather than mandatory for its members. He admitted that individuals might interpret the words as commanding the practice of polygamy, but insisted that the revelation itself did not warrant such an interpretation. Furthermore, Richards insisted that the church was willing to conform to the requirements and demands of the law, which was passed to punish actual offenders.

In arguing the case against priesthood domination, Richards focused on the charge that tithing constituted a tax on church members exacted under priesthood sanctions. He said that members paid tithing as a voluntary contribution and not as a church tax. From this example he deduced the freedom of the members to follow or ignore the advice of church leaders. Richards's testimony provided an important rationale for redefining Mormon doctrine within the spiritual arena and limiting the scope of religious authority within the temporal. Nevertheless, unconvinced of the Saints' sincerity, Congress rejected the petition.[61]

In 1887, the church leadership also recognized the challenge they faced from Gentiles who were excluded from politics, and they began tentative efforts to share power in Salt Lake City—in part from necessity, in part from conviction. Several of the Twelve, particularly Heber J. Grant, believed that the church had been far too closed in its political relationships with others. As early as December 1887, Grant wrote that the church ought to be more "liberal before we are forced to be for considerations of policy. . . . I am," he wrote, "as much opposed to aiding and supporting our enemies as it is possible for a man to be, but I am willing to grant them representation in our City, County and Territorial government where they are good and substantial citizens."[62] On December 29, Woodruff, Cannon, Joseph F. Smith, Grant, and John W. Taylor of the Twelve and a number of local People's party leaders, including Mayor Francis Armstrong and members of the city council, met at Woodruff's office. They discussed the advisability of inviting a number of Liberal party members to run for the Salt Lake City council on a joint ticket. The group approved the proposal, some arguing that it was good policy under the circumstances, and others like Grant favoring it "because they thought it just."[63]

A committee of William W. Riter, John Clark, and Samuel P. Teasdel left the meeting to contact a number of the Liberal party leaders. After discussing the matter with Gentiles like Governor Caleb West, U.S. Marshal Frank H. Dyer, Joseph L. Rawlins, U.S. Attorney William H. Dickson, and J. R. McBride, they agreed to nominate for positions on the city council four prominent businessmen: William S. McCornick, John E. Dooley, M. B. Sowles, and Bolivar Roberts. The church leadership also considered having the legislature redistrict the city so certain areas with a predominance of Gentiles would elect Liberal party representatives, but the 1888 legislature met too late to effect the change for that year. In the February 1888 election, however, the coalition slate, styled the Citizen's Ticket, won quite handily.[64]

Following the victory of the Citizen's Ticket in Salt Lake City in February 1888, a number of Latter-day Saints favored the breakup of the People's party and perhaps even its amalgamation with the Democratic party.[65] The effort failed at the time, but the church leadership had already opened a series of initiatives with national Democratic and Republican political leaders aimed at securing amnesty for themselves and admission of Utah as a state.

Still, conflict drove the process of modernization through the reconsideration of doctrines and practices in both the temporal and spiritual arenas. For example, an adverse decision by federal judge Thomas J. Anderson in late 1889 to a petition for citizenship from John Moore, a Mormon immigrant from Great Britain, prompted an official reconsideration of much that had transpired. Concerning itself with the loyalty of members of the church to the United States government and collective disdain for the law, the court ruled Mormons unfit for citizenship. Anderson issued a sweeping indictment of the church, citing public statements of church leaders, particularly their emphasis on millennialism, the imminence of the apocalypse, and doctrines like blood atonement and polygamy. Beginning with the premise that the church taught that their organization was the actual kingdom of God on earth with political authority vested in the priesthood, Anderson ruled that it perceived itself as a temporal and spiritual kingdom holding authority to control all aspects of the lives of its members. He cited the church's millennial doctrines that the kingdom of God would eventually overthrow the United States and all other governments and showed that church leaders had preached blood atonement for certain sins. He pointed out also that the church believed that polygamy was a commandment of God and cited statements of General Authorities taking issue with the Reynolds decision and insisting that all laws interfering with religion were unconstitutional.[66]

The naturalization case became the catalyst for an official statement on church doctrine and policy that further widened the separation between the temporal and spiritual spheres.[67] In response to the ruling, President Woodruff, his counselors, and the Twelve Apostles agreed to prepare and sign "a dignified paper . . . setting forth our doctrines, and denying the . . . charges of our murderous character and disloyalty to the government."[68]

The paper, labeled an "Official Declaration," generally called "the Manifesto of the Apostles," was drafted by Charles W. Penrose. The leadership read and edited the document on December 12, 1889, then those present signed it.[69] The declaration began by setting the events in the context of the recent naturalization hearings. Denying that the church preached blood atonement, it argued that the charges had been rendered "plausible by culling isolated passages from old sermons without the explanatory context." It denied also that church courts had the right to "supersede, annul or modify a judgment of any civil court," and said that the church "does not claim or exercise the right to interfere with citizens in the free exercise of social or political rights and privileges." It claimed the right, however, to offer advice to its members. Furthermore, it said, nothing in the endowment ceremony or in any doctrine of the church was "hostile to the Government of the United States." The ruling sustaining charges of disloyalty and sedition, they said, had resulted from the selection and grouping out of context of "Utterances of prominent men in the Church" made during the Utah War and it conveyed an erroneous impression about the present leadership. The early sermons, the apostles argued, were aimed at "traitorous officials who were prostituting the powers of their positions to accomplish nefarious ends." Moreover, they pointed out, criticism of acts of federal officials "was not considered," then or now, "as treason against the nation nor as hostility to the Government." Furthermore, the declaration said, although the Latter-day Saints proclaimed that "the kingdom of heaven is at hand," other Christians did the same thing. Most importantly, the church did not constitute itself a provisional government trying to overthrow the United States or any other civil government.[70]

Following Judge Anderson's ruling, the federal government began the confiscation of church property under the Edmunds-Tucker Act while continuing to imprison large numbers of Mormon men. As a result, between mid-1890 and December 1893, Woodruff presided over what he called, quite appropriately, a "Revolution" since it effectively completed the separation of the temporal from the spiritual in all relevant areas.

In the meantime, conservative efforts like offering fusion tickets coupled with continued control over party machinery were doomed to failure. A major crack in Mormon political control appeared in the fall of 1888 as several Liberal party candidates won election to the territorial legislature. Hard on the heels of this loss, the Mormon people suffered another major setback in February 1889 when the Liberal party captured control of the city government in Ogden, Utah's second largest city. In 1890, the Mormons lost control of Salt Lake City.[71]

Both in public and in private, Woodruff saw the broader implications of the loss of political power. At the end of 1889, he confided to his diary that "the word of the Prophet Joseph Smith is beginning to be fulfilled that the whole Nation would turn against Zion & make war upon the Saints."[72]

In practice, however, the enemies of the church prospered as God seemed to intensify his controversy with the Mormon people. Throughout 1888, in proceedings before a special examiner, the Territorial Supreme Court compiled a list of property belonging to the LDS Church that it had confiscated—the legal term was escheat—for the benefit of the territorial schools. Church attorneys Franklin S. Richards and James O. Broadhead worked out an agreement with U.S. Solicitor General George Jenks to exempt temples, the tabernacle, and meeting houses.[73] The Utah Territorial Supreme Court confirmed that agreement in its decree of October 8, 1888, which ordered the receiver, Frank Dyer, to return the temple block to the Presiding Bishopric, since it ruled that the church used the property exclusively for religious purposes as stipulated in the Edmunds-Tucker Act.[74] The United States Supreme Court confirmed in May 1890 the right of the federal government to confiscate the property. An opinion by Justice Joseph Bradley ruled that the church had engaged in illegal activities, holding the federal government completely justified in escheating the property.[75]

Contrary to the expectations of church leaders, however, the Supreme Court's ruling had left open the possibility that the federal government might legitimately confiscate religious property on the ground that since the church promoted illegal activities, it did not use such properties exclusively for religious purposes. In July 1890, the federal courts removed Dyer and appointed Henry W. Lawrence, "a bitter apostate," as receiver. A Godbeite who had testified against the church in the Moore hearings, Lawrence sought to confiscate the religious properties.[76]

Throughout the negotiations between late 1888 and July 1890, the church had come under increasing public pressure to renounce the practice of polygamy.[77] The Saints in Idaho faced disabilities beyond imprisonment and the loss of church property since the Gem State had disfranchised all Latter-day Saints.[78] Only some rather vigorous lobbying with a number of local Republicans like Francis E. Warren had saved Wyoming Saints from a similar fate.

National political leaders urged the Saints to give in. They refused to do so. In an effort to temporize, the church leadership issued a confidential ruling ordering church leaders not to perform plural marriages in the United States, though they might do so in Mexico if "the contracting parties, or at least the female has resolved to remain in that country." They had already urged members to live only with one wife, and they began to discipline church leaders who publicly advocated plural marriage.[79]

In September 1890, however, these measures proved inadequate. After a trip for consultation with church leaders in Arizona, Colorado, New Mexico, and Utah in August 1890, Woodruff learned in early September that the federal court had issued a subpoena for his testimony in a suit seeking to confiscate the church's temples.[80] Evading service, Woodruff and a group of associates left for California, where they consulted with a circle of political leaders including Isaac Trumbo, Morris Estee, and Alexander Badlam, all interested in business in Utah and in Mormon goodwill, who favored amnesty for the Mormons and statehood for Utah.[81]

After returning from California, on September 24 and 25 Woodruff discussed with his counselors and members of the Twelve a fundamental change in church policy that defined the spiritual sphere more carefully. In his diary, he said that he had

> arrived at a point in the History of my life as the President of the Church of Jesus Christ of Latter Day Saints whare I am under the necessity of acting for the Temporal Salvation of the Church. The United State Governmet has taken a Stand & passed Laws to destroy the Latter day Saints upon the Subjet of poligamy or Patriarchal order of Marriage. And after Praying to the Lord &

feeling inspired by his spirit I have issued . . . [a] Proclamation which is sustained by my Councillors and the 12 Apostles.[82]

The proclamation—generally called the Manifesto—Woodruff labeled an "Official Declaration." In the Manifesto, Woodruff denied that the church had continued to solemnize plural marriages. Indicating that since the Supreme Court had declared the laws forbidding polygamy constitutional, he intended to "submit to those laws and to use . . . [his] influence with the members of the Church . . . to have them do likewise." He denied that the church encouraged members to enter polygamy and insisted that church leaders had "promptly reproved" those elders who had done so.

In fact, while the Manifesto facilitated the process of modernization within the Mormon community and accommodation with general American society, it conceded only a little more in public than the church leadership had already implemented in private.[83] Still, on the day after the general membership approved the Manifesto in conference, Utah Supreme Court Justice Charles S. Zane essentially freed the church from any fear of further action aimed at confiscating the church's religious properties by announcing his belief in the honesty and sincerity of the church's "solemn declaration."[84]

In practice, the difficult effort to define the Manifesto's meaning and secure its full implementation continued well into the first decade of the twentieth century. New plural marriages continued on a reduced scale and eventually two apostles lost their positions in the Quorum of the Twelve over the question. Nevertheless, Woodruff had laid the intellectual groundwork for compromise by redefining the scope of the spiritual sphere.[85]

Conclusion

In sum, the real and threatened religious sanctions, especially the loss of the temples, when coupled with pressure caused by the jailing of church leaders and the loss of temporal property, eventually forced the church into separating the temporal from the spiritual, restricting the scope of the spiritual sphere, and completing the process of modernization. In the absence of such pressure, the church might well have continued to function even with the loss of temporal properties. Adherence by church members to the rules allowing plural marriages only among parties who agreed to remain in Mexico might have stopped the parade of priesthood holders through the Utah and other territorial and state penitentiaries. Eventually, however, continued monitoring by Evangelical Protestants would undoubtedly have uncovered the continued plural marriage and precipitated renewed conflict.

Subsequent changes further defined church doctrine within the spiritual arena and established pluralistic and modern practice within the temporal. Although the process of political modernization caused extreme trauma, punctuated by the expulsion of a member of the Quorum of the Twelve Apostles in 1896, the church pressed its membership to divide into the two national political parties beginning in 1891. This division facilitated the extension of political pluralism and modernization begun earlier with the inclusion of Gentiles in the constitutional conventions and fusion with Liberal party elements. The federal government recognized the changes in 1894 by authorizing Utah to draft a constitution and admitting the state to the Union in January 1896. Economic pluralism continued in the 1890s as the church leadership cooperated with non-Mormons in the development of various enterprises, including a sugar company, power companies, and mining ventures.

What of the strident apocalyptic characteristic of Woodruff's 1880 Wilderness Revelation and of subsequent pronouncements? By 1889, although Woodruff still anticipated the judgments of the Lord upon the nation and on those who warred against the Latter-day Saints, he no longer expected the imminent fulfillment of these prophecies.

Nevertheless, the church continued to perceive itself as the restoration of primitive Christianity. Modernization had not changed that. During the 1890s and into the first decades of the twentieth century, church leadership, academics, and publicists such as James E. Talmage, John A. Widtsoe, B. H. Roberts, and Charles W. Penrose reviewed and reconsidered church doctrine, defining the doctrines of God and people, clarifying the relation of humankind to Christ, and defining Mormondom's relationship to science as essentially friendly.[86]

In summary, then, sixty years of conflict, most particularly the intensive prosecutions and confiscations together with the threatened seizure of the church's temples, played the same role in bringing about a reconsideration of Mormon doctrine and practice and the adoption of modern attitudes toward the temporal and spiritual spheres in the nineteenth century as the Thirty Years' War had in the seventeenth. Responding through revelations that their view of Christian primitivism facilitated and through restatements and reconsideration of policy, the LDS leadership separated the temporal and spiritual arenas and rethought essential doctrine and practice. In the process, they reconstructed the temporal sphere into a pluralistic arena in which they could function without unmanageable conflict in the modern American society with which they had previously waged unrelenting warfare. At the same time, they rethought the spiritual sphere, abandoning bizarre doctrines like blood atonement and suppressing offensive practices like polygamy. These changes allowed the Mormons to retain the essential features of both the temporal and spiritual spheres while dividing the two, and at the same time to maintain a satisfactory relationship with their community and their God in the modern world.

Notes

1. In general, the term *modernization* encompasses a complex of features including technological improvement, popular and generally democratic government, widespread education, and intellectual and cultural pluralism. Some authors have also included the secularization of religion. For a study of the development of modernization in the United States, see Richard D. Brown, *Modernization: The Transformation of American Life, 1600–1865* (New York: Hill and Wang, 1976).

2. Max Weber, *From Max Weber: Essays in Sociology,* ed. H. H. Gerth and C. Wright Mills (New York: Oxford University Press, 1958), 307. Emile Durkheim, in *The Elementary Forms of the Religious Life,* trans. Joseph Ward Swain (New York: Free Press, 1965), 477, wrote: "Scientific thought is only a more perfect form of religious thought. Thus it seems natural that the second should progressively retire before the first, as this becomes better fitted to perform the task.

"And there is no doubt that this regression has taken place in the course of history. Having left religion, science tends to substitute itself for this latter in all that which concerns the cognitive and intellectual functions."

Peter Berger, in *The Sacred Canopy: Elements of a Sociological Theory of Religion* (Garden City, N.Y.: Doubleday, 1967), 107–8, has argued, "Put simply, this means that the modern West has produced an increasing number of individuals who look upon the world and their own lives without the benefit of religious interpretations." He locates the phenomenon more in men than in women, more among industrialized countries than among traditional, and less in the United States, except he believes that the churches here have become "highly secularized themselves, so that the European and American cases represent two variations on the same underlying theme of global secularization."

Another example is Mircea Eliade, in *The Sacred and the Profane: The Nature of Religion,* trans. Willard R. Trask (San Diego: Harvest, 1959), 17: "We need only compare their existential situations [of nomadic hunters and sedentary cultivators] with that of a man of the modern societies, living in a desacralized cosmos, and we shall immediately be aware of all that separates him from them."

3. Andrew M. Greeley, *Unsecular Man: The Persistence of Religion* (New York: Schocken Books, 1972).

4. Henry F. May, in *The Enlightenment in America* (New York: Oxford University Press, 1976), esp. xiv–xv, xviii, and chaps. 3, 4, argues that Enlightenment culture in America, contrary to the situation in Europe, included exceptional religious vitality; see also Peter W. Williams, *Popular Religion in America: Symbolic Change and the Modernization Process in Historical Perspective* (Englewood Cliffs, N.J.: Prentice Hall, 1980), 2; Robert N. Bellah, Richard Madsen, William M. Sullivan, Ann Swindler, and Steven M. Tipton, *Habits of the Heart: Individualism and Commitment in American Life* (New York: Harper, 1986), 219–49.

5. Stan L. Albrecht and Tim B. Heaton, "Secularization, Higher Education, and Religiosity," *Review of Religious Research* 26 (Sept. 1984): 43–58.

6. For three of the most recent studies of Christian Primitivism and the relationship with Mormonism, see Richard T. Hughes, ed., *The American Quest for the Primitive Church* (Urbana: University of Illinois Press, 1988), especially Jan Shipps, "The Reality of the Restoration and the Restoration Ideal in the Mormon Tradition," 181–95; Richard T. Hughes and C. Leonard Allen, *Illusions of Innocence: Protestant Primitivism in America, 1630–1875* (Chicago: University of Chicago Press, 1988), especially 133–52; and Marvin S. Hill, *Quest for Refuge: The Mormon Flight from American Pluralism* (Salt Lake City: Signature Books, 1989).

7. Grant Underwood, "Primitivism and the Latter-day Saints," paper presented at the conference "Christian Primitivism and Modernization: Coming to Terms with Our Age," Pepperdine University, Malibu, Calif., 1991.

8. On this point, see particularly Nathan O. Hatch and Mark A. Noll, eds., *The Bible in America: Essays in Cultural History* (New York: Oxford University Press, 1982), especially Mark A. Noll, "The Image of the United States as a Biblical Nation, 1776–1865," 39–58, and Nathan O. Hatch, "Sola Scriptura and Novus Ordo Seclorum," 59–78.

9. On some of these groups, see Stephen A. Marini, *Radical Sects of Revolutionary New England* (Cambridge, Mass.: Harvard University Press, 1982); and Clarke Garrett, *Spirit Possession and Popular Religion: From the Camisards to the Shakers* (Baltimore: Johns Hopkins University Press, 1987).

10. On the basis for this doctrine, see the Articles of Faith of the Church of Jesus Christ of Latter-day Saints, articles 5, 6, 7, 8, and especially 9, and the Book of Mormon, the Doctrine and Covenants, and the Pearl of Great Price.

11. Stephen Toulmin, *Cosmopolis: The Hidden Agenda of Modernity* (New York: Free Press, 1990).

12. Doctrine and Covenants 29:34–35.

13. For detail on these experiences, see Wilford Woodruff, *Wilford Woodruff's Journal, 1833–1898*, typescript ed., ed. Scott G. Kenney, 9 vols. (Midvale, Utah: Signature Books, 1983–85), 1:128–29, 130–31, 132, 137 (Apr. 3–6, 1837).

14. Leonard J. Arrington, *Great Basin Kingdom: An Economic History of the Latter-day Saints, 1830–1900* (Cambridge, Mass.: Harvard University Press, 1958), 5–6. I thank Richard Lambert for suggesting the word *holistic*.

15. For a general study of community building, see Arrington, *Great Basin Kingdom,* especially 39–194; and Arrington, Feramorz Y. Fox, and Dean L. May, *Building the City of God: Community and Cooperation among the Mormons* (Salt Lake City: Deseret Book, 1976).

16. On Young's talk, see Woodruff, *Journal,* 4:45 (July 6, 1851).

17. Alexis de Tocqueville, *Democracy in America,* ed. Richard D. Heffner (New York: Mentor Books, 1956), 198.

18. Universal Scientific Society, "Minutes, 1854–1855," 19, MS 5942, Archives of the Church of Jesus Christ of Latter-day Saints, Salt Lake City, Utah (hereafter cited as LDS Archives). The organization included such luminaries as Ezra T. Benson, Robert L. Campbell, David Candland, James Coudy, Albert Carrington, Charles Derry, Amos Fielding, William France, David Fullmer, James Galley, Thomas Hawkins, John Hyde, John V. Long, John Lyon, Philip Margetts, A. F. McDonald, Richard V. Morris, W. W. Phelps, Orson Pratt Jr., Albert P. Rockwood, Phineas Richards, Samuel W. Richards, George A. Smith, Lorenzo Snow, Orson Spencer, John Taylor, Walter Thompson, George D. Watt, and George B. Wallace.

19. Universal Scientific Society Minutes, loose pages, Feb. 17, 1855, LDS Archives.

20. Ibid.

21. The meeting of November 10, 1855—the last recorded—indicated that few attended and those in attendance adjourned without holding a lecture.

22. Wilford Woodruff to George A. Smith, May 28, 1856, Wilford Woodruff unprocessed correspondence, folder 6, LDS Archives; Woodruff, *Journal,* 4:446 (Sept. 9, 1856), 5:345 (June 14, 1859).

23. Woodruff to Asa Fitch, July 31, 1856, Wilford Woodruff unprocessed correspondence, box 7, folder 6, LDS Archives; Journal History of the Church of Jesus Christ of Latter-day Saints, July 31, 1856, LDS Archives, microfilm, Special Collections, Harold B. Lee Library, Brigham Young University; Woodruff, *Journal,* 4:446 (Sept. 8. 1856).

24. Wilford Woodruff to Thompson Woodruff, Salt Lake City to Holmesville, Oswego County, New York, July 31, 1856, Wilford Woodruff correspondence, box 7, folder 6, LDS Archives; Thompson Woodruff to Wilford Woodruff, Nov. 23, 1856, Wilford Woodruff unprocessed correspondence, box 1, folder 2, LDS Archives; Wilford Woodruff to Thompson Woodruff, June 1, 1857, Wilford Woodruff unprocessed correspondence, box 7, folder 7, LDS Archives; Journal History, July 4, 1857. The grafting in 1857 was much more extensive than in 1852, and he got Charles Oliphant, a local orchardist, to help him. Woodruff, *Journal,* 5:31 (Mar. 9, 10, 11, 12, 1857), 32 (Mar. 14, 15, 1857), 47–48 (Apr. 14, 1857), 50 (May 4, 1857); 4:418 (May 6, 1856).

25. Arrington, *Great Basin Kingdom,* 116–29; J. Kenneth Davies, *Mormon Gold: The Story of California's Mormon Argonauts* (Salt Lake City: Olympus, 1984); Kimberly Day, "Frederick Kesler, Utah Craftsman," *Utah Historical Quarterly* 56 (Winter 1988): 55–74; Morris A. Shirts and William T. Parry, "The Demise of the Deseret Iron Co.: Failure of the Brick Furnace Lining Technology," *Utah Historical Quarterly* 56 (Winter 1988): 23–35; Frederick M.

Huchel, "The Box Elder Flouring Mill," *Utah Historical Quarterly* 56 (Winter 1988): 75–87; Journal History, Oct. 12, 1861; Woodruff, *Journal*, 4:384 (Jan. 9, 1856), 430 (July 17, 1856), 432 (July 29, 1856), 5:106 (Oct. 9, 10, 1857), 594 (Sept. 17, 19, 1861); Arrington, *Great Basin Kingdom*, 162–69, 195–96.

26. Woodruff, *Journal*, 4:25 (May 16, 1851), 51 (July 27, 1851).

27. Ibid., 4:162–70 (Sept. 8, 1851).

28. See ibid., 5:67 (July 12, 1857) for an example of central nomination. On the Council of Fifty, see Klaus J. Hansen, *Quest for Empire: The Political Kingdom of God and the Council of Fifty in Mormon History* (East Lansing: Michigan State University Press, 1967); Marvin S. Hill, "Quest for Refuge: An Hypothesis as to the Social Origins and Nature of the Mormon Political Kingdom," *Journal of Mormon History* 2 (1975): 3–20; and D. Michael Quinn, "The Council of Fifty and Its Members, 1844–1945," *BYU Studies* 20 (Fall 1979): 163–97.

29. For a discussion of the linking of these matters, see Paul H. Peterson, "The Mormon Reformation" (Ph.D. diss., Brigham Young University, 1981), 40–45. Peterson also believed that the grasshoppers of 1855, the harsh winter of 1855–56, the drought of early 1856, and the consecrations of the mid-1850s were linked to the reformation as well. Woodruff, however, did not see these links. See Woodruff, *Journal*, 4:316 (May 5, 1855), 398 (Feb. 2, 1856), 421 (June 1, 1856). On the possibility of applying Anthony F. C. Wallace's revitalization model to Mormonism, see Cherel Jane Ellsworth Olive, "Mazeway Reformulation and Revitalization Movements: the Wallace Model as Applied to the Development of Mormonism" (M.A. thesis, University of Nevada at Las Vegas, 1977).

30. Woodruff, *Journal*, 4:506 (Dec. 8, 1856).

31. Ibid., 4:451 (Sept. 21, 1856). For a discussion of the preaching and practice of the doctrine, see Peterson, "The Mormon Reformation," chap. 9.

32. In March 1857, William Parrish and several of his family and friends decided to leave the church and the community at Springville. They were murdered under suspicious circumstances, and although the perpetrators were never found, a number of commentators associated the deeds with the doctrine of blood atonement. See Norman Furniss, *The Mormon Conflict, 1850–59* (New Haven, Conn.: Yale University Press, 1960), 88–89; Brigham H. Roberts, *Comprehensive History of the Church of Jesus Christ of Latter-day Saints, Century 1,* 6 vols. (Salt Lake City: Deseret News Press, 1930), 4:176n.

33. On the Utah war, see Furniss, *The Mormon Conflict*.

34. For examples of the violence, see Woodruff, *Journal*, 5:217, 225–26 (Sept. 10, Oct. 23, 1858).

35. Woodruff, *Journal*, 5:233 (Nov. 7, 1858).

36. Ibid., 5:337 (May 21, 1859), 5:247 (Nov. 29, 1858). Woodruff approved Cumming's activity and Cradlebaugh's removal. Woodruff to Ilus F. Carter, Salt Lake City, May 25, 1859, Historian's Office Letterpress Copybook, LDS Archives.

37. For these events, see Furniss, *Mormon Conflict*, 230–31, and E. B. Long, *The Saints and the Union: Utah Territory during the Civil War* (Urbana: University of Illinois Press, 1981).

38. Brigham Young told Woodruff on August 10 that he did not want to call public meetings on any subject. Woodruff, *Journal,* 5:207, 269 (Aug. 10, 1858, Jan. 2, 1859). Members of Wilford Woodruff's prayer circle were Edward Hunter, Leonard Hardy, Jesse C. Little, Abraham Hoagland, Abraham O. Smoot, Seth M. Blair, Elijah F. Sheets, George D. Grant, Robert T. Burton, Jonathan Pugmire, Robert L. Campbell, Wilford Woodruff Jr., David O. Calder, Arza Hinckley, John T. Caine, and an otherwise unidentified brother Willey. Woodruff, *Journal,* 5:202–3 (July 25, 1858). For a discussion of prayer circles, see D. Michael Quinn, "Latter-day Saint Prayer Circles," *BYU Studies* 19 (Fall 1987): 79–105. Quinn argues that various prayer circles established by certain members of the Quorum of the Twelve met each night of the week and that the prayer circles of the Twelve combined with those of six apostles to meet with a circle of the First Presidency on Sunday nights. Woodruff's diary indicates, however, that he perceived his prayer circle and the circle of the apostles and presidency as separate. Moreover, with the exception of the early Wednesday meetings, he ordinarily met with his circle in the morning or at noon on Sunday and met separately with the First Presidency and Twelve in a prayer circle on Sunday evening. Woodruff's journal provides no indication that other church members beside the First Presidency and the Twelve met in the Sunday evening circle. See Woodruff, *Journal,* 5:269–70 (Jan. 2, 1859).

39. For the discussion, see Woodruff, *Journal,* 6:307–8 (Dec. 26, 1866). For the Second Anointings, see all entries for 1867, especially those for Saturdays.

40. Woodruff, *Journal,* 6:477 (June 2, 1869). See also 6:478, 485 (June 7, July 11, 1869).

41. Ibid., 5:607–8 (Dec. 15, 1861).

42. Ibid., 6:9–13 (Jan. 22–23, 1862).

43. Ibid., 6:92 (Jan. 19, 1863).

44. Journal History, April 7, 1869. On the organization of the first school of the prophets, see Woodruff, *Journal,* 6:378–79 (Dec. 2, 1867). See also Arrington, *Great Basin Kingdom,* part 3; and Arrington, Fox, and May, *Building the City of God.*

45. This interpretation is at variance with that of Robert J. Dwyer in *The Gentile Comes to Utah: A Study in Religious and Social Conflict (1862–1890),* 2d ed. (Salt Lake City: Western Epics, 1971).

46. For this discussion, I have relied on work by Ronald W. Walker, especially "The Godbeite Protest in the Making of Modern Utah" (Ph.D. diss., University of Utah, 1977); "The Liberal Institute: A Case Study in National Assimilation," *Dialogue* 10 (Autumn 1977): 74–85; "When the Spirits Did Abound: Nineteenth Century Utah's Encounter with Free-Thought Radicalism," *Utah Historical Quarterly* 50 (Fall 1982): 304–24; "The Commencement of the Godbeite Protest: Another View," *Utah Historical Quarterly* 42 (Summer 1974): 217–44; and Davis Bitton, "Mormonism's Encounter with Spiritualism," *Journal of Mormon History* 1 (1974): 39–50.

47. On Mugwumps, see Richard Hofstadter, *The Age of Reform from Bryan to FDR* (New York: Vintage Books, 1960), sect. 4; Robert Crunden, *Ministers of Reform: The Progressives' Achievement in American Civilization, 1889–*

1920 (New York: Basic Books, 1982), 3–15; and John G. Sproat, *"The Best Men": Liberal Reformers in the Gilded Age* (New York: Oxford University Press, 1968).

48. Books indexing properties owned, book 1, 41 and 42, MS, United States Smelting, Mining, Refining, and Mining Company records, Sharon Steel Site, Midvale, Utah.

49. Woodruff, *Journal,* 6:499 (Oct. 16, 1869).

50. Harrison's response is quoted in Leonard J. Arrington, *Brigham Young: American Moses* (New York: Knopf, 1985), 358. My discussion of the trial is based on 358–61.

51. Woodruff, *Journal,* 6:501 (Oct. 25, 1869); See Walker, "The Godbeite Protest," 243.

52. On this affair, see Thomas G. Alexander, "'Federal Authority versus Polygamic Theocracy': James B. McKean and the Mormons, 1870–1875," *Dialogue* 1 (Autumn 1966): 85–100.

53. For general studies of polygamy and Mormon polygamous lifestyles, see Richard S. Van Wagoner, *Mormon Polygamy: A History,* 2d ed. (Salt Lake City: Signature Books, 1989), and Jessie L. Embry, *Mormon Polygamous Families: Life in the Principle* (Salt Lake City: University of Utah Press, 1987).

54. For detailed discussions of these matters, see Alexander, "Polygamic Theocracy"; Edwin Brown Firmage and R. Collin Mangrum, *Zion in the Courts: A Legal History of the Church of Jesus Christ of Latter-day Saints, 1830–1900* (Urbana: University of Illinois Press, 1988); and Thomas G. Alexander, "The Utah Federal Courts and the Areas of Conflict, 1850–96" (M.A. thesis, Utah State University, 1961).

55. Woodruff, *Journal,* 7:63 (Mar. 9, 1872).

56. Brigham Young to Wilford Woodruff and Erastus Snow, July 16, 1877, Brigham Young Letterbook no. 15, 22–25, LDS Archives.

57. Woodruff, *Journal,* 7:363 (July 25, 1877).

58. On the Protestant beliefs, see George Marsden, *Fundamentalism and American Culture: The Shaping of Twentieth-Century Evangelicalism, 1870–1925* (New York: Oxford University Press, 1980), esp. 51–54. For the Latter-day Saint view, see Louis Reinwand, "An Interpretive Study of Mormon Millennialism during the Nineteenth Century with Emphasis on Millennial Developments in Utah" (M.A. thesis, Brigham Young University, 1971); Grant Underwood, "Seminal versus Sesquicentennial Saints: A Look at Mormon Millennialism," *Dialogue* 14 (Spring 1981): 32–44; Grant Underwood, "Millenarianism in the Early Mormon Mind," *Journal of Mormon History* 9 (1982): 41–51; Grant Underwood, "Early Mormon Millenarianism: Another Look," *Church History* 54 (June 1985): 215–29; Grant Underwood, *The Millenarian World of Early Mormonism* (Urbana: University of Illinois Press, 1993); and David J. Whittaker, "Early Mormon Use of the Book of Daniel," unpublished essay in the author's possession.

59. For the text of the revelation, see Fred C. Collier, ed., *Unpublished Revelations of the Prophets and Presidents of the Church of Jesus Christ of Latter Day Saints* (Salt Lake City: Collier's, 1979), 1:123–29.

60. On the question of the constituencies of the Republican party, see Richard J. Jensen, *The Winning of the Midwest: Social and Political Conflict, 1888–1896* (Chicago: University of Chicago Press, 1971); and Paul Kleppner, *The Cross of Culture: A Social Analysis of Midwestern Politics, 1850–1900*, 2d ed. (New York: Free Press, 1970).

61. Franklin S. Richards to Wilford Woodruff and George Q. Cannon, Feb. 28, Mar. 22, 1888, Franklin S. Richards Correspondence, Utah State Historical Society Library, Salt Lake City. In August 1887, Richards had made similar points in a letter to George Ticknor Curtis. He pointed out that when the revelation was first received many entered the practice because they believed the revelation made the practice mandatory. Many who did not enter did so on the plea that it was permissive, not mandatory. The difference of opinion as to the construction still exists. Still, he pointed out, the people are united in believing that the prohibitory clauses of the 1887 constitution ought to be enforced. Richards to George Ticknor Curtis, Aug. 27, 1887, Richards Correspondence. For the complete hearings, see U.S. Senate, Committee on Territories, *Admission of Utah: Report of a Hearing before the Committee on Territories of the United States Senate in Regard to the Proposed Admission of the Territory of Utah as a State in the Federal Union*, 2 parts (Washington, D.C.: GPO, 1888). Wilford Woodruff to William M. Paxman, Apr. 2, 1888, and Woodruff to George Teasdale, Apr. 4, 1888, First Presidency, Letters sent, LDS Archives.

62. Heber J. Grant, journal, Dec. 29, 1887, LDS Archives.

63. Ibid.; Woodruff, *Journal*, 8:473–74 (Dec. 29, 1887).

64. Woodruff, *Journal*, 8:482 (Jan. 24, 1888); Roberts, *Comprehensive History*, 6:201.

65. See Edward Leo Lyman, *Political Deliverance: The Mormon Quest for Utah Statehood* (Urbana: University of Illinois Press, 1986), 100–103; Franklin D. Richards, journal, May 7, 1888, LDS Archives; Grant, journal, Oct. 22, 1888.

66. Abraham H. Cannon, journal, Nov. 30, 1889, Manuscripts Department, Harold B. Lee Library, Brigham Young University, Provo, Utah.

67. Woodruff also received a new revelation in connection with this incident. The revelation reaffirmed the basic principles that the church leadership had taught previously, but in a much less strident or apocalyptic tone than the 1880 Wilderness Revelation. The church leadership was told not to "deny my word or my law." The revelation said they should not place "yourselves in jeopardy to your enemies by promise." The revelation promised further that the Lord would remain with the Saints and that he would pour out his judgments "upon all nations under the heavens which include great Babylon." The judgments stood "at the door," and the Lord promised to deliver the Saints from the wicked "in mine own due time and way." Woodruff, *Journal*, 9:67–69 (Nov. 24, 1889). Apparently, the revelation was well received by members of the Twelve. See Brigham Young Jr., journal, Nov. 24, 1889, LDS Archives; Cannon, journal, Dec. 19, 1889.

68. Cannon, journal, Dec. 6, 1889; Grant, journal, Dec. 6, 1889.

69. Cannon, journal, Dec. 12, 1889; Grant, journal, Dec. 28, 1889. The First Presidency telegraphed those apostles who were available for permission to attach their signatures and Woodruff authorized the signatures of those who were not available.

70. James R. Clark, *Messages of the First Presidency of the Church of Jesus Christ of Latter-day Saints,* vol. 3 (Salt Lake City: Bookcraft, 1966), 184–87.

71. The information on the 1890 election in Salt Lake City is based on Cannon, journal, Oct. 11, 17, 18, 19, Nov. 12, Dec. 28, 1889, Jan. 8, 14, 20, 23, 27, 29, 31, Feb. 3, 6, 7, 9, 1890; Wilford Woodruff to George Q. Cannon, Feb. 3, 1890; Wilford Woodruff and Joseph F. Smith to George Q. Cannon, Jan. 21, 1890; Wilford Woodruff (per James Jack) and Joseph F. Smith to Moses Thatcher, Jan. 23, 1890; Wilford Woodruff and Joseph F. Smith to George Teasdale, Jan. 27, 1890; First Presidency to George Q. Cannon, Jan. 29, 1890; and Wilford Woodruff to Abraham O. Smoot, Jan. 30, 1890, all in First Presidency, Letters sent, LDS Archives. Wilford Woodruff and Joseph F. Smith to George Q. Cannon, Jan. 29, 1890; James Jack to John T. Caine, Jan. 29, 1890; and Wilford Woodruff to George Q. Cannon, Feb. 3, 1890, all in Wilford Woodruff Letterbooks, LDS Archives; Grant, journal, Jan. 8, 9, 20, 21, 23, 25, 29, Feb. 3, 5, 8, 10, 1890.

72. Woodruff, *Journal,* 9:74 (Dec. 31, 1889).

73. Grant, journal, July 23, 1888; Lewis Allen (Woodruff) to William Atkin, July 26, 1888, Woodruff-Atkin Correspondence, Utah State Historical Society Library, Salt Lake City; Wilford Woodruff to John Henry Smith, Aug. 9, 1888, Wilford Woodruff Letterbooks; Wilford Woodruff to W. B. Dougall, Sept. 10, 1888, First Presidency, Letters sent; Young, journal, Sept. 19, 1888.

74. Lewis Allen (Woodruff) to William Atkin, May 23, 1888, Woodruff-Atkin Correspondence; Wilford Woodruff to George Teasdale, May 23, 1888, First Presidency, Letters sent; First Presidency to John T. Caine, June 16, 1888, Wilford Woodruff Letterbooks; Wilford Woodruff to Daniel H. Wells, June 19, 1888, First Presidency, Letters Sent; Arrington, *Great Basin Kingdom,* 372.

75. See Late Corporation of the Church of Jesus Christ of Latter-day Saints v. U.S. (136 U.S. 1, 1890). Woodruff heard the decision read on June 9, 1890, Woodruff, *Journal,* 9:97 (June 9, 1990).

76. Cannon, journal, July 16, 1890.

77. On October 5, 1888, shortly before the church completed the settlement with Utah Territory and appealed the suit to the U.S. Supreme Court, Woodruff met with representatives of the church leadership, the church attorneys, and some of the federal officials. Frank Dyer and George Peters urged him to renounce polygamy as part of the settlement and save the church's property in the bargain. Woodruff told them he "would see the whole Nation D——d first." Woodruff, *Journal,* 8:520 (Oct. 5, 1888). Lewis Allen (Woodruff) to William Atkin, Nov. 2, 1888, Woodruff-Allen Correspondence. See also Young, journal, Oct. 5, 1888, and Grant, journal, Oct. 5, 1888.

78. Woodruff, *Journal,* 8:520 (Oct. 8, 1888). Lewis Allen (Woodruff) to William Atkin, Nov. 2, 1888, Woodruff-Allen Correspondence. See also Young, journal, Oct. 5, 1888, and Grant, journal, Oct. 5, 1888.

79. On June 12, 1890, Secretary of State James G. Blaine gave a paper to George Q. Cannon, who was then visiting in Washington, for the "leading authorities of the Church to sign in which they make a virtual renunciation of plural marriage." Cannon's son Abraham said that he felt "revolt at signing such a document." Cannon, journal, June 12, 1890, see also July 10, 1890; Jan Shipps, "The Principle Revoked: A Closer Look at the Demise of Plural Marriage," *Journal of Mormon History* 11 (1984): 71.

80. Cannon, journal, Sept. 1, 1890; Woodruff, *Journal*, 9:109 (Sept. 2, 1890); Lyman, *Political Deliverance*, 135.

81. This story has been told elsewhere. See Thomas G. Alexander, *Things in Heaven and Earth: The Life and Times of Wilford Woodruff, a Mormon Prophet* (Salt Lake City: Signature Books, 1991), 265–66.

82. The original spelling is retained.

83. On this point, see Thomas G. Alexander, "The Odyssey of Latter-day Prophet: Wilford Woodruff and the Manifesto of 1890," *Journal of Mormon History* 17 (1991): 169–206.

84. Thomas G. Alexander, "Charles S. Zane, Apostle of the New Era," *Utah Historical Quarterly* 34 (Fall 1966): 312.

85. On the problems involved, see D. Michael Quinn, "LDS Church Authority and New Plural Marriages, 1890–1904," *Dialogue* 18 (Spring 1985): 9–105.

86. On these matters, see Thomas G. Alexander, *Mormonism in Transition: A History of the Latter-day Saints, 1890–1930* (Urbana: University of Illinois Press, 1986); Thomas G. Alexander, "The Reconstruction of Mormon Doctrine: From Joseph Smith to Progressive Theology," *Sunstone* 10 (May 1985): 8–18; and Thomas G. Alexander, "The Manifesto: Mormondom's Watershed," *This People* (Fall 1990): 21–27.

10

Renewal and Modernization among American Mennonites, 1800–1980: Restorationist?

THERON F. SCHLABACH

In the early 1950s Harold S. Bender, the leading Mennonite interpreter of sixteenth-century Anabaptism, objected when a fellow scholar named Franklin H. Littell presented Anabaptists as restorationists. "However brilliant and challenging" that interpretation, Bender rejoined, Littell had rooted Anabaptism too much in a cultural idea and not enough in religious impulses. He thought Littell should have made more of Anabaptists' emphasis on "obedience to Christ and personal attachment to Jesus as Lord"; for, Bender insisted, Anabaptists' most central idea was radical discipleship. Wrote he: "I am still inclined to make discipleship the central controlling idea more than primitivism and restitution."[1] Since that exchange, other scholars have explored the early European Anabaptists' views of history and the questions of their primitivism, restorationism, and restitutionism;[2] but there has been less such study of the later Mennonites and Amish of America.[3]

Had Littell made his point about Mennonites and Amish in America, especially those before the midtwentieth century, someone would need to dissent even more. Yet, many scholars have operated with precisely this assumption, largely because of a widespread tendency to equate present-day Mennonitism with the writings of Mennonite scholar John Howard Yoder, who, throughout much of his career, has emphasized this theme. In light of that tendency, and after two generations' talk of a "Recovery of the Anabaptist Vision," it is understandable that scholars might see Mennonites as restorationists.

Yet, the theme of primitivism hardly helps one to understand American Mennonites and Amish for most of their history. For Mennonites and Amish in America certain ideas that we may once again label radical discipleship were central—while restorationism, carefully defined, seldom was. Also very important were more sociological impulses: *denominationalism,* the American pattern which, like the state-church pattern in Europe, put pressure on smaller groups to meld into the larger civic-religious community; *acculturation,* often via patterns that were or appeared to be quests for religious renewal; and *modernization,* especially as expressed in the building of denominational institutions, activism, and programs.

Defining Terms

There are the usual problems of definition. First of all, *radical discipleship.* In this essay the term implies more than simply a determination to follow the Lord Jesus faithfully. Presumably all earnest Christians strive for that, by one formula or another. The core ideas of radical discipleship among Mennonites in America, at least among the less acculturated, were more specific. Those Mennonites had an understanding of Christianity that emphasized the ethical fruits of regeneration somewhat more than the removal of guilt and alienation. They understood God's grace as enabling right living as much as offering forgiveness; while they trusted grace and ultimately not works, they had little of the Protestant fear that to emphasize ethics, deeds, outward symbols, and quality of being necessarily implied a religion of works. In their radical discipleship they tended strongly to treat the New Testament as qualitatively different from the Old in God's revelation and to treat Jesus' teachings and the Gospels as more essential than Pauline theology and the Epistles. And they assumed that there were two kingdoms sharply at odds in human affairs. On earth, quite literally and visibly (albeit still imperfectly), the church of the truly faithful represented God's kingdom. The other kingdom, of course, was that of the fallen, unregenerated "world." The world's governments ruled by sub-Christian ethics. Yet those governments derived their authority from God. God instituted government to keep some semblance of justice and order in the realm of the unregenerate and to protect the true Christians as the Christians went about vulnerably to do God's work. The Christian way, the vulnerable way, will ever be the narrow way. Radical discipleship will never be popular. The true church will always be the "little flock." Ipso facto, any church that is or tries to be popular or to embrace the whole society must be false.

This concept of radical discipleship is embedded in works such as the 1632 Dordrecht Confession, the *Martyrs Mirror,* and Menno Simons's *Foundation Book*—writings that Mennonites brought with them to North America from the time they first arrived in the seventeenth century. More or less, this concept lasted among Mennonites in America into the twentieth century. Deep inroads of Pietism and then American revivalism partly competed with it but did not destroy it. Sometimes they even reinforced commitment to radical discipleship.[4]

The second idea needing definition is of course that of *Christian primitivism* or *restorationism.* I am a novice to the concept's subtleties, but I seem to find definitions at three confusing levels.[5]

At one level scholars use the terms *primitivism* and *restorationism* very casually. Any favorable reference to a past age, any admiration of a religion's founders, or any serious biblicism becomes evidence that primitivism and restorationism are at work. The net is so broad that even Episcopalian reformers fall into it.[6] Richard T. Hughes, surely an authority on primitivism as I am not, has seemed to approve; but he then has had to struggle with the danger that, in his own words, "if all are primitivists, then none are primitivists," because the term loses all meaning. To my mind the broad definition catches too many. The nets strain, the boat sinks, and even the savior on the shore—Hughes—can scarcely rescue it.[7]

At the next two levels the definitions are more careful. There we find primitivism or restorationism only if a thinker or a group really tries to imitate a time of founding—that of the apostles, the sixteenth century, or whenever. From this view, the founding time cannot have been an era of immaturity and imperfection; it must represent considerable purity. Such a criterion has a problem: it may have little place for history and tradition. It may treat history and tradition as irrelevant or, again using a word from Hughes, as lacking "jurisdiction."[8] Must we, then, try to turn the calendar back? If that hardly seems possible, one solution is to try to recapture no more than the seminal spirit and beliefs of the original, rather than the primitive church's whole structure. In that case we seek only the essence and do not say that Christians can transplant a model from one historical time to another.[9] With that caveat, we have a second level of definition.

Finally, there is the third level. It is more literalist and is even more pessimistic about the course history has taken.[10] At worst history and tradition are a sad story of falling away.[11] According to an analysis in 1977 by John H. Yoder, this view is not ahistorical as historian Sidney Mead and others have charged; it takes history seriously but treats history's outcomes as needing critique rather than as traditions to invest with authority.[12] Yoder seemed to imply a largely negative critique; and it seems that such a judgment on the outcome of history implies that restorationists should aim to reproduce not merely the essence and the seminal beliefs of the normative age but also the age's outlook and social structure. In the extreme, those who operate at this third level of definition seem to imply that we should reverse history or leap across it. Apparently they hope to capture not only the original faith's essence but also much of its mood, its doctrines, its practices, its polity, its application, its worldview.[13]

By one or more of these definitions, is the idea of primitivism useful for understanding Mennonites in America?

By the casual, first-level definition we might make an apparent case for restorationism among American Mennonites and Amish. From their arrival in the seventeenth century until well into the nineteenth, Menno Simons's *Foundation Book* and Thieleman van Braght's *Martyrs Mirror* shaped their view of the Bible and of Christian faith. Each book used a basic paradigm of the Christian church's apostasy and the preservation of the faithful church of the New Testament. Van Braght, especially, offered an alternative history. His *Martyrs Mirror* posited a chain of faithful, dissenting groups throughout the centuries, groups who for Mennonites comprised a kind of apostolic succession—spiritually if not organically and institutionally. Mainline church tradition and history, as carried by the Catholics and continued too much by the Reformers, held virtually no authority. At least until the midtwentieth century, this general view of history informed American Mennonites and their Amish cousins, although scholarship in the twentieth century altered the details.

Moreover in the eighteenth century and through much of the nineteenth, Mennonites and Amish often spoke of keeping to the "old foundations" or the ways of the fathers. And very often they looked back to New Testament precedents for specific practices, for instance the rite of feet washing, the lot for selecting ministers, and formulas for church discipline. And certainly they were biblicists. Thus, by the casual, first-level definition they surely appear to have been primitivists. At points those Mennonites appear to have been restorationists even by the second- and third-level definitions. Indeed, in 1763 a posthumous book by the first Mennonite author in America to publish original work, Bishop Heinrich Funck of the Skippack region north of Philadelphia, appeared with the title *Eine Restitution . . .*, or *A Restitution . . . .* However, that book's subtitle as later translated was *An Explanation of Several Principal Points of the Law; How It Has Been Fulfilled by Christ, and Will Reach Its Perfect Consummation in His Great Day.* And indeed, the book was not mainly a plan for restoring Christ's original church in Funck's day; instead it was an elaborate discussion of how Old Testament symbols pointed forward to Christ and Christian eschatology.[14] Nor did it begin any notable changes or renewal movements among Mennonites in America.

A careful analysis of major renewal movements and changes in Mennonite and Amish thought and outlook until about the midtwentieth century creates doubt that primitivism was a major theme among Mennonites and Amish in America. There were five such major developments: (1) about 1800, a shift from suffering to humility as the organizing idea for church-world dualism and radical discipleship; (2) in the midnineteenth century, emergence of a more progressivist branch, first with a schism in 1847 centering around John H. Oberholtzer, a minister in eastern Pennsylvania, and then more broadly with the founding, in Iowa, of the General Conference Mennonite denomination in 1860; (3) in the late nineteenth century, in the so-called "old" Mennonite and Amish Mennonite fellowships, adoption and adaptation of American revivalism and of Protestant denominationalism—in some instances deeply altering the theology and styles of those who stayed Mennonite and in other cases creating new groups even more attuned to American evangelicalism; (4) meanwhile, in the mid- to late nineteenth century, emergence of smaller "Old Order" Mennonite and Amish communions both for renewal and in reaction to progressivist, revivalist, and denominationalist developments; and (5) not least, in the midtwentieth century, the impact of "Anabaptist vision" scholarship.

Humility Theology

In 1804, with the endorsement of other key eastern Pennsylvania Mennonite ministers, Christian Burkholder, a bishop in Lancaster County, published a small book of Christian instruction he had composed in 1792. Written as a conversation between a kindly pastor and an inquiring youth, the book carried a title that translates as *Useful and Edifying Addresses to Youth on True Repentance and Saving Faith in Jesus Christ, Pure Love to God and Our Neighbor, Obedience to the Word of God, and a Full Surrender of the Soul.*[15] By 1900 the volume had appeared in ten German and four English printings. The most historic feature of Burkholder's book was that it articulated fully and well what may be called "a Mennonite theology of humility." In it the ultimate mark of faithfulness was no longer suffering but a deep attitude and practical lifestyle that eschewed all marks of pride. Whether because of the book's influence or due to larger forces, for eight or nine decades after 1804 humility theology dominated the main bodies of Mennonites and Amish in America. Why that theology appeared is a question needing more study. One answer may be some impact of Pietism; another may be that in America, Mennonites were not doing much suffering.[16] In either case the new theology suited the tolerant American environment far better than did the old suffering theology. And it repaired the foundations of radical discipleship.[17]

The book was also a response to denominationalism. Burkholder wrote that Scripture indicated "the Lord has a church, and has given it a law, and that primitive Christians were under one bond of communion" but that now the church seemed confused and declining.[18] Still, Burkholder advised his fictional youth not to be too concerned; instead, "direct your mind's eye to Jesus," the true church's cornerstone.[19] He had the youth ask explicitly whether "one church [was] to be preferred to another." The answer: "I do not venture to say that our church has any preference," and we are not to commend ourselves. Jesus had advised that when we have done all, we are still unprofitable servants.[20] Again he had his youth ask why not marry across denominational lines. "Are there not many pious, discerning Christians" outside of our own church?[21] On that practical question Burkholder advised that intermarriage would tempt youths to pervert marriage into an unhumble quest for reputation and power. Also, intermarriage would make church discipline difficult. And, in a point more ingenious than convincing, Burkholder recalled that God had enjoined the Israelites not to intermarry even with other Israelite tribes. This was in order to prevent various temptations. But, said Burkholder, the command did not mean that God necessarily preferred one tribe over another.[22]

Burkholder did not embrace other churches, but neither did he put them outside the Christian pale. Not quite all Mennonites walked so fine a line. In 1812, in Burkholder's own county, a certain John Herr broke away to begin the "Reformed Mennonites," a group that still exists as a tiny denomination; and that group was so radically exclusive that it said no other denomination, Mennonite or other, was really Christian.[23] But the vast majority of Mennonites dealt with denominationalism much as did Burkholder. In 1841 Benjamin Eby, a bishop in Ontario, suggested that God let other Protestants divorce, swear oaths, and wage war because of the "hardness of their hearts." Yet, he said, "we do not blame them very much. . . . [Since] God has patience with [both them and us] . . . we should all abstain from any hard judgment."[24]

The thought patterns of humility-era Mennonites and Amish were quite different from the restorationism of Thomas Campbell and Alexander Campbell. Scholars seem to agree that the Campbell response to denominational confusion had strong elements of, or at least much affinity with, Lockean thought and rationalism. The Campbells thought that applying human reason and taking Scripture at face value would lead Christians to agree rationally on the New Testament model of the church; and by a rational return to that model, they would eliminate the confusion of denominational and sectarian quarreling.[25] The response of Burkholder and other Mennonites in the next seven or eight decades did not rest on such rationalism. In the previous century, while Anglo-Saxons had been imbibing John Locke or Common Sense philosophy, Germanic Mennonites had been taking the sweet, gentle milk of Continental Pietism.[26] Burkholder's answers were those of a gentle pastor and tribal elder, not the reasoned arguments of rational debate. Even though he and nineteenth-century Mennonites who followed quoted Scripture after Scripture, they were not proof-texting since "proof" implies tight argument.[27] Like Burkholder, who pointed to the tribes of Israel to offer an answer about interdenominational marriage, humility-era Mennonites used Scriptures for types and analogies, not tight argument. Scripture was a guide to practical living rather than a set of rational proofs.

Similarly, Burkholder and those who followed did not rationalize an earlier age to imitate. Burkholder might use language that a translator rendered into English in 1857 as the unity of "primitive Christians."[28] Or, on the question of baptism, he might advise his youth to "examine the doctrine of Christ and his apostles . . . and rather follow them than all other received customs."[29] Even in that last statement, however, he was trying to continue Mennonite tradition as much as trying to restore something lost. By shifting from suffering to humility, Burkholder and others, such as midnineteenth-century Ohio bishop John M. Brenneman, altered the tradition. But the change was evolutionary and unconscious, not an effort to sweep away present patterns in order to go back to an earlier one. Overall, humility-era thought patterns were a reworking of the radical-discipleship tradition, not restorationism.

The Progressivism of John H. Oberholtzer and the Early General Conference Branch

In 1847, Mennonites of the Franconia Conference, living in counties about thirty to fifty miles north of Philadelphia, divided. The division occurred around one John H. Oberholtzer, a schoolteacher, printer, locksmith, and recently ordained minister. Oberholtzer and his supporters thought that conference authorities were high-handed and arbitrary; the conference's partisans thought the issue was the dissenters' prideful resistance to church decisions. Modern historians easily see the

stresses and strains caused by acculturation, by quarrels in the larger
national culture, and by change from traditionalism to modernity. In
addition to being slow to put on a certain kind of coat required of ministers—certainly a question of church tradition, not primitivism—Oberholtzer wanted a shift from traditional oral authority to the rationalized kind. He did not put the issue exactly that way, but almost: he
demanded that the conference begin to keep formal minutes and he
wrote a constitution though the conference had never had one before.
In such demands, modernization was at work, as well as in other points
Oberholtzer favored. Nurture- and print-minded, Oberholtzer began
a modern institution-building process by starting a kind of Sunday
school and a printing press. One article of Oberholtzer's constitution
tended to open the way for modern business, by allowing for members to resort to lawsuits for just cause. Other broad influences surely
at work and closely related to modernization were growing wealth
among Mennonites in an economically developing region, the attrac-
tions of political participation, and several decades of debate about
public education.[30]

Denominationalism was also a factor. In their new constitution or
in early decisions of a new conference that they formed, Oberholtzer's
supporters quickly showed themselves ready to reciprocate in various ways with neighboring Protestant congregations. They specifically
allowed marriage across denominational lines and accepted other
churches' baptisms if performed upon confession of faith.[31] Within
five years they decided that worthy Christians of other churches could
commune in the "new" Mennonite congregations, even if baptized as
infants.[32] They opened their congregations' pulpits to all Christian
ministers deemed to be evangelical, of sound doctrine, and "in regular standing in their [own] Synods and churches."[33] And they began
building institutions: supporting a kind of Sunday school Oberholtzer
had begun and a printing press and paper that he started and showing interest in missions.

In 1860 a meeting took place at West Point, Iowa, that launched
another new Mennonite group usually known as the General Conference Mennonite church, eventually the second largest Mennonite body
in North America. Oberholtzer attended and his conference joined. But
the main promoters were recent immigrants from provinces along the
Rhine River in Germany. Since they were newcomers, their motives,
compared to Oberholtzer's, had less to do with negative reaction against
American Mennonite traditionalism; nor were they attracted as much
to American denominationalism. Instead they hoped to promote Mennonite unity by allowing congregationalism and diversity. Such plural-

ism smacked of modernity. So also did another goal, that of starting institutions and programs, especially for mission and for education. The new conference soon established a mission fund and by 1868 it founded a college at Wadsworth, Ohio—short-lived, but important as the first institution of higher education in America sponsored by a Mennonite church body. Neither the conference nor the college put any notable emphasis on humility or keeping the "little flock" in tension with the world. Various progressive Mennonite congregations joined the conference, including some relatively recent immigrants from Switzerland and then, in the 1870s, quite a few who arrived from the Russian empire and took up life on the prairies.[34]

Students of the Oberholtzer and General Conference movements will have to look long and hard to find traces of primitivism. Efforts for vitalization and renewal, yes, but not via restorationism or primitivism. Oberholtzer's group set its constitution up as an authority alongside Scripture; for instance, the constitution said that a person who believed the church had exercised discipline wrongly had no case "if the complainant cannot prove that the decision is in contradiction to the Holy Scriptures or to this constitution."[35] Certainly what emerged was not primitivism by the third definition, and it was scarcely so, if at all, by the second. The models were not from some past age; rather, they were those of well-established Protestant denominations and of modern Protestant enterprises for education and mission. The impulses of institution building, and in Oberholtzer's case denominationalism and acculturation, are clear.

Further, if these progressives hoped to promote radical discipleship, they pursued it without great emphasis on suffering, humility, or the two-kingdom analysis. As for other traditional points, the Oberholtzer group and the new General Conference branch taught Mennonite pacifism; but oddly, the founding document of the new General Conference did not mention that principle.[36] Moreover, one leader later reported that in early sessions of the General Conference, held during the U.S. Civil War, pacifism was a "delicate" issue.[37] And while Oberholtzer's constitution reaffirmed pacifism, during the Civil War the conference founded under that constitution made discipline for military service a matter for each congregation to decide. Also, the constitution contained the clause that partly relaxed the rule against suing at law.[38] Such changes began to blur the sharp line between church and world and between God's ethic for Christians and God's more permissive ethic for government. Coupled with acceptance of denominationalism, the blurring undermined the idea of the "little flock" in a fallen and hostile world.

Nor did the progressive reformers refer notably to a normative time in the past. They could have argued quite correctly that sixteenth-century Anabaptists had been activist and zealous at evangelism; but at that time, Anabaptism was not particularly a model for Mennonites. Radical discipleship in its traditional forms was beginning to yield. But it was not yielding to primitivism.

The Impact of Revivalism

Oberholtzer and the new General Conference were not revivalist. But in the "old" and Amish Mennonite churches, beginning slowly in the 1860s and reaching a crescendo from about 1890 to 1910, there was a historic quickening. (Most of the "old" and Amish Mennonites would later merge to form the largest of the Mennonite denominations, often called the "old" or the "MC" Mennonite church.) Partisans who favored the new tempo usually called it by the revivalists' term, *awakening; quickening* is a more neutral term.[39] Stimulating that tempo were various Protestant influences, including the Sunday school movement of the time, the mission movement, church publications, and revivalism, especially the Wesleyan variety. Also, many commentators then and later have pointed to reaction against traditional Mennonite and Amish leaders' legalism, formalism, and preoccupation with old ways. Such comments have usually been quite partisan, but partisan comments can carry truth. Finally, secular forces may have been at least as important as religious impulses. Modern historians are likely to point to the way that nationhood was dissolving particularism, to processes of acculturation and of modernization, to the power of American denominationalism, and to specific factors such as the influence of public schools and the younger generations' use of English.[40]

In any case the tempo of "old" and Amish Mennonite church life quickened. Beginning slowly in the 1860s and reaching its speed from about 1890 to 1910, the quickening induced "old" and Amish Mennonites to begin publications, Sunday schools, tract societies, missions, Bible conferences, ministers' meetings, youth activities, charitable homes, colleges, more centralized conference structures, women's organizations, and more. It was a progressive, denomination-building[41] movement that borrowed heavily from Protestant models, and thus on the surface it may appear much like developments that produced the General Conference church. In fact, there were deep differences. In the General Conference story there was virtually no revivalism; but the "old" Mennonites accepted a subdued version of that American phenomenon, due largely to the leadership of evangelist John S. Coffman from Virginia. Virginia had long been a frontier area for Mennonites where United Brethren and other brands of revivalism were strong, even among German speakers.

On the other hand, just as the "old" and Amish Mennonite quickening was at peak tempo and just as it was opening Mennonite windows to outside breezes and greater pluralism, some new young leaders, led especially by an editor named Daniel Kauffman, began a kind of countermovement. That movement used the new, more modern structures to centralize control over institutions and beliefs and to shore up church discipline. The result was that as a church the "old" Mennonites clung firmly to traditional Mennonite nonresistance and they codified and strengthened their nonconformity—even though they combined it with a more revivalistic soteriology and even though they now made activism, rather than humility, the central mark of Christian faithfulness.[42] As they clung to such key doctrines as nonresistance and nonconformity, they sharpened the boundaries between themselves and other denominations. The "old" Mennonite reformers from about 1880 to 1930 were sufficiently acculturated to share in an American and Western penchant for building larger-scale, more rationalized institutions, and to a degree they adopted Protestant forms and soteriology.[43] They therefore borrowed massively. But paradoxically, in the end they turned their borrowings and their new denominational institutions into stronger Mennonite separatism.[44]

Once more, the dynamic was not primitivism.[45] To be sure, the quickening's publisher, John F. Funk of Elkhart, Indiana, published Anabaptist works, including an English edition of founder Menno Simons's complete writings and a new English-language edition of the *Martyrs Mirror.* Occasionally a Mennonite might recall that the Anabaptists had been missionary.[46] And Mennonites remained as biblicist as ever. However, their biblicism was no doubt a matter of tradition more than clear evidence of primitivism; moreover, by the 1920s to some degree they were biblicist in a new way, having been influenced by Protestant Fundamentalism.[47] Also, surely more from tradition than from primitivism, the stronger discipline and sharper separatism meant that the concepts of radical discipleship and the "little flock" remained; but due to revivalistic soteriology those concepts too survived in somewhat altered forms. In any case restoration was not the central motif of those decades: restoration neither of Anabaptism[48] nor of the New Testament church, restoration neither of structure nor in any explicit way of essence. Certainly a central motif and indeed a central reality was renewal: but the devices for renewal were using more rationalism, becoming more Protestant, and building new denominational programs and structures.

Old Orders

Long before Daniel Kauffman's day there was another kind of renewal that rejected progressivism and quickening. This kind brought forth
the Old Order fellowships, both Mennonite and Amish. As early as the
1840s a prototype appeared around Jacob Stauffer, a relatively literate
and articulate Mennonite minister of Lancaster County, Pennsylvania.
Groups fully recognized as Old Order Mennonites emerged in Indiana and Ohio in the 1870s, in Ontario in 1889, in Pennsylvania's Lancaster County in 1893, and in Virginia's Shenandoah Valley about
1900. They emerged around various issues, especially opposition to
Sunday schools and revival meetings. Meanwhile Amish congregations
sorted themselves between Old Order and the more progressive. This
occurred especially from 1862 to 1878 through a series of specially
called, almost-annual Amish ministers' conferences. The ministers
failed to resolve Amish differences. A few formed new, usually revivalistic churches. Some of the progressives took steps that eventually
led into the General Conference Mennonite church. Most Amish were
soon moving toward the "old" Mennonite church, with whom they
merged early in the twentieth century. But a sizable minority became
Old Order Amish and retained the Amish name.[49]

Surely a great temptation for Old Orders has been legalism; yet the
idea that theirs is a religion of works and not of grace is simply wrong.[50]
Often, critics make that mistake because they look through an intellectually rigid Protestant lens. Nor have Old Orders simply been reactionaries. There was a great deal of reactionism among Old Order
founders, but to dismiss them merely as reactionary is not helpful. Nor
is the central issue a resistance to modernity and technology. Old Orders have become highly visible by resisting certain technologies, but
that resistance has been a means rather than an end. It is a means to
control the groups' sociologies in order to preserve the all-important
qualities of community and church.[51] Old Orders are not necessarily
holdouts against modernity; at least one sociologist, Marc A. Olshan,
has argued that they are true moderns, for instead of being fatalistic
they have taken control and made their own choices.[52]

Finally, the Old Orders have not stood merely against. Their fellowships began as movements for renewal as certainly and perhaps as
thoughtfully as did the progressive movements. Their founders believed
that spirituality can come through rigorous discipline. Their framework
of discipline was the idea of *Ordnung*, an idea difficult to express apart
from that German word. No doubt for many Old Order people the idea
is essentially legalistic. But among more thoughtful Old Order spokes-

persons, the scholar can detect a wide-ranging, philosophical ideal. *Ordnung* captures the moral design that the creator God has structured into the universe. It puts the Christian in touch with divinely created natural law. To violate it is to walk away from the blessings, that is, from the *Gottseligkeit,* the God-blessedness or salvation, that a loving God intended for his people. The punishment for violation is intrinsic, not imposed.[53]

As to whether the Old Order founders in the late nineteenth century were restorationists, they were essentially traditionalist, not primitivist.[54] They, of course, meant to be very biblical, but for authority on how to be so they looked to a series of eighteenth- and nineteenth-century documents and conference decisions. The Amish cherished a set of oft-copied manuscripts, mostly letters, known as *Ordnungsbriefe.* These told of decisions of various ministers' conferences in Europe and in America, conferences called ad hoc to decide very practical questions of church discipline. For the untrained farmers and craftsmen who became Amish ministers, such documents also told how to proceed with key rituals such as baptisms and weddings.[55] Meanwhile, Old Order Mennonite founders tried to follow their perceptions of key district conference decisions or of teachings by key Mennonite leaders of a generation or two earlier.[56] Neither Old Order Amish nor Old Order Mennonite founders tried in any systematic way to reconstitute the New Testament church or sixteenth-century Anabaptism or any other distant golden age. Implicitly, they accepted the authority of Amish or Mennonite tradition as it had been evolving. Thus they were not primitivists.

The Midtwentieth-Century "Recovery of the Anabaptist Vision"

The "old" and Amish Mennonite "quickening" of the late nineteenth century produced a quickening of thought as well as new colleges to accelerate that thought. Meanwhile General Conference Mennonite progressivism, programs, and colleges made for similar acceleration in that branch. So also did the presence of education-minded immigrants from the Russian empire and of erstwhile "old" Mennonites who found the General Conference branch to be intellectually more free than were the "old" Mennonites. As a result, from about 1925 to the 1960s there occurred among Mennonites in America a kind of intellectual renaissance, or at least a scholarly naissance. If one slogan came to dominate that naissance it was "The Recovery of the Anabaptist Vision." Worldwide, Mennonites became conscious of their Anabaptist forebears as they had never been since the sixteenth century. Eventually a Mennonite scholar could write sardonically,

> In Mennonite lore,
> We need not say more;
> One word is always the aptest.
> Whate'er we construe,
> To be good and true,
> We name with the word Anabaptist.[57]

Such is the case at least with many North American Mennonites. Mean-while some scholars other than Mennonites, some in major American and European universities, added their findings. An idea generated by scholars in colleges and universities penetrated remarkably deeply to less-lettered, grass-roots Mennonites in the congregations.

If recovery of a sixteenth-century ethos or set of ideas was the dom-inant slogan, was not the scholarly naissance ipso facto a primitivist or restorationist movement? And was it not even more so because two major ingredients of the ideal vision were thought to be radical bibli-cism and imitation of the New Testament church?

The case is not quite so simple. To test the hypothesis we need to look not only to verbal constructs but even more at what models the leaders of the naissance actually followed. The key leader was Harold S. Bender.

The name of Bender, churchman and educator based at Goshen College in northern Indiana, is all but synonymous with the recovery slogan. In 1943 he used the phrase *The Anabaptist Vision* as the title of his presidential address to the American Society of Church History. That address has been variously reprinted as the classic statement of how Goshen school scholarship defined the essence of Anabaptism. In 1957 *The Recovery of the Anabaptist Vision* became the title of a book of essays in Bender's honor.[58] Was Bender a primitivist?

In recent decades the scholarship growing out of that naissance has produced considerable dissent from important points in Bender's and the Goshen school's interpretation. As yet, however, there have not been many attempts to analyze and develop categories to describe the essential structure of Bender's thought. In recent years, a committee of scholars has initiated work on a life-and-times biography of Bender and has engaged Albert N. Keim of Eastern Mennonite College to be its chief researcher and writer. That work will soon appear. Until it does, any statement about whether Bender and the Goshen school represent-ed primitivism must be only sketchy and at best suggestive.

One relevant analysis, sketchy and suggestive, has existed for some time. In a lecture he gave and published in 1969,[59] John H. Yoder in-cluded Bender in a seminal discussion of innovators in the "MC" Mennonite branch since the late nineteenth century. Contrasting Anabaptist vision with Mennonite reality, and with those concepts in his title, Yoder argued that Mennonitism in modern times has been a "small *Christendom*" whose essence is all too much like the Corpus Christianum synthesis of religion and culture that the sixteenth-century Anabaptists rejected. Within that synthesis, "form determines substance." About Bender specifically, Yoder concluded:

1. Bender's rearing and education were not typical of his church.
2. He borrowed heavily, taking concepts of seminary education and reformation studies especially from Presbyterianism.
3. In adopting new ideas Bender himself exercised the Anabaptist principle of free choice; but most of his fellow Mennonites, living within their small Christendom, did not exercise free choice.
4. Bender arrived when Mennonite borrowing had proceeded so far that he did not have to deal with his church as a peoplehood or convince congregations to accept ideas. By Bender's time, Yoder said, Mennonite institutions and Mennonite power were centralized enough that Bender could and did impose new ideas from the top down.
5. The result, therefore, was more Protestant than Anabaptist.[60]

If Yoder was even half correct, then according to our definitions of *primitivism* Bender and the Goshen school certainly did not meet the third-level definition: determination to recapture the whole of a pristine era, structures and all. And if we accept Yoder's premise that the structural form reveals more substance than does the verbalized idea,[61] then Bender and his colleagues were not successful primitivists even by the second-level definition: aiming to recapture at least the essence. So despite the restorationist sound in the ringing phrase *Recovery of the Anabaptist Vision,* by this analysis the leader of the so-called "recovery" was hardly a primitivist or restorationist at all. At least he was not a successful one.

Bender and his generation were successful in other ways, one of which was to attract and motivate a number of very able students. Those students largely made up an illustrious second generation of Anabaptist-vision scholars. Ironically, despite the vision's emphasis on communalism and church, the second-generation scholars often were (and are) strong individuals; so they went various intellectual directions, which helped break down the Goshen-school consensus.[62] But in the late 1950s and in the 1960s some of the more prominent second-generation scholars such as John H. Yoder, now of Notre Dame University, and sociologist Paul Peachey, of Catholic University, took the tack of trying to recapture true Anabaptism where their mentors had failed. Yoder typically qualified his remarks to the point that it is difficult to determine just how restorationist he was.[63] But obviously more than the first generation, key members of the second generation used the criterion of recapturing not only the Anabaptist essence but also its approach to structure.

What of the historical problem? Had not so much history flowed under the bridge of time that recovery of sixteenth-century Anabaptism could be only a dream? In a 1964 paper Yoder in effect said no, for he declared that the situation facing modern Christians was essentially the same as that of the sixteenth century. At least in Western countries, Christians still lived against "a background of 'Christianized' conformity"; Western peoples still confused church and society. Internally, the church's main challenge was still to exercise a "redemptive yet binding personal discipline," including in economic life; externally its challenge was still to be independent of the state, to reject war, and to be missionary.[64]

Such an analysis informed much of Yoder's writing of that period and much of a key pamphlet series published by a loosely formed circle of second-generation scholars now remembered as the Concern group.[65] The main strategy was to turn the Anabaptist critique against midtwentieth-century Mennonitism itself, that is, against cultural and ethnic Mennonitism and against Protestantlike institutions and instruments of coercive power that Mennonite modernization had produced. Structurally, sixteenth-century Anabaptism had been anti-institutional. At least that was a key theme in some prominent second-generation voices. Those voices spoke out well ahead of the anti-institutionalists among American protesters of the 1960s. And intertwined with their anti-institutionalism was criticism of the ethnic church. In any case, one criterion was whether modern Mennonitism was at all like sixteenth-century Anabaptism, either structurally or in terms of ideas. The Anabaptist pattern, in the view of a John Yoder or a Paul Peachey, had been rejection or at least constant remaking of structure.

In 1957, in the final essay of the book honoring Bender, Peachey admitted that "certain historical situations or achievements" were "irreproducible." Scholars could never retrace the Anabaptists' steps.[66] So, at the outset, Peachey seemed to reject primitivism, at least at the third level of definition. But as his essay unfolded, Peachey reiterated that the essence of Anabaptism was to "confront Christendom ever anew with the call to radical discipleship." That, he said, was what Bender's generation had emphasized; and he suggested that the same confrontation was still the Anabaptist mission.[67] But to carry on that mission, radical Christians had to understand that the work of God in gathering a people is "self-authenticating, not bound or determined by ecclesiastical institutions."[68]

According to Peachey the important point of Anabaptism was "the rediscovery that the church is ever the continuously created fellowship of the people of God in Christ through the Spirit."[69] Did such a concept of the church mean "anarchy"? It was true, Peachey answered, that to rely "on culture and ecclesiastical structure" seemed safer. But, he asked, "in so far as we build upon a carefully guarded cultural continuity, on objectively formulated creeds or theology, [and] on uniform social institutions and cultural traits," then whence, in the new age, would come "the valiant leap of faith, the eschatological expectancy, and the radical walk of discipleship"?[70] Others of Peachey's generation asked essentially the same question—for instance, John W. Miller, chief founder of an intentional community in Evanston, Illinois. His was a radical-discipleship community who tried quite literally to translate the Sermon on the Mount into a visible fellowship and to practice sharing of goods as in the book of Acts.[71]

Thus in the end prominent members of the Anabaptist vision's second generation were restorationists at both the second and the third levels. Whatever their disclaimers,[72] they attempted to leap across history and recapture both the essence of Anabaptism and its structural pattern. The essence was radical discipleship and the ever-renewing church. The structural pattern was nonstructure, really: to transcend the cultural and ecclesiastical structures that history had produced and to be a Spirit-led, constantly recreated people of God rather than an institution. In that antistructural quest, Peachey was at least partly consistent: he continued in a local Mennonite congregation, but for his career he moved out of Mennonite institutions and hence to Catholic University of America.[73]

Conclusion

Restorationism or primitivism by any meaningful definition was significant among Mennonites in America only for a time in the midtwentieth century. Prominent members of the second generation of Anabaptist-vision scholars were restorationists, at least in the 1950s and 1960s, but their position was something new. Far more helpful than primitivism or restorationism for understanding Mennonite and Amish history in America is the concept of radical discipleship, plus sociological motifs such as acculturation, denominationalism, and the modernizing process. There have been various attempts at renewal, ranging from progressive to Old Order, but hardly any of those attempts have been essentially restorationist. At least not by any useful definition of that word.

Notes

1. Franklin H. Littell, *The Anabaptist View of the Church* (Chicago: American Society of Church History, 1952); Harold S. Bender, Review of *The Anabaptist View of the Church: An Introduction to Sectarian Protestantism* by Franklin H. Littell, *Mennonite Quarterly Review* 27 (July 1953): 249–53.

2. See esp. John H. Yoder, "Anabaptism and History: 'Restitution' and the Possibility of Renewal," in Hans-Jürgen Goertz, ed., *Umstrittenes Täufertum, 1525–1975: Neue Forschungen* (Göttingen: Vandenhoek and Ruprecht, 1975), 244–307. Yoder's footnotes offer a considerable bibliography for the topic. See also Frank Wray, "History in the Eyes of the Sixteenth Century Anabaptists" (Ph.D. diss., Yale University, 1953); Wray, "The Anabaptist Doctrine of the Restitution of the Church," *Mennonite Quarterly Review* 28 (July 1954): 186–96; H. W. Meihuizen, "The Concept of Restitution in the Anabaptism of Northwestern Europe," *Mennonite Quarterly Review* 44 (Apr. 1970): 141–58; Hans J. Hillerbrand, "Anabaptism and History," *Mennonite Quarterly Review* 45 (Apr. 1971): 107–22; Franklin H. Littell, "Research Note: In Response to Hans Hillerbrand," *Mennonite Quarterly Review* 45 (Oct. 1971): 377–80; Richard T. Hughes, "A Comparison of the Restoration Motifs of the Campbells (1809–1830) and the Anabaptists (1524–1560)," *Mennonite Quarterly Review* 45 (Oct. 1971): 312–30; Cornelius J. Dyck, "The Place of Tradition in Dutch Anabaptism," *Church History* 43 (Mar. 1974): 34–49; and Dennis D. Martin, "Nothing New under the Sun?: Mennonites and History," *Conrad Grebel Review* 5 (Winter 1987): 1–27, plus comments on Martin's article from Willard M. Swartley and from Stanley K. Johannesen, *Conrad Grebel Review* 5 (Spring 1987): 147–53, and Martin's reply in *Conrad Grebel Review* 5 (Fall 1987): 260–62. Most of these sources use the term *restitution* more than *primitivism*; they use *restorationism* hardly at all.

3. In the Martin-Swartley-Johannesen exchange (see note 2), Swartley commented on the love of tradition and institutionalism evident in two manuscripts in progress for the series Mennonite Experience in America. Those manuscripts have since been published as Theron F. Schlabach, *Peace, Faith, Nation: Mennonites and Amish in Nineteenth-Century America* (Scottdale, Pa.: Herald Press, 1988), and James C. Juhnke, *Vision, Doctrine, War: Mennonite Identity and Organization in America, 1890–1930* (Scottdale, Pa.: Herald Press, 1989).

4. Theron F. Schlabach, "Mennonites and Pietism in America, 1740–1880: Some Thoughts on the Friedmann Thesis," *Mennonite Quarterly Review* 57 (July 1983): 222–40.

5. I detect these levels especially as I read the various chapters in Richard T. Hughes, ed., *The American Quest for the Primitive Church* (Urbana: University of Illinois Press, 1988); Yoder, "Anabaptism and History"; Martin, "Nothing New under the Sun?" and the comments on it.

6. See David L. Holmes, "Restoration Ideology among Early Episcopal Evangelicals," in Hughes, ed., *American Quest*, 170.

7. Richard T. Hughes, "Introduction: On Recovering the Theme of Recovery," in Hughes, ed., *American Quest*, 5–6, 7.

8. See Grant Wacker, "Playing for Keeps: The Primitivist Impulse in Early Pentecostalism," in Hughes, ed., *American Quest*, 197; Hughes, "Introduction," esp. 4–7; Martin, "Nothing New under the Sun?" and Swartley's comment (note 2). See also Holmes, "Restoration Ideology." Hughes and Holmes manage to reconcile restorationism and respect for history; Martin sets them sharply against each other; Swartley seems to suggest that because of the restoration versus history problem, *restorationism* is not very useful.

9. Schlabach, "Mennonites and Pietism," 222–40.

10. Yoder, "Anabaptism and History," 248–49.

11. Ibid., 247. See also Hughes, "Introduction," esp. 4–7, and Holmes, "Restoration Ideology," 157. Hughes and Holmes, of course, find a way out of this rejection of history and tradition. But it seems to me their solution is to operate at what I am calling the first level of definition.

12. Yoder, "Anabaptism and History," 249–53.

13. See ibid., 249. I am using *social structure* broadly enough to include trying to be countercultural, counterinstitutional, and counterestablishment, as implied in Yoder's phrase "an alternative to the social shape of the fallen Christendom."

14. Heinrich Funck [Henry Funk], *A Restitution; or, An Explanation of Several Principal Points of the Law; How It Has Been Fulfilled by Christ, and Will Reach Its Perfect Consummation in His Great Day* (Elkhart, Ind.: Mennonite Publishing, 1915), a translation of his *Eine Restitution, oder eine Erklärung einiger Haupt-punckten des Gesetzes; wie es durch Christum erfüllert ist* (Philadelphia: Anton Armbrüster, 1763).

15. Christian Burkholder, *Useful and Edifying Address to the Young*, bound with [Gerrit Roosen], *Christian Spiritual Conversation on Saving Faith, for the Young, in Questions and Answers* (Ephrata, Pa.: A Committee of Mennonites, 1974), 173–301. This is a translation of Burkholder's *Nützliche und Erbauliche Anrede an die Jugend, von der wahren Busse, von dem Seligmachenden Glauben an Jesu Christo, und der reinen Worte Gottes, und der reinen Übergab der Seelen, an die Hand Gottes; Vorgestellt in Frag und Antwort* (Ephrata, Pa.: Bauman and Cleim, 1804).

16. Richard K. MacMaster, *Land, Piety, Peoplehood: The Establishment of Mennonite Communities in America, 1683–1790* (Scottdale, Pa.: Herald Press, 1985), 177–79.

17. For the fullest treatments of humility theology, see Schlabach, *Peace, Faith, Nation*, esp. 31–32, 87–105, 319–21; and Joseph C. Liechty, "Humility: The Foundation of Mennonite Religious Outlook in the 1860s," *Mennonite*

Quarterly Review 54 (Jan. 1980): 5–31. For another key primary source, see John M. Brenneman, *Pride and Humility: A Discourse, Setting Forth the Characteristics of the Proud and the Humble* (Elkhart, Ind.: John F. Funk, 1867). Brenneman was the midcentury's most-traveled Mennonite bishop and pastor in America and almost certainly the one with the broadest influence.

18. Burkholder, *Useful and Edifying*, 218.

19. Ibid., 218–19.

20. Ibid., 243.

21. Ibid., 237–38.

22. Ibid., 238–40.

23. Daniel Musser, *The Reformed Mennonite Church: Its Rise and Progress, with Its Principles and Doctrines* (Lancaster, Pa.: Elias Barr, 1873), 179; John Herr, *Life of John Herr* (LaSalle, N.Y.: David N. Long, 1890), reprinted from *John Herr's Complete Works* (Buffalo, N.Y.: Peter Paul and Bro., 1890), 429; Kathleen Kern, "The Reformed Mennonite Self-Conception as Christ's Sole Church; or, Heaven Won't be Crowded," Archives of the Mennonite Church, Goshen College, Goshen, Ind.

24. Benjamin Eby, *A Concise Ecclesiastical History and Doctrinal Theology of the Baptists or Mennonites* (Elkhart, Ind.: Mennonite, 1901), 98–100. This printing, however, must have been made much later. Page 7 refers to a 1938 edition of *Martyrs Mirror;* the preface is dated Berlin, Canada, August 30, 1841. The original German edition is *Kurzgefasste Kirchen Geschichte und Glaubenslehre der Taufgesinnten-Christen oder Mennoniten: Verfasst und herausgegeben von Benjamin Eby, Mennoniten Prediger* (Berlin, Canada: Heinrich Eby, 1841).

25. See Hughes, "A Comparison," 317–19; Bill J. Humble, "The Restoration Ideal in the Churches of Christ," in Hughes, ed., *American Quest,* 221; and Yoder, "Anabaptism and History," 255. See also Richard T. Hughes, "Recovering First Times: The Logic of Primitivism in American Life," in Rowland A. Sherrill, ed., *Religion and the Life of the Nation: American Recoveries* (Urbana: University of Illinois Press, 1990), 193–218. Humble and Yoder made explicit reference to Lockean and Enlightenment contexts of the Campbells' thought. However, these authors did not rule out spirit as well as reason in that thought.

26. The classic study of Mennonites and Pietism is Robert Friedmann's *Mennonite Piety through the Centuries: Its Genius and Its Literature* (Goshen, Ind.: Mennonite Historical Society, 1949); for a critique of that book, see Theron F. Schlabach, "Mennonites and Pietism," 222–40. See also MacMaster, *Land, Piety, Peoplehood,* esp. chap. 6, and Schlabach, *Peace, Faith, Nation,* esp. 87–95. Further study of Pietism and Mennonites in America is in order.

27. A good example is Brenneman's *Pride and Humility.*

28. Burkholder, *Useful and Edifying*, 218.

29. Ibid., 222.

30. See esp. Samuel Floyd Pannabecker, *Open Doors: The History of the General Conference Mennonite Church* (Newton, Kans.: Faith and Life Press,

1975), 16–29; John L. Ruth, *Maintaining the Right Fellowship: A Narrative Account of Life in the Oldest Mennonite Community in North America* (Scottdale, Pa.: Herald Press, 1984), chaps. 9 and 10; Schlabach, *Peace, Faith, Nation,* 117–27. For primary documents, including Oberholtzer's constitution, see esp. "The Oberholtzer Division," a special issue of *Mennonite Quarterly Review* 46 (Oct. 1972): 326–430.

31. John H. Oberholtzer, "Constitution of the Mennonite Brotherhood," trans. Elizabeth Bender, in "The Oberholtzer Division," special issue of *Mennonite Quarterly Review* 46 (Oct. 1972): 396, 394. The constitution is available in various other translations.

32. East Pennsylvania Mennonite Conference minutes, May 1, 1851, 17, Oct. 23, 1851, 22. The conference's minutes are available in German in Mennonite historical libraries, e.g., at Goshen College, Goshen, Ind. (used for this study), and at Bethel College, North Newton, Kans.; for English translations, see "Minutes of the Eastern District Conference of the General Conference of Mennonites of North America, 1847–1902," trans. S. M. Grubb, and "Minutes of the Eastern District Conference of the General Conference of Mennonites of North America, 1847–1902," trans. N. B. Grubb, both in typescript, with copies in various Mennonite historical libraries. (The East Pennsylvania Mennonite Conference eventually became the Eastern District Conference of the General Conference Mennonite church.)

33. East Pennsylvania Mennonite Conference minutes, May 6, 1852, 23.

34. See esp. Pannabecker, *Open Doors,* chaps. 3–5, and Schlabach, *Peace, Faith, Nation,* 127–40, 283–88.

35. Oberholtzer, "Constitution of the Mennonite Brotherhood," 392.

36. Translation in Pannabecker, *Open Doors,* 47–48.

37. Christian Krehbiel, *Prairie Pioneer: The Christian Krehbiel Story* (Newton, Kans.: Faith and Life Press, 1961), 67.

38. Oberholtzer, "Constitution of the Mennonite Brotherhood," 395, 396; East Pennsylvania Mennonite Conference minutes, Oct. 1861, Oct. 1862, May and Oct. 1863.

39. See Theron F. Schlabach, "Reveille for *Die Stillen im Lande:* A Stir among Mennonites in the Late Nineteenth Century," *Mennonite Quarterly Review* 51 (July 1977): 213–15.

40. Ibid., 213–26; Schlabach, *Peace, Faith, Nation,* chap. 11. For the traditional "Awakening" interpretation, see, e.g., J. S. Hartzler and Daniel Kauffman, *Mennonite Church History* (Scottdale, Pa.: Mennonite Book and Tract Society, 1905); Guy F. Hershberger, "Historical Backgrounds to the Formation of the Mennonite Central Committee," *Mennonite Quarterly Review* 45 (July 1970): 218–21; and Harold S. Bender, *Mennonite Sunday School Centennial, 1840–1940: An Appreciation of Our Sunday Schools* (Scottdale, Pa., 1940), reprinted as "New Life through the Sunday School," in J. C. Wenger, ed., *The Mennonite Church in America: Sometimes Called Old Mennonites* (Scottdale, Pa.: Herald Press, 1966).

41. Denomination-building is a strong theme of Juhnke's in *Vision, Doctrine, War.*

42. Schlabach, *Peace, Faith, Nation*, 316–21.

43. J. Denny Weaver, "The Quickening of Soteriology: Atonement from Christian Burkholder to Daniel Kauffman," *Mennonite Quarterly Review* 61 (Jan. 1987): 5–45.

44. Theron F. Schlabach, "Paradoxes of Mennonite Separatism," *Pennsylvania Mennonite Heritage* 2 (Jan. 1979): 12–17.

45. Dennis Martin thought it was restitutionism; I disagree, unless *restitutionism* is simply a word for revitalization or renewal. See Martin, "Nothing New under the Sun?" 10.

46. Theron F. Schlabach, *Gospel versus Gospel: Mission and the Mennonite Church, 1863–1944* (Scottdale, Pa.: Herald Press, 1980), 44, 49.

47. C. Norman Kraus, "American Mennonites and the Bible," *Mennonite Quarterly Review* 41 (Oct. 1967): 309–29; Juhnke, *Vision, Doctrine, War;* for a key primary document, see "Report of Committee on Fundamentals," *Gospel Herald* 14 (Nov. 10, 1921): 627.

48. Schlabach, "Reveille for *Die Stillen im Lande*," 220–26.

49. Schlabach, *Peace, Faith, Nation*, chap. 8. For Old Order Mennonite documents and articles, see Amos B. Hoover, comp. and ed., *The Jonas Martin Era: Presented in a Collection of Essays, Letters, and Documents That Shed Light on the Mennonite Churches during the Fifty Year Ministry (1875–1925) of Bishop Jonas H. Martin* (Denver, Pa.: Amos B. Hoover, 1982); and J. C. Wenger, "Jacob Wisler and the Old Order Mennonite Schism of 1872 in Elkhart County, Indiana," *Mennonite Quarterly Review* 33 (Apr.–July 1959): 108–31, 215–40. For the Amish story, see Paton Yoder, *Tradition and Transition: Amish Mennonites and Old Order Amish, 1800–1900* (Scottdale, Pa.: Herald Press, 1991).

50. See Schlabach, *Peace, Faith, Nation*, 212–13; Yoder, *Tradition and Transition*, 72–82, esp. 76–79.

51. Schlabach, *Peace, Faith, Nation*, chap. 8; Donald B. Kraybill, *The Riddle of Amish Culture* (Baltimore: Johns Hopkins University Press, 1989), chap. 7.

52. Marc A. Olshan, "Modernity, the Folk Society, and the Old Order Amish: An Alternative Interpretation," *Rural Sociology* 46 (Summer 1981): 297–309.

53. Schlabach, *Peace, Faith, Nation*, chap. 8; James N. Gingerich, "Ordinance or Ordering: *Ordnung* and Amish Ministers Meetings, 1862–1878," *Mennonite Quarterly Review* 60 (Apr. 1986): 180–99.

54. This is a point on which Dennis Martin and I agree; see Martin, "Nothing New under the Sun?" 10.

55. Harold S. Bender, trans. and ed., "Some Early American Amish Mennonite Disciplines," *Mennonite Quarterly Review* 8 (Apr. 1934): 90–98; Harvey J. Miller, ed. "Proceedings of Amish Ministers Conferences, 1826–31," *Mennonite Quarterly Review* 33 (Apr. 1959): 132–42. Handwritten copies of the *Ordnungsbriefe* are, for instance, among the papers of nineteenth-century Iowa Amish bishop Jacob Schwarzendruber, in Daniel B. Swartzendruber Papers, Hist. Mss. 1–144, Archives of the Mennonite Church, Goshen College, Goshen, Ind.; for an inventory of Schwarzendruber's papers, see John

Umble, "Catalog of an Amish Bishop's 'Library,'" *Mennonite Quarterly Review* 20 (July 1946): 230–39.

56. Hoover, *Jonas Martin Era;* Wenger, "Jacob Wisler," esp. 108–31, 215–40; Schlabach, *Peace, Faith, Nation,* 201–10, 223–29.

57. The poem is by Theron Schlabach, circa 1980.

58. The three major printings are Harold S. Bender, "The Anabaptist Vision," *Church History* 13 (Mar. 1944): 3–24; *Mennonite Quarterly Review* 18 (Apr. 1944): 67–88; and Appendix 1 in Wenger, *Mennonite Church,* which is a slightly revised version. See also Guy F. Hershberger, ed., *The Recovery of the Anabaptist Vision: A Sixtieth Anniversary Tribute to Harold S. Bender* (Scottdale, Pa.: Herald Press, 1957).

59. John H. Yoder, "Anabaptist Vision and Mennonite Reality," typed and multilithed paper prepared for a forum at Goshen Biblical Seminary, Goshen, Ind., 1969, copy in Mennonite Historical Library, Goshen College, Goshen, Ind., 11 pp. A printed version is in A. J. Klassen, ed., *Consultation on Anabaptist Mennonite Theology: Papers Read at the 1969 Aspen Conference* (Fresno, Calif.: Council of Mennonite Seminaries, 1970), 1–46; this version omits some paragraphs, but it has a supplement, obviously added to respond to discussion that followed the original reading.

60. In a 1964 paper in which he gave a similar but less-developed analysis, Yoder at least conceded that Mennonites of the 1930s and 1940s had been sincere in thinking that institutions such as Mennonite colleges and the Mennonite Central Committee embodied the Anabaptist vision; in the 1969 paper he did not even make that point. See John Howard Yoder, "The Recovery of the Anabaptist Vision," typed and multilithed paper for a summer seminar at Elkhart, Ind., Aug. 1964, sponsored by the Student Services Committee of the Mennonite Board of Missions, copy in the Mennonite Historical Library, Goshen College, Goshen, Ind., later printed as Concern pamphlet 18. See p. 22 of the pamphlet for Yoder's concession. See also Yoder, "Anabaptist Vision and Mennonite Reality."

61. In his 1977 article "Anabaptism and History," Yoder still made the recapture of ideas about structure a key test. For restitution of the Radical Reformation, he argued, one criterion had to be "an alternative to the social shape of the fallen Christendom."

62. For an introduction to a core group of these scholars, known as the Concern group, see the special issue of *Conrad Grebel Review* 8 (Spring 1990) and Ronald S. Kraybill, "The 'Concern Group': An Attempt at Anabaptist Renewal," ms., 1967, Mennonite Historical Library, Goshen College, Goshen, Ind.

63. See esp. the supplement to his "Anabaptist Vision and Mennonite Reality" in Klassen, *Consultation.*

64. Yoder, "The Recovery of the Anabaptist Vision," 20–21.

65. See note 62; Concern pamphlets are available in various Mennonite libraries and elsewhere.

66. Paul Peachey, "The Modern Recovery of the Anabaptist Vision," in Hershberger, ed., *The Recovery of the Anabaptist Vision,* 328.

67. Ibid., 335–36.

68. Ibid., 337.

69. Ibid.

70. Ibid., 338.

71. Among Miller's various writings, see, e.g., "The Renewal of the Church," typed and multilithed paper for a summer seminar at Elkhart, Indiana, Aug. 1964, sponsored by the Student Services Committee of the Mennonite Board of Missions, copy in the Mennonite Historical Library, Goshen College, Goshen, Ind.

72. In addition to Peachey's opening disclaimer, see Yoder's reply to what he considered to be Franklin Littell's charge that the Anabaptist-vision school represented a naive ideal of restoring the New Testament church in "The Recovery of the Anabaptist Vision," 18–19.

73. I know from personal conversations with Peachey in (I believe) the late 1960s and the 1970s that he saw his career choices in light of his rejection of Mennonite ethnicism and institutionalism.

Contributors

THOMAS G. ALEXANDER is the Lemuel Hardison Redd Jr. Professor of Western American History at Brigham Young University. He has written *Mormonism in Transition: A History of the Latter-day Saints, 1890–1930* (1986); *Things in Heaven and Earth: The Life and Times of Wilford Woodruff, A Mormon Prophet* (1991); and "The Reconstruction of Mormon Doctrine: From Joseph Smith to Progressive Theology" (1980).

R. SCOTT APPLEBY is an associate professor of history and the director of the Cushwa Center for the Study of American Catholicism at the University of Notre Dame. He has written two books and several articles on religious modernisms and fundamentalisms. With Martin E. Marty, he edited *Fundamentalisms Observed* and four additional volumes in the Fundamentalism Project series published by the University of Chicago Press.

DAVID EDWIN HARRELL JR. is the Daniel F. Breeden Eminent Scholar in the Humanities at Auburn University. He previously was University Scholar at the University of Alabama, Birmingham, and Distinguished Professor of History at the University of Arkansas. He has written *Quest for a Christian America: The Disciples of Christ and American Society to 1866* (1966); *The Social Sources of Division in the Disciples of Christ, 1865–1900* (1973); *All Things Are Possible: The Healing and Charismatic Revivals in Modern America* (1975); and *Oral Roberts: An American Life* (1985).

RICHARD T. HUGHES is Distinguished Professor of Religion at Pepperdine University. He previously taught at Southwest Missouri State

University and Abilene Christian University. With C. Leonard Allen, he has written *Illusions of Innocence: Protestant Primitivism in America, 1630–1875* (1988). He has also written *Reviving the Ancient Faith: The Story of Churches of Christ in America* (1996) and has edited *The American Quest for the Primitive Church* (1988).

FRANKLIN H. LITTELL is an emeritus professor of religion at Temple University. He has also served as the Robert Foster Cherry Distinguished Visiting Professor at Baylor University (1993–94) and the Ida E. King Distinguished Visiting Professor at Richard Stockton College of New Jersey (1989–91). He has written *The Anabaptist View of the Church* (1952), *The German Phoenix* (1960), *From State Church to Pluralism* (1962), *The Free Church* (1957), and *The Crucifixion of the Jews* (1975).

JAMES WM. MCCLENDON JR. is a professor and Distinguished-Scholar-in-Residence at Fuller Theological Seminary. His books include *Biography as Theology: How Life Stories Can Remake Today's Theology* (1990); the three-volume *Systematic Theology*, written from a baptist perspective (1986, 1994, and forthcoming); and, with James M. Smith, *Convictions: Defusing Religious Relativism* (1994). He has taught at a variety of institutions, including Golden Gate Baptist Theological Seminary, Church Divinity School of the Pacific, and the University of San Francisco.

GEORGE MARSDEN is the Francis A. McAnaney Professor of History at the University of Notre Dame and previously taught in the Divinity School at Duke University and at Calvin College. He has written *The Soul of the American University: From Protestant Establishment to Established Nonbelief* (1994); *Reforming Fundamentalism: Fuller Seminary and the New Evangelicalism* (1987); and *Fundamentalism and American Culture: The Shaping of Twentieth-Century Evangelicalism, 1870–1925* (1980).

MARTIN E. MARTY is the Fairfax M. Cone Distinguished Service Professor of the History of Modern Christianity at the University of Chicago. A senior editor of the *Christian Century*, a co-editor of *Church History*, and Senior Scholar in Residence of the Park Ridge Center for the Study of Health, Faith, and Ethics, Marty has written more than forty books, most recently the multivolume *Modern American Religion*. He is past president of the American Academy of Religion (1988), the American Society of Church History (1971), and the American Catholic Historical Association (1981).

THERON F. SCHLABACH is a professor of history and department chair at Goshen College, where he has taught since 1965. Editor-in-chief of the series Studies in Anabaptist and Mennonite History, he has written *Peace, Faith, Nation: Mennonites and Amish in Nineteenth-Century America* (1988); *Gospel versus Gospel: Mission and the Mennonite Church, 1863–1944* (1980); and a variety of scholarly articles on Mennonite history in such publications as *Church History* and the *Mennonite Quarterly Review*.

SUSIE C. STANLEY is a professor of historical theology at Messiah College and taught at Western Evangelical Seminary. She is the author of *Feminist Pillar of Fire: The Life of Alma White* (1993), the compiler of *Wesleyan/Holiness Women Clergy: A Preliminary Bibliography* (1994), and has written numerous articles on the Wesleyan/Holiness tradition.

GRANT WACKER is a professor in the Divinity School at Duke University. He has published widely on a variety of aspects of American religion including the Protestant encounter with world religions and the history of pentecostalism and evangelicalism. His books in progress include "Heaven Below: Primitive Pentecostalism in America" and "But Why Christianity?: American Protestants and the Confrontation with World Religions."

JOHN HOWARD YODER is a professor of theology and fellow of the Joan B. Kroc Institute of International Peace Studies at the University of Notre Dame. He previously served as a professor of theology and president of Goshen Biblical Seminary. His many books include *The Politics of Jesus* (1972), *The Priestly Kingdom: Social Ethics as Gospel* (1985), and *The Royal Priesthood* (1994).

Index